A Boy Without Hope

CASEY WATSON

A Boy Without Hope

The heartbreaking
true story of a
troubled boy with
a terrible past

HARPER
element

This book is a work of non-fiction based on the author's experiences.
In order to protect privacy, names, identifying characteristics,
dialogue and details have been changed or reconstructed.

HarperElement
An imprint of HarperCollins*Publishers*
1 London Bridge Street
London SE1 9GF

www.harpercollins.co.uk

First published by HarperElement 2018

19 20 21 22 LSCC 10 9 8 7 6 5 4

A catalogue record of this book is
available from the British Library

PB ISBN 978-0-00-829855-5
EB ISBN 978-0-00-829859-3

Printed and bound in the United States of America by
LSC Communications

Find out more about HarperCollins and the environment at
www.harpercollins.co.uk/green

This book is dedicated to the army of passionate foster carers out there, each doing their bit to ensure that our children are kept as safe as possible in such a changing and often scary world. As technology is reinvented and becomes ever more complicated for those of us who were not brought up amid such advances, we can only try to keep up, in the hope that we continue to learn alongside our young people.

Acknowledgements

I remain endlessly grateful to my team at HarperCollins for their continuing support, and I'm especially excited to see the return of my editor, the very lovely Vicky Eribo, and look forward to sharing my new stories with her. As always, nothing would be possible without my wonderful agent, Andrew Lownie, the very best agent in the world in my opinion, and my grateful thanks also to the lovely Lynne, my friend and mentor forever.

Chapter 1

Some things are set in stone. That's as true for me as for anyone. Those little anchor points of life that provide stability and reassurance. The perfect way to make coffee. Tyler's special breakfast porridge. The fact that Christmas wouldn't be Christmas without at least a dozen strings of fairy lights. Mike's bear hugs. My many cleaning routines.

Birthdays, too, of course. Not to mention all the associated parties. Particularly those of my grandkids, in which my role was unchanging: chief entertainment officer, chief caterer and, invariably, chief bouncer as well.

I held two hot, sticky hands in mine – those of my two darling granddaughters, whom I was about to lead, suitably subdued, back into the dining room.

'Now, girls,' I said in my strictest grandmother voice, 'are you sure you can go back into the party without arguing?'

Marley Mae, my daughter Riley's youngest, opened her mouth in indignation. She was never one to shy away from giving the world the benefit of her opinion, but clearly thought better of it having caught my expression. So instead she sighed heavily, as if having been forced to concede a great military defeat.

'Well?' I asked.

'Yes, Nan,' she said finally, reaching around to wrap her cousin in a bear hug and mumbling the requisite 'sorry' as she did so.

My son Kieron's daughter Dee Dee, now three, was a year younger than her bossier cousin, and though they loved one another, they were both very competitive, so managed to find an argument in just about anything. Today's anything was a pink balloon, which both had laid claim to, and, in the ensuing scuffle, it was a miracle it hadn't already popped. Perhaps better that it had, to stop them squabbling over it. As it was, I had tethered it to the bannisters instead, telling them that if they couldn't share nicely then neither of them could have it. 'And I don't want to hear any more about it,' I told them sternly. 'This is Jackson's birthday party. Which means it's *his* special day. So no more of this arguing. You both got that?'

They both duly nodded, keen to rejoin the party. So I opened the door and ushered them back into the dining room, where a game of musical bumps had just started.

'You should have left both of them on the naughty step, Mum,' Riley said as I rejoined her in the kitchen area. 'Marley Mae gets four minutes at home when she carries on like that. She needs to learn to share better.'

'Oh, she will,' I told my daughter. 'School will sort her out in no time. It's only because she has two older brothers who give into her all the time because they want a quiet life.'

'Maybe,' she said, though she sounded unconvinced. 'I wish she could go full-time. She's more than ready. And so am I! September seems a very long way away still.'

'Problems?' Kieron asked, as he passed me his empty coffee mug. 'Well, they all look as if they're having fun. I can't believe Jackson is ten already. Can you?'

Kieron has Asperger's, which is a mild form of autism, and one of his special talents is asking questions, making statements and issuing instructions all at once. It's been the same since he was little; as if he makes these mental lists of every passing thought, before opening his mouth.

'No problems we can't handle,' I told him. 'And yes, they are having fun. And, yes, time flies – I can't believe Jackson is ten already either. And yes, I'll make more coffee. Anything else?' I added, laughing at his confused expression.

'Oh, yes,' he said, handing me my mobile, which I hadn't spotted. 'Here you go. John Fulshaw's on the phone.'

'Oh Kieron, *honestly*,' I said, snatching it from him. 'You could have started with that, couldn't you? Sorry, John,' I added, as I put the phone to my ear. 'As you probably noticed, you've caught me mid-party. Hang on, let me find somewhere quieter to talk.'

I wove a path through a dining room full of small people, and some unfamiliar adults, into the conservatory, en route to the back garden – the one place, because of a heavy April shower earlier, we had opted to make out of bounds. I'd happily agreed to Riley's suggestion that we hold Jackson's party at our house – it was a good bit bigger, so it made sense – but I'd forgotten just how many friends the average ten-year-old simply *must* invite to their parties. These days, a whole form's worth, plus a couple of extras, seemed to be the norm. Throw in a couple of cousins, and friends from various clubs and activities, plus half their parents (did they not have anything better to do?), and there didn't seem an inch of our downstairs that wasn't occupied by a human, and the house seemed to be creaking under the strain of it all.

Literally, I thought, as I clacked across the squeaking floorboards.

'You sound a bit ruffled, Casey,' John said, once I'd shut both the door and noise behind me. 'I could always call back later if you'd rather?'

'No, no,' I said, perching myself on an upturned log at the bottom of the garden. 'It's just a birthday bash for one of the grandkids, and it's a good excuse to escape for a few minutes, to be honest. I think I'm getting a little old for all this mayhem. But nothing that won't be over within the next hour or so. Anyway, long time no speak. To what do I owe the pleasure? Have you got a child for us?'

In reality, it had been no more than three weeks or so, but John, being our fostering link worker, was so much a part of the regular fabric of our lives that three weeks was actually quite a while. We'd been in limbo for the last three months or so – 'recuperating', for want of a better word, after our last long-term child had left us.

Though Keeley hadn't been a child, quite. She'd turned sixteen while she was with us. And had taken us down some intense, uncharted waters. Since then, Mike and I had quite enjoyed being on the back burner. We'd been doing respite work – where you step in short term to support other full-time foster carers – a few days here, a week there, nothing too challenging. And though we had experienced the odd trauma (one weekend visitor, for instance, was so fond of absconding that she arrived complete with a tracking bracelet on her ankle, and decided to abscond anyway), these were short bursts of fostering activity in a largely calm, family-orientated landscape, for a change. And with four grandchildren now, I was kept pretty busy as it was.

I never thought I'd say it, but I wasn't feeling the usual tug that always used to happen when I didn't have a child in. And I also had Tyler, our permanent foster son, to think about. He had GCSEs coming up in a few weeks now, and we wanted to support him as well as we could.

'Actually, no,' John said, surprising me. 'It's news of a slightly different kind. News I wanted to share with you and Mike before it becomes public knowledge. So I was wondering if I could pop round for half an hour in the next day or so.'

'What kind of news?' I demanded.

He chuckled. 'I'd rather tell you face-to-face.'

'Oh, don't go all coy on me, John. What?'

'When are you free?'

'Oh, for goodness' sake,' I said. 'But okay, you win. This evening?' I looked at my watch. 'Mike will be home within the hour – on pain of death, I might add – and we should have cleared everyone out soon after. Why don't you come over around seven? Assuming you're in the office, that is?' John was famous for never leaving work much before that.

'Perfect,' he said. 'Now I'll let you get back to the party.'

His tone was bright and chirpy, so why did I fear bad news so much?

* * *

'Because it will be?' Mike said, as he shovelled the last of the paper plates into the recycling.

He had narrowly avoided being hung, drawn and quartered by showing up a full twenty minutes before the designated end time and entertaining the kids with some high-octane rough and tumble, while Riley and I divvied up the birthday cake and wrapped sticky slices to shove into the thirty-five-odd party bags. Yes, they'd leave hitting the ceiling with over-excitement, but once they'd calmed down they would all sleep well tonight.

Now it was just a case of sluicing down and tidying up. 'He didn't sound as if it was,' I said. 'But my antennae are twitching.'

'And definitely not a new child?' Mike asked.

'He said not. Though there's a thought. Perhaps an old one?'

This did happen sometimes; you thought a child had moved on from you successfully, only to have things break down – perhaps at home, or with a 'forever' foster family

– months or even years down the line. It hadn't happened to us, but that wasn't to say it couldn't.

'Well, there's no point in speculating,' Mike said, as he knotted the green bag. 'It will be what it will be. And he'll be here any minute to put you out of your misery. In fact …' We heard the bing-bong of the doorbell simultaneously. 'Speak of the devil. Get the kettle on. I'll go and let him in.'

Mike did so, and moments later John was standing in my kitchen in his 'lucky' jacket. A raggy tweed number, which couldn't have screamed 'public sector' louder, and which he'd had for as long as I'd known him. For all his teasing earlier, he shrugged it off and came straight to the point. 'I'm leaving,' he said. 'End of this month.'

'Whaaaatttt?' I said, teaspoon of coffee in mid-scoop. 'As in *leaving*? As in two weeks from now? Just like that?' I knew my face was probably reflecting my emotions a little too much, but I couldn't help it. How could this be happening so suddenly, and so *soon*?

Or, more accurately, why didn't I already *know*? Jobs like John's weren't the kind that you just walked away from with a couple of weeks' notice. They had long notice periods, and complex, structured handovers. John *was* the fostering agency as far as I was concerned. He knew everything and everyone; how could it possibly cope without him? Yes, a bit melodramatic, maybe, but not too far from the honest truth.

'I know it's a bit out of the blue,' he said, 'and it's not how I'd planned it. It's just that my dad's not well, as you know, and we really need to relocate, and –'

'Oh, God, John, I'm sorry,' I said, feeling awful. I knew his dad had been ill. I knew he lived alone, some way distant. 'I didn't mean it like that. Of course, you must. Just ignore me. Sorry – but, God, it's just so sudden.'

'So leaving the service entirely?' Mike asked, pulling out a chair and gesturing that John should sit on it. 'Quite a big life change for you, then.'

'Yes and no,' John said. 'And, Casey, really, don't worry. I'm not dashing off to attend him on his death bed or anything. He's getting a kidney transplant and all being well it's going to revolutionise his life, so it's all positive. And the truth is that I've been offered this promotion twice already and have always said I'm not interested – not least because we're so settled here. But with Dad and that, well, it seemed fate was telling me something, and as there's someone unexpectedly available who can slot in pretty easily …'

Promotion. Of *course*. Why wouldn't he want promotion?

'So what's the new job?' I asked, recovering my equilibrium a little.

'I'm taking over as Senior County Manager. You know, mixing with all the big wigs and overseeing some of the regional teams.'

'So just leaving the area,' Mike said.

John nodded. I put his coffee in front of him. 'And they already have a replacement for you?' I asked. 'How can they? You're irreplaceable. Everyone knows that.'

John grinned. 'Thanks for the vote of confidence, Casey. That's so nice of you to say. But it's still absolutely not true.

8

That's why we're able to rush things through. I know it sounds as though I'm deserting a sinking ship, what with all the budget cuts, and politics, and extra stress everyone's been facing just lately, but I'm hoping I'm going be in a position of greater influence.' He grinned. 'Speaking truth to power, and lots of other noble stuff like that.'

'Well, congratulations,' Mike said, raising his own coffee mug. 'Good on you. Lovely as it's been to have you all to ourselves for so long, if the call comes, why wouldn't you take it? Cometh the hour, cometh the man and all that. The state that social services are in these days, we need some sort of shake-up. Casey, we will *cope*,' he added, seeing my ill-concealed stricken face.

'Thanks, Mike,' John said. 'I have to say I'm really looking forward to it. It's going to be very different – not to mention very challenging, I don't doubt – but I'm not going to miss working the ridiculous hours I do. And neither will 'er indoors, as I'm sure you can imagine. Well …' He smiled. 'You two, of all people, know all about that, don't you?'

Didn't we just. And we'd never minded. It was the nature of what we did. But to do it without John? Calm, capable, unflappable, always-at-the-end-of-the-phone, supportive, lovely John? I simply couldn't imagine it.

'I'm really, really pleased for you,' I told him, and, despite my shock, I meant it. It was because he had always been all of those things that he needed, and deserved, to have a break from it. We all knew the saying that on your death bed you never wish you'd spent more time at the office. But how many of us forget it till it's all too late? This was absolutely his time to remember and act on it. And there was no doubt about it. He should.

'Thanks, Casey,' he said. 'I knew you would understand. I was worried about a general foster-carer exodus – I still am – but I knew I could rely on you two. Change is always hard, but I'm sure you'll get on brilliantly with Christine Bolton once you get to know her, and –'

'Christine? So it's a woman taking over from you?' I asked him. 'The name doesn't ring a bell. Should it?'

'No,' John said, 'she's not from round here. She's relocating too. She's currently based in Liverpool. Doing pretty much the same job as me. And the reason it's all fallen into place the way it has is that she wants to move fairly quickly for family reasons, too. I don't know all the details, but I believe her partner needs to return here. Another elderly parent situation.'

'Twas ever thus …' mused Mike.

But I had fixed on something else. 'Once we get to know her?' I asked John, whom I knew better than perhaps he realised. 'Why "once you get to know her"? Come on. What aren't you telling us?'

He looked slightly uncomfortable. 'I shouldn't have put it like that. She's really nice. And *very* professional.'

'But?' I was like a dog with a bone now.

'There aren't any buts,' he said. 'Honestly, Casey. I've already met up with her a couple of times, and we're obviously liaising closely re the handover and everything. *Seriously.* Don't look like that. She's fine. I just meant –

well, you know how it is – different people have different ways of doing things, don't they? That's all I meant. That everyone will have to adjust to everyone's different … um … peccadillos. That goes with the territory when you're part of a multidisciplinary team, and –'

'Blinding me with science now – I get it. Come on, spill, John Fulshaw. Is she an overbearing battle-axe? If so, we need to know.' I pushed up the sleeves of my top. 'Forewarned is forearmed, and I need some ammo.'

John burst out laughing. 'Oh, God,' he said, winking at Mike once he'd recovered his composure. 'I am *so* going to miss this one! I'm going to miss all of you,' he added, more seriously. 'D'you know, I was thinking on the way here – it's been so many years, hasn't it? So many children. And your two all grown up – and both now with their own kids. Your *grand*kids. How is that even possible? And Tyler sixteen now. How did that happen?'

Tyler had come to us as an eleven-year-old, with a terrible, tragic background: a dead heroin-addict mother, a father who didn't want him, and, after all sorts of heart-breaking emotional abuse, he'd ended up going for his step-mother with a kitchen knife. I still remembered the day I'd gone to fetch him from the local police station, immediately afterwards. Hard not to, given that, during that first memorable meeting, he'd spat at a police officer, kicked a chair around the interview room, called his stepmother a witch, called another officer a 'dick brain' and, for good measure – he was obviously keen to make a good impression – told his social worker to fuck off. Though I didn't know it as that then – I'd been tickled by him more than anything – what I'd actually felt had been love at first sight.

'He's going to miss you,' I told John.

'I'm going to miss him too – a lot. *All* of you. And' – he chuckled again – '*how* many house moves has it been now? It really does feel like the end of an era, doesn't it?'

'Oh, God,' I said, reaching for the kitchen roll. 'Don't set me off.'

But, of course, he already had.

* * *

Change. Change is good. Change is necessary even. And, as a resilient foster carer, one might imagine it was something I coped with brilliantly. And, in the main, for most of the time, one would have imagined right, because I did. Especially given that on the surface, our household never had a routine, not in the conventional sense.

But, deep inside, I knew I shared some of the traits of my Asperger's son. Yes, I could cope with chaos easily, but only as long as certain things were set in stone. It wasn't necessarily visible, because my real routine simply hummed away in the background. The forefront of my life could be as messed up as it liked, as long as some things never changed; as long as what really mattered was set in stone.

Now one of those things, those reassuring rocks, had begun to crumble, and I wasn't sure this change was going to be one that I could easily cope with. Wasn't sure, given everything, if I even wanted to try.

Plus John still hadn't answered my question.

Chapter 2

Because time was short, and he had a lot to tie up before leaving us, we had two days to reflect on John's bombshell. Which wasn't really that much of a bombshell – why on earth wouldn't he get promoted? – but since I'd obviously had my head stuffed deep into the sand, it still took a fair bit of getting used to.

Mostly I chuntered on, uncharacteristically negative, unable to do the one thing Mike deemed to be the *only* thing – to stop wondering what John's replacement was like and simply wait and see. But we both knew there was actually a bit more to it than that, because it wasn't just a case of whether we bonded with her or didn't – it was also the timing, coming along at precisely the point when I was seriously considering a change in direction myself. Was this the catalyst that would make me jump one way or the other? It certainly felt like fate had arranged it that way.

I was also nervous, those words 'very professional' running round and round my brain. I had visions of a sharp-suited, shoulder-padded dynamo – the sort of vision of a high-flying, glass-ceiling-smashing career woman that many of us can so easily call to mind. Which was ridiculous. She might equally be gentle and mumsy. Being professional isn't about the clothes you choose to wear, particularly when you're in the line of work we were, dealing with messy domestic dramas and troubled, angry children, sometimes in the small hours, having tumbled blearily out of bed. John had certainly done his share of that and it was odds-on that this Christine Bolton would have too.

But, having worked myself up, I still felt a bit intimidated, so much so that on the day itself I had ants in my pants. Big soldier ants, with big pincers, trying to chew me up. Which was probably why I was so irritable.

'Come on,' I snapped at Tyler, who was wading through his cereal on slo-mo. 'You're going to be late if you don't hurry up.' I pointed at the kitchen clock. 'Look at the time! The bus'll be here in two minutes, and you don't even have your shoes on. Arrgh!'

Being the bright teenager that he was, Tyler had obviously seen this coming. He looked straight past me at Mike, who was leaning against the kitchen counter, reading the paper while waiting for the kettle to boil. He'd had some changes of his own, in his job managing a warehouse, having reached a height lofty enough to delegate some of his duties, one being the relentless ridiculously early starts. For a couple of days a week now, he was still at home at breakfast time.

Which was presumably why they always seemed to be in cahoots these days. 'See, Dad,' Tyler said, 'I told you she'd be like this, didn't I? It's alright though,' he added, reaching for the offending trainers. 'My shoulders are broad. Calm down, Mum,' he said, smiling at me as he leaned down to put them on. 'The woman will be just fine, everything is sparkly clean, and she won't fail to be impressed that you've got the bone china out.'

I swiped him with the tea towel. 'Bone china? As if!' I huffed. 'She's lucky she's not drinking cheap coffee out of a mug, and for your information, young man, I *am* calm. Now hurry up and get yourself sorted rather than nit-picking at me.'

I saw the exchange of raised eyebrows between my husband and foster son and was at least able to manage a bit of a grin myself. They were right, of course. Considering how many years I'd been fostering and the amount of social workers I had met, it made no sense that I was getting so strung up about meeting Christine Bolton. After all, she was simply an agency link worker, like John was, or, at least, used to be, and hadn't he said that she'd moved over from Liverpool? Yes, he had. So she probably wouldn't have that clipped, cut-glass accent that usually made me feel so nervous. It was ridiculous of me to get myself in such a state. So why was I?

'Don't worry, Casey,' Mike said after Tyler had at last set off for his bus. 'Remember what I said? If you decide it's time to hang up your fostering apron, then so be it. That's completely *fine*. After all, it's you who has all the day-to-day stuff to contend with. If you've had enough, you've had enough and I'll support you whatever you decide.'

We had talked long into the night after John's news about this and I think it was the first time I had ever voiced the notion and actually meant it. I'd even drifted off to sleep thinking that I'd phone my sister, Donna, and ask her if she could guarantee me a few shifts at her tea rooms, Truly Scrumptious. One thing I really lacked these days, especially with my own kids long flown, was the ridiculously simple pleasure of daily adult company. Perhaps it was time to put that right.

I stared into my posh china cup, which I hated. Truth was, I didn't know what to do. On the one hand, I loved my job. I loved most of the children that entered our lives, and felt privileged to be able to play a small part in helping them towards a better future. On the other hand, I recognised that I often felt tired and disillusioned with all the red tape.

Because fostering had changed over the years. That was a fact. Financial cuts meant that social workers these days often barely knew the kids they were responsible for. They might have as many as twenty children on their caseloads and just didn't have the time to build a meaningful relationship with them, so the all-important trust just didn't seem to be there. Statutory visits, meant to take place at least every six weeks, often got cancelled at the last minute, which compounded it. As a consequence, relationships, period, just weren't the same any more. It deeply bothered me that it seemed to be all about counting the pennies out, and less about the actual children.

'I'm still not sure, love,' I told Mike. 'I think it might depend on how settled I feel when we meet this new woman. I mean, we've been so lucky to have had John for so many years, and that he felt the same as we do. I'm just hoping she's of a similar mindset, that's all.'

'And if she isn't?' Mike asked

'Well, we'll just have to see,' I said. And I meant it. 'I know I'm impulsive. I know I sometimes act first and think later. But I really will put a lot of thought into it before deciding.'

'Well, that'll be a first,' he said. 'But you know what? I don't think you'll need to. This is one of those times where I think your instinct will – and should – lead the way. Hey,' he added, reaching for the matches so he could light the scented candle I'd dug out. 'Maybe she'll be a tea drinker! Then you won't have to think at all, will you?'

Which comment made it all but impossible for me not to explode into nervous laughter, when, ten minutes later, our new visitor responded to my usual opening gambit of 'Drink? Tea or coffee?' with 'Oh, tea for me, please – every time.'

I might have done, too, had John not beaten me to it, along with a jaunty 'Forgot to tell you, Casey – Christine hails from the dark side.'

Though in truth, a tea drinker was exactly what she looked like. Which, bizarrely, given my prejudices, was something of a comfort. Yes, she was dressed in a sharp skirt and jacket suit, and there was no denying that she looked ready for business, with her fair hair perfectly blow-dried and her big leather laptop case, and the label – *Ms C.*

Bolton – on a folder she'd pulled out, but there was at least something approachable about her that I hadn't anticipated, enhanced by her soft Liverpudlian accent, and her readiness to accept a chocolate chip cookie, which she dunked in her tea while John went through his spiel. You couldn't mistrust a dunker, could you?

Having never been through a change-over of fostering link worker before, I had no idea how these things usually went. Though I didn't doubt there would be a protocol – there was a protocol for *everything*. But it turned out there wasn't – not in my house, at any rate. Such official handing over of responsibilities as needed to happen had already happened. And would continue to do so, John explained, over the next couple of weeks, during which time Christine would shadow him in his various duties.

And this was one such – no more than an unofficial 'meet and greet', really. One where I had the bizarre notion that the poor woman was having to repeat herself endlessly, in a series of thinly veiled 'pitches' to John's stable of carers, as if she was on *The Apprentice* or something, having to go from house to house, laying out her credentials over endless cups of tea. I wondered how far along the line we were. She certainly seemed to have memorised her script.

'John speaks very highly of you both,' she said as she daintily sipped her tea. 'So I'm very much looking forward to us working together. I'm also hoping that both of you might be something of a crutch for me, while I'm finding my way around the way things work here. All those boring procedures and so on.'

I laughed politely. 'Likewise,' I told her. 'But I'm sure John's also told you I'm a bit of a scatterbrain, so I doubt I'd be much use as a crutch. In fact, if I'm honest,' I rattled on, 'I'm usually the one who's battling *against* procedure' – I grinned at John – 'more often than the other way around.'

John spluttered slightly. 'That's not true at all, Christine,' he said. 'Yes, Casey does sail a little close to the wind at times, as I'm sure she'll be the first to admit. But as I explained on the way here' – he grinned back at me – 'that's only because she cares. She's fiercely protective of the children she looks after for us, and will fight tooth and nail to be their advocate if she feels there's any injustice. But that's one of her great strengths. Am I right, Mike?'

Mike nodded. I blushed, feeling Christine's eyes on me. Feeling scrutinised. I wondered what else they'd already discussed. 'And I'm sure you'll soon get the hang of things, Christine,' Mike said. 'And you'll love working over this end. We're not a bad bunch round here. What about your own family? How are they finding the relocation?'

'No family. Just myself and my husband Charles,' she answered. 'He's an accountant, and he does a lot of work from home, which makes it easier. Which it needs to be, given how erratic my hours can be, of course.'

She smiled. I smiled back. So it looked like they were childless. Which didn't make any difference. It shouldn't, and it wouldn't. Some of the most remarkable advocates for and defenders of children were able to be so precisely because they *didn't* have their own. I judged her to be in her mid-forties or thereabouts. I wondered if it was a case of

not wanted, not yet, or not able. Then checked myself –
these were thoughts that wouldn't have even occurred to
me had a man been sitting across from me – and that was
food for thought in itself. But perhaps being female made
it difficult not to have them. As a person blessed (or cursed)
with a strong maternal urge, I was always interested in
women's choices, and how they made them. Or, in the case
of so many of the kids we had fostered, how those choices
were taken away from them. I wondered what had brought
Christine Bolton into the world of care and children.

It sounded as if she had other things to worry about,
however. 'The main thing is that we're closer to my
husband's parents,' she said. 'He's an only child and his
father has Alzheimer's,' she explained. 'Being closer means
he'll be able to help his mum out a lot more. You probably
know what it's like.' We all nodded, in unison. Was there a
family around not impacted by dementia? I counted my
blessings that my own parents, both now in their late
seventies, had so far been spared.

'That must be tough,' I said. 'But, as you say, being
closer will make things easier. And here's hoping you'll
have the space to ease into work gently, so you can get
yourself orientated and settled in.'

At which point John coughed. And Christine Bolton
looked across at him. I'm no Sherlock Holmes, but I
clocked it immediately. I caught his eye.

'So,' he said, 'does anyone have any questions?'

Only one unspoken one, I thought. *What's going on?* I
looked across at Mike, who was rising from his chair, ready

to say his goodbyes and head for work. And I could tell he was wondering that too. And when John retrieved his case from where he'd parked it under the table, Mike sat down again. 'I have,' he said to John. 'And it's "And?"'

John had the grace to look guilty. Though, actually, not that guilty. Because, given that he was leaving, why would he? He pulled a manila file, smooth as silk, from his trusty bag.

He looked at me. 'You don't have to say yes, Casey,' he said as he held it up. 'And I'm not playing games with you, I promise,' he added, having read my expression (something he was obviously good at) and correctly interpreting it as one of irritation that what he'd been doing was *exactly* that.

'A child,' Mike said, nodding towards the unopened file.

'A twelve-year-old boy,' John said. 'Name of Miller Green. And this literally landed on my desk only this morning, or of course I'd have phoned you and told you both. We've barely even had a chance to have a read through of all the notes, have we?' he added, glancing at his now professionally grim-faced successor. 'And I obviously didn't want to welly straight on into it till you and Christine had had a chance to get acquainted. So ...'

'Sounds fair enough,' Mike said mildly. 'What's the story?'

'First thing is that this doesn't sound like an easy one,' John admitted. 'So you'll have to think hard before agreeing to it, okay? And I mean that.' He tapped the file. 'This looks like one challenging kid.'

At which point I'd have normally thought *bring it on*. I didn't. 'So?' I asked instead. 'What's his background?'

John donned his reading glasses and skimmed through what he'd obviously identified at the key facts. 'A really sad case, it seems. Poor kid was first known to social services when he was found playing on a railway crossing, adjacent to a busy road, almost seven years ago. Almost naked, etc., etc., police called to investigate, parents didn't want him – they're both long-term substance abusers, apparently. The boy's been in care ever since. But a huge number of placement breakdowns. And I mean huge. From what I can gather, there's also a pattern. Always seems to feel the need to destroy it almost before it starts.' John glanced at me from over his glasses. 'Frequently described as being "difficult to like".'

He'd freighted the last three words with heavy, deliberate meaning. 'And where is he now?' I asked.

'Currently with a foster couple called Jenny and Martin in another county,' John said. 'Martin works away during the week, and Jenny can no longer cope. The boy has been excluded from – it says here – "yet another school, and is not at the moment in education". Jenny wants him gone as soon as possible. Ideally today.'

'Wow!' I said. 'I know you're not trying to put me on the spot, but this really is a decision that needs making, like, now, isn't it?'

'Yes, it does,' John admitted. 'Though, given what we do know about the boy, and his previous history, plus the fact that he's currently out of education, we don't expect you to make a long-term commitment right away. All we're after is a commitment to giving it a proper shot. See how things go, say, for starters, on a month-by-month basis. Well supported, of course. You know you can depend on that.'

A proper shot, I thought. As if we'd ever commit to anything less! But well supported? Without John? And by this brisk, slightly stiff woman?

'Well, of course,' I said. 'Obviously. But –'

Then Christine jumped in. 'But we completely understand if you think it might be too big an ask for you. I mean given his age – and let's face it, none of us are getting any younger, are we? Please feel free to say no, and we can keep the door open for you to take on a child who doesn't come accompanied with quite so many challenges.'

I stared at John in disbelief. In fact, I think my mouth hung open for a good twenty seconds. Too big an ask? None of us were getting any younger? Take on a child *without quite so many challenges*? Cheeky mare!

A part of me accepted that she was just covering the bases. If she sensed any hesitation, it was right that she did, too. It would be insane to place a child with carers any less than 100 per cent willing. Placement breakdowns were damaging. And it seemed this kid had already suffered quite a few.

But, whether she was aware of it or otherwise, her words had hit a nerve. Needless to say, if there was one thing I always rose to, it was a challenge. In this case, the challenge of correcting *Ms* Bolton in the matter of the impression she had obviously already formed about me. So it was that I opened my mouth before engaging my brain. 'We'll do it,' I said firmly. 'He sounds right up my street.'

Chapter 3

They'd said they'd be with us at 6.30 p.m., and it was now almost seven. So my initial reservations about Christine Bolton had now been replaced with the familiar feeling of nervous anticipation I always had before a new child arrived.

Though she had indeed ruffled my feathers earlier in the day, even if not in the way I had expected. It was only after she and John had left us that it occurred to me that I might have been 'played' – as Tyler might put it. That her gestures of concern about whether Mike and I felt up to such a challenge might have been expressly designed to ensure that I couldn't *help* but rise to it. A laying down of a gauntlet that I couldn't resist picking up. If so, she already knew me better than she realised.

So I'd put myself here, in short. Just as I had convinced myself that I could easily walk away from fostering and find something else to keep me occupied, a huge spanner had consequently been thrown in the works – one which would certainly force me to put any thoughts of leaving on the back burner. And for me, that wasn't an ideal situation to be in at all. I hated having a 'should I, shouldn't I' scenario playing out somewhere in the back of my mind. It would gnaw away at me during any quiet moments, I just knew it.

The truth was, of course, that I could, and perhaps should, have said no. I could have explained that I'd been having doubts about our future as foster carers, and that at this point – at least till I'd worked my concerns through in my head – I wasn't ready to take on another child, particularly one flagged as particularly difficult to manage. They would have understood. I knew that. They would have offered to support me. There was no point in less than 100 per cent commitment, after all. That was true for them as much as me.

But even knowing little about this child they were so desperate to place, the fact that he was real now – no longer a potential child, but an actual one – was already messing with my head. It would no longer be a case of turning down a hypothetical child. I'd be turning down a specific one, which felt very different. My decision to do so wouldn't just be removing us from the agency register. It would mean refusing to take a *real* child, with very real, possibly grave, consequences for him. No, he wouldn't know that, but *I* would.

Which was my right. And, given my ambivalence, perhaps the right thing to do anyway, but I couldn't help my mind from returning to Justin, the very first child we'd agreed to foster, over a decade back and, in some ways, one of the most challenging, because of that. We had helped turn his life around, and back when we were still very inexperienced. Now we had all that experience under our belts, wouldn't we be even better placed to offer the support and guidance this child clearly needed? The similarities between the boys resonated too. Here was another lad knocking on the door of that 'last chance saloon', with another string of failed placements making him increasingly hard to place. Abandoned, both by his parents, and – at least as good as – by the system. Did I want my name to be added to the growing list of people who'd turned away? *Could* I? I wasn't sure I could. Perhaps I just needed to meet him. Perhaps my gut would tell me. I hoped so.

'A case of *que sera*, I suppose,' I said aloud, even if more to myself than anyone else. But it caused both Mike and Tyler to grin in mild amusement. '*What*?' I said, going to peep out of the window for the umpteenth time. 'Don't the pair of you ever talk to yourselves these days?'

We'd bought Tyler a guitar for his sixteenth birthday, the better to further his dream of becoming a famous singer-song-writer (well, in his free time from being a famous footballer, obviously), and in the few months he'd had it, he'd already become quite good. He was also having lessons, and had impressed us with his diligence in practising; we'd often hear the sound of repetitive twanging coming from his bedroom, accessorised by the odd curse when he played a wrong chord. He was strumming it now, swaying on a dining chair as he played, channelling Ed Sheeran, as was his current habit. 'And we all watched ... as she slowly went insane, yeah, yeah ...'

Mike roared with laughter. 'Is that the new song you're writing, son?' he asked, quickly taking refuge in the dining area, where he'd be safely out of my reach.

'Oh, very funny,' I said, shaking my head at the two of them. I glanced at the clock again. 'It's now *gone* seven,'

I pointed out. 'What's going on?'

'Maybe the kid's run off,' Tyler suggested. 'Didn't you say that was one of his things, running away? Maybe he's decided he doesn't want another move and has run away to join a circus.'

As opposed to this circus, I thought. Then caught myself half hoping it might be true, so that it was a decision that wouldn't be mine to make. I silently berated myself. I had to do this wholeheartedly, or not at all.

And Tyler was right. Since the morning's meeting I had been receiving bits of information all day. Christine had been busy; I'd had several phone calls and emails, and the bigger picture was now becoming clear. Absconding appeared to be one of Miller's favourite activities. And he didn't do things by halves either. He'd run from classrooms, meetings, various foster homes and cars. At one point, it was recorded, he'd even leapt from a *moving* car. It seemed clear that if he wasn't in a secure area, and constantly watched, it was odds-on that he'd try to escape.

But he always came back. And, to me, that seemed key. Just as a half-hearted suicide attempt was often a cry for help, so this lad seemed not to really want to disappear – which he could do, should he want to – but simply to cause maximum inconvenience and stress for all concerned.

Which, of course, was a cry for help too. I left my vigil at the dining-room window, and went into the kitchen, where I slapped the switch down on the kettle for about the sixth or seventh time. Ridiculous, really, because I could boil it when they arrived. It was just a nervous tic I couldn't shake.

'I imagine he probably has,' I said to Tyler. 'But you'd have thought they'd have at least phoned me! John knows what I'm like,' I harrumphed. 'He should have phoned.'

'But it's not John who's bringing him, love,' Mike reminded me. 'It's the boy's social worker, isn't it? John probably doesn't even know what's going on, truth be known. It will be Christine taking the lead on this one, won't it?'

I was just about to say 'Whatever' when, as if on cue, my mobile phone rang, showing an unknown number in the display. I snatched it up, mouthing *Finally* at Mike.

'It's Libby Moran,' a female voice said. 'I'm Miller Green's social worker?'

She sounded bright enough, but I could tell that the brightness was forced, as if her tone was for the benefit of someone else. 'I'm just, um, calling to let you know that we should be with you in about half an hour, if that's okay? Sorry about the delay. Miller was a little bit afraid of another move so quickly, so we had a teeny bit of a job convincing him to get into the car … but it's all okay now,' she trilled. 'We're finally on the road.'

'That's fine,' I trilled back, imagining I'd be coming through the loudspeaker. 'We'll see you when you get here, but please do tell Miller that he has *nothing* to be afraid of. We're all really looking forward to meeting him. Oh, and you might want to let him know that we've put a TV in his bedroom, and I've managed to borrow a PlayStation from my sister for him, too.'

'Oh, that sounds wonderful,' she replied, but, as she hung up the call, I was sure I could hear manic laughter.

I kept that to myself, however. Best not to pre-judge. 'Half an hour,' I told Mike and Tyler. 'He was just a bit reluctant, that was all.'

'I can understand that,' Tyler said. 'I mean, he's bound to be scared, isn't he? Specially if he's been on the move all the time. Must be crap for him.'

'Rubbish.' I corrected. 'It must be "rubbish" for him. You'll have to try to curb your language, Ty – he's at an impressionable age, remember.'

Though whether we'd be able to make any sort of impression on him was quite another matter. I had my doubts. Miller, it seemed, liked to be the one calling the shots. The half-hour stretched. Then stretched some more. Then became a full hour. It was gone ten past eight by the time the doorbell eventually buzzed, and I wondered what had held them up now.

Though it wasn't a 'them' that was standing on the doorstep. It was just a young, flustered-looking woman – no sign of Miller – with a suitcase in one hand and a bin bag in the other.

'He's still in the car,' she explained, as I peered past her into the street. 'Won't get out at the minute – this is a bit of a thing with him, I'm afraid – but I'm sure if we go inside, curiosity will get the better of him, and he'll come and join us.'

With little choice but to go with her assessment of the situation, I stood aside to let her in and put the door on the latch. She looked to be in her late twenties, and put me in mind of a 1960s hippy; long floral skirt, bright orange oversized jumper and her dyed red hair hung in long dreadlocks. Conventional social worker she wasn't, at least in appearance. She also had a lip piercing, which surprised me, even in these enlightened times. Though less surprising, I decided, as I ushered her into the living room, would be to find out that under the maxi-skirt she had heavy workmen's boots.

I wasn't disappointed. As she took the seat I proffered, and hitched up her dress, I spied a pair of chunky ten-eyelet Dr. Martens. I hoped she was as robust as they looked.

'Bless him,' she said, accepting the mug of coffee Mike handed her. 'He's such a little monkey. After all he put Jenny and Martin through, you wouldn't credit it, would you? Decided he was going nowhere. Refused point blank to get into my car. And then of course he ran off and it was ages before we found him. Up a tree as it turned out, watching us all running around looking for him.'

Running rings round them, more like, I thought but didn't say. There was also the small matter of him still being *in* the car. He was only twelve, after all, and with a long history of absconding. For all we knew, he could already be halfway down the street.

Mike was on a different tack, however. 'And, if he refuses, how do you propose we get him back *out* of your car?'

'Or more to the point,' Tyler said, before Libby had a chance to answer, 'how are you going to get back *into* your car?' He'd been keeping watch, out of the window, and now motioned for us to look. 'Because he's sitting in the driving seat and, if I'm not mistaken, I think those are your car keys he's waving?'

Libby Moran's hands flew into the canvas bag she had across her shoulder. 'Oh, for heaven's *sake*!' she groaned, rummaging in it fruitlessly. 'The little …!'

And the next word was definitely not 'monkey'.

Chapter 4

'How on earth …?' Libby Moran said, getting up and joining Tyler at the front window. She was still rummaging in her bag, seemingly unable to accept the evidence of her own eyes.

'My thoughts exactly,' I said, pulling Tyler away. If it was attention Miller was after, then perhaps best if we didn't give him any.

'Did you leave them in the *ignition*?' Mike asked, unable to hide his astonishment.

She shook her head. 'No, it's a wireless ignition. 'But I put them in my bag … God, he must have got them out again while I was getting his stuff from the back seat.' She clapped a hand to her forehead. 'God, I'm so *stupid*!'

Miller was still gurning at us, sticking his tongue out and pressing it against the car window, so I suggested we all come away. He clearly wanted us out there so he could taunt us a little further. 'Why don't we leave him to it and get started on the paperwork?'

'Good idea,' she said, visibly trying to regain a sense of order. She took her seat again. I felt a bit sorry for her.

'Have you been his social worker for a long time?' I asked as we joined her.

She pulled out a bunch of papers from the large canvas bag. 'I'm afraid not.' She sounded apologetic, as if that was a personal failing. 'In fact, I don't know Miller very well at all. His previous social worker left two months ago – she's gone on maternity leave – and she'd only been with him for a year. I've only had two visits since I got assigned to him, to be honest. I don't think he likes me very much,' she finished.

Looking at her doleful expression, I wondered if the feeling might be mutual. 'Well, I imagine he's gone through social workers as regularly as he's gone through carers, so I expect he finds it difficult to build up meaningful relationships with any of them. I wouldn't take it personally,' I added reassuringly. 'It just is what it is.'

'I suppose,' she said, gesturing towards the paperwork she'd got out. 'And I'm afraid I've not had time to get everything together at such short notice, but what I do have is his last care plan, his last risk assessment and a minuscule paragraph about his education, such as it is. I should be able to pull some more bits together for you over the next few days, but in the meantime I'm afraid what I've got on him is all a bit sketchy.'

Plus the small matter of us not actually having the 'him' in question inside the house yet. 'That's absolutely fine,' I said. 'We'll just take him as we find him. On which note, do you think it might be worth Mike going out to try and entice him in?'

A Boy Without Hope

Libby looked at Mike with such hope in her eyes that I wondered what sort of stand-offs they'd already had. Forget forging a 'relationship'. I suspected she'd yet to even exert basic control. 'It could be worth a shot,' she said. 'Thank you. If you don't mind, that is.'

'Of course not,' Mike said. 'But let's give it another five minutes first, eh? I don't want to antagonise him on his first day with us if I don't have to. The kid might just decide to join us on his own accord.'

He was probably right. I leaned in to pick up the risk assessment document. 'Well, we may as well use the time to take a look through some of this,' I said, scanning the main points.

It was a document that I was very familiar with, though at first glance they can seem very confusing. They are all different, obviously, because every child in care is, but, structurally, they were all pretty much the same: a grid of rows and columns, each of which represents an area of risk that a child might either pose or be exposed to. It covers areas such as risk of absconding, of self-harming, of exploitation and so on. There are many different areas, too, so it can be quite a long list, and for each there is a column that goes on to explain the potential risk, and how it might play out in reality. This is then followed by a third column that explains how the risk is currently being managed – what is being done, and by whom, in order to minimise that risk. Then, finally, there's a column that is all about suggestions; ideas about what further actions could be taken.

Miller's risk assessment document was detailed, to say the least, and I noticed immediately that there was something about monitoring his medication, and checking that he actually swallowed his nightly tablets as he apparently had a tendency not to take them. I recognised them too. They were a brand of melatonin. 'So he's on medication to help him sleep then?' I asked Libby.

'Oops – glad you spotted that,' she said, delving once again into her capacious bag, and pulling out a plastic bag with a tablet box inside it. 'Don't want to land you with another load of problems, do I? Though there's only a few days' supply in there, I'm afraid. You'll need to get in touch with your GP to get some more organised. He takes the maximum adult dose.' She consulted her notes. 'Three per night, 7 p.m.'

Before I had the chance to point out that it was already a lot later than that, Tyler, who'd been keeping a discreet eye-out anyway, called us once again to the window.

'Well, that's ... *interesting*,' he said, as we all went to join him. 'Is it a boy? Is it a T-Rex? *You* decide ...', he added, laughing.

It appeared to be the latter. Some sort of dinosaur, at any rate. Miller, who was dark-haired, and slighter than I'd expected, was currently striding up and down on the grass outside the window, with his neck craned forward, his shoulders hunched, and his arms close to his chest with his hands bent and hooked to look like claws. 'What the hell is *that* about?' Tyler observed, transfixed.

'Language!' I reminded him, trying not to smile myself. It was really quite an impressive impersonation. 'Perhaps time to go out and rein him in?' I said to Mike.

'Literally, by the look of it,' he said, chuckling and shaking his head. 'I'll just go and dig out my patented dinosaur net, shall I?'

Libby, however, looked far from amused. And something else struck me – was she actually afraid of this child? 'I think you'd better,' she said. 'Before he gets even worse. The thing is with Miller is that he's all about control. Likes to think he's in charge. Pulling everyone's strings, you know? Definitely something to bear in mind.'

'Oh, we will,' I said, watching him strut back and forth, completely focused on his performance.

Or perhaps she was just embarrassed about having left her car keys in the car, with Miller – clearly a challenging child – still in there. Whatever the reason, she was certainly uncomfortable. 'Would you like a top-up?' I asked, nodding towards her empty mug.

'No thank you,' she said. 'I need to rush off as soon as I can, actually. I have to get across the county to pick my husband up, and I'm already late.'

I heard the front door go. 'Okay, well let's hope Mike can manage to get your car keys off Miller, then. And we're happy to settle him in ourselves if you need to get off. I'll have a read-through of what you've brought and hopefully you can dig up some more information for us tomorrow. I understand he's excluded from mainstream education. Any news on an alternative yet?'

Again, the poor woman shook her head. 'As far as I know, they've exhausted all the usual routes and there's nothing on the horizon at the moment. However, I do know the ELAC team are on the case.' (ELAC was education of looked-after children.) She turned back to the window. 'I do hope Mike can get him inside. Maybe I should go out, too, and just try to get my car keys? I could jump in and drive off then, couldn't I? I'm just thinking you'd have more of a chance of settling him if I weren't here. Like I said, I don't think he likes me.'

I had no answer to that, and I really didn't know what to think. But she was right about one thing: I did think she was better off hopping into her car the first chance she got and just leaving us to it. If control and attention were the driving forces behind Miller, then the fewer people there were around to witness his provocative behaviour, the better.

After telling Tyler to stay put, I followed Libby out of the front door. Miller was continuing his bizarre behaviour and was also making squealing noises, presumably for added effect. I raised my eyebrows at Mike, who'd as yet to make a move, though he'd obviously been talking to him. 'Come on, just chuck us those car keys, will you, mate,' he said, 'so that Libby can get her other bag out of her boot. It's stuff she's brought over for Casey and we need it. Our Tyler is waiting to show you his new PlayStation games as well. I think he's got a dinosaur one, come to think of it.'

Miller stopped his pacing and regarded us all suspiciously. Then, bizarrely, like something out of a comedy movie, he stomped up and roared at me. Right at my face. I could almost taste the warm sweetness of his breath. He then placed the car keys on the window ledge by the front door, and returned to making exaggerated steps across the lawn.

Libby had clearly spotted her moment. Quick as a flash, she snatched up her keys and darted to the car – there really was no other word for it. Not until she was inside it, and had locked it, did she lower the window. And then, I noted, by no more than an inch.

The engine sprang to life. 'I'll give you a call in the morning, Casey,' she shouted through the gap. 'And, Miller, you be good, okay? I'll see you soon.'

If we were aghast – which we were – Miller was galvanised. 'Noooooo!' he yelled, running full pelt towards the car, even kicking it as it moved out into the road. 'Get back here, you lying bitch!' he yelled. 'You fucking *liar*! Get *back* here!' He then bent down and snatched up a handful of gravel, and threw it hard at the car as it drove away. 'Get *back* here! I'm not staying!' he screamed up the street.

Everything became clear in an instant. I didn't know what had been said between them, but between Miller's fury, and the social worker's hasty escape, I suspected no firm agreement had been reached about him actually staying with us tonight. If so, why on earth hadn't she warned us?

Mike walked up to Miller's side, making the most of the disparity in their sizes. Mike was a big man – six foot three – and Miller was short and skinny. 'Come on, lad,' he said, standing close but being careful not to touch him. 'Forget social workers for tonight, hey? Let's go in and meet Tyler. Then you can have a look at your room before settling in for the night. How does that sound?'

Some kind of switch must have flipped because Miller then turned to look up at Mike. For a moment, I thought he was going to kick him as well, for good measure, but he didn't. He just inspected him, looking him up and down, calmly and minutely. Then he nodded, as if decided. 'Okay,' he said. 'Can I have a drink?'

Then he swivelled and trotted back down the front path towards me.

Miller was definitely on the small side for twelve. He looked more like ten, in fact, an impression already heightened by his strange, child-like antics and apparent lack of self-consciousness. And he had strange darting eyes that never quite looked directly into mine. His hair was dirty and matted, and in need of a good trim, and his clothes were far too small for him. Not for the first time – and I'd seen a lot of kids, from all sorts of backgrounds – I wondered how a child who had been in care for so many years could look so urchin-like and dishevelled.

'So, do I come in?' he asked me. There was a note of challenge in his voice.

'Of course,' I said, smiling, but still wary. I stood aside to let him pass.

'Up here, then?' he asked. Then headed straight up the stairs as if he owned the place. And was now, at least, in it. Mike shut the door firmly behind him.

* * *

The bedroom we had hastily prepared for Miller was the one opposite Tyler's. There was a double bed, the usual furniture of wardrobe, drawers and bedside table, and, as I'd promised, we had added a new television and a borrowed PlayStation, as well as a selection of books, and a bright green rug and matching cushions. I'd normally have chosen and bought a new duvet cover in a theme I thought the new child would like, as well as posters and a matching lightshade, but having had no time, I'd had to plump for something plain and pastel from the pile in the airing cupboard, and just hope it suited. Apparently it did.

'Yeah, I really like it,' Miller said, surprisingly brightly, once we'd trooped up the stairs after him, so he could make his inspection. I wondered how many homes he'd done this exact same thing in. 'So is it okay if I set up the PlayStation?' he asked me. 'And can I please have the code for the internet, too? I usually play online.'

I noted the 'please'. But looked quizzically at Tyler. Play online? I had no idea what that meant.

'It's just so he can join other players, Mum,' Tyler explained. 'Then you're not just playing alone, and you can get into tournaments and stuff.'

'Ah, I see,' I said. 'Fine. But first, love, find yourself some pyjamas out of your suitcase, then, once you're ready for bed, come down for your tablets and a drink, and I'll give you the password. You can't be on it for too long, though. It's already late. So just an hour then it goes off until tomorrow. Okay?'

'Okay,' Miller said, smiling up at me. 'Deal.' Then he sank down to his knees and began unzipping his case, humming to himself as if he didn't have a care in the world. A very different child to the one who'd screamed abuse and thrown gravel. Different too, to the Shakespearean-level dinosaur impersonator.

I wondered what other characters would emerge from beneath his shell.

Chapter 5

I woke up the following morning in an irritable, scratchy mood. Which is par for the course when you've barely slept a wink, obviously, but still unexpected, since the child currently residing in the spare room was apparently medicated to ensure that he *did* sleep.

But he hadn't. Though that likelihood wasn't obvious initially. In fact, after the fun and games in the front garden when he'd arrived, Miller had appeared to have accepted his new reality. I wasn't naïve about first impressions. I was too long in the tooth for that. But, for the moment, it seemed he was happy to play ball. He'd come down in his pyjamas (Lego Batman ones, which, unlike the clothes he'd had on, fitted), eaten his supper without complaint and taken his pills. Upon which, I had kept my promise, and given him the WiFi password, so he could spend an hour playing his game before going to sleep – something I had a hunch had no small bearing on his cheerful demeanour.

He was also happy for Tyler to accompany him back upstairs to set everything up. Though it was only a matter of some ten or fifteen minutes before Ty reappeared in the kitchen, arms spread wide in wonderment, shaking his head.

'I tell you what, Mum,' he said, 'that kid is some kind of computer genius. I mean, *seriously*. I have absolutely no idea what he's just done, but it's, like, something I've never seen before. He's opened up all kinds of new levels – levels I never knew even *existed*. It's like he's a hacker or something, I swear!'

I had several good reasons to be wary of what kids could get up to on computers these days, not least the teenager we'd most recently cared for, Keeley. It still concerned me that she'd been able to run a whole cottage industry – and of a kind that still made me blanche when I thought of it – out of nothing more than the smartphone in her bedroom.

Smartphones, generally, were becoming the bane of our working lives. As foster carers, we had always had a plethora of 'training' documents, one of which was obviously about online safety. But in recent years, recognising that a document produced a decade ago no longer applied in the fast-moving virtual world, we'd been expected to attend regular sessions to make good the lack. In truth, however, we had little hope of keeping up. The advice was sound enough: to teach children about how to stay safe online, to not give out personal information, to only accept 'friends' that they knew in the real world and to put parental controls on any device used by younger children. But modern kids are extremely savvy, and Miller was obviously no exception. They had ways and means to counteract many of the filters we put in place.

But by far the biggest problem today is that most kids of around the age of twelve, and often younger, already have their own smartphones when they come to us. Which they naturally keep private, even if they have nothing to hide, and if the phone belongs to them we have no legal right to remove them. So, both legally and practically, we have our hands tied. It's a growing problem, and one social services are still struggling to cope with.

So I understood exactly what Tyler meant. You were a fool if you didn't understand just how many streets children were ahead of you when it came to the virtual world these days. Whereas even being 'online' was an alien concept for those of us who grew up in the last century (and a science we had to learn, and keep learning), kids nowadays were around computers and tablets almost from birth; what was often extremely taxing for fifty-somethings like me and Mike was as natural to modern kids as breathing. It truly was a whole new world, and a changing one too – that this kid was twelve and apparently already knew more than a sixteen-year-old said it all.

I patted Tyler reassuringly. 'Well at least we've discovered two things that he appears to like,' I pointed out. 'Gaming and dinosaurs. So that's a positive, isn't it? And who knows – perhaps him being able to teach you a thing or two about computers will be a great way to break the ice between you.'

'Hmm,' he said, looking decidedly unconvinced. 'I mean, I know he's clever and that, but I'm not sure we're going to have much in common. Mum, he freaks me out a bit to be honest. He's *weird*.'

'Early days, love,' I said, patting him again. 'Early days.'

But clearly not early nights. Not without a battle of wills. When I popped back upstairs to let Miller know his hour was over, he didn't even seem to hear me. He certainly didn't take his eyes off the screen, or stop his thumbs flying across the control pad. 'Ten more minutes,' he said finally, when I asked him a second time. 'I need to get these guys out of this warehouse first.'

I digested this, dithered briefly, but then shook my head. Yes this was his first night, but, knowing what I knew about his control issues, I felt it best that we start as we meant to go on. 'No, Miller, I'm afraid you'll have to pause it, or whatever it is you need to do, and finish it off in the morning. I told you we had a cut-off time, and this is it.'

Miller dragged his eyes from the screen long enough to look at me in astonishment and, if I wasn't mistaken, contempt. 'You can't just *pause* it!' he said, still tapping furiously on the control pad. 'That's not how it works. I need notice. If you didn't want me to have ten minutes at the end, then you should have given me ten minutes' notice. Don't you know *anything*?'

I hadn't noticed Mike follow me up, but he now appeared in the bedroom doorway. 'Okay, lad,' he said, before I could. 'I'm sure you've lived in enough houses to realise that each family has their own rules. In the morning we can go over our house rules with you, but for now the one that matters is that electronics go off at bedtime.' A short pause. 'So go on, do as Casey says. Switch it off, please.'

Miller continued to tap away, and this time he didn't look up. 'And I suppose bedtime is just whenever you say it is, right? And that's because *you're* a grown-up and *I'm* a kid. Nothing to do with it being correct or anything. Anyway, I only need five minutes now, so it's not like the end of the world, is it?'

There was no aggression in his tone. Just an invitation to keep the discussion going. Where no discussion should be happening in the first place. I knew a stalling tactic when I saw one.

But Mike wasn't in the mood to play games, so he didn't answer. Simply took two strides and switched the TV off at the plug socket.

'Why did you do that?' Miller yelled. 'You complete *idiot*! Now I've lost everything!'

'Rule two,' Mike added mildly, 'is that we do not speak to each other like that in this house. We don't scream and yell and we certainly don't call people idiots. Now I strongly suggest you get yourself into bed. I will then put the television back on for you – quietly – but *not* the console. And you will try to get some sleep. And then we will start afresh in the morning.'

Which seemed to be the end of it, even if he was cross about it, which he was – throwing the controller down, jumping into bed and burrowing under the duvet, huffing noisily as he rolled himself across the bed to face the wall. Which we took to be a signal for us to leave, so we did.

And silence reigned then, and continued to, when we went to bed ourselves, both agreeing that first nights were, more often than not, difficult. That we'd all sleep on it. Regroup. That tomorrow was another day.

But a day that would be a very long time coming.

It was just before two when I was awoken by the sound of banging. And as I sluggishly dragged myself from sleep into alert mode I soon worked out it was coming from Miller's room. I lifted the duvet back and padded across the landing to investigate, only to find he was bouncing up and down on his bed, fully upright, as if practising for a trampoline tournament. He giggled like a toddler when he saw me.

'What on earth are you doing?' I asked him.

He grinned at me. 'I'm bouncing.'

'I can see that,' I said. 'But, love, it's two in the morning. Come on, back into bed and go to sleep.'

'I can't sleep,' he said. He continued to bounce.

'Well, you have to try,' I said, reaching a hand out to stop him. 'Come on, into bed, before you wake the whole house up.'

'But I can't sleep,' he whined, as I took hold of his wrist.

'But you have to,' I told him, taking his other wrist and stilling him. 'Everyone needs to sleep.'

'I don't,' he said.

'Well, in that case, you must at least get into bed, and be still now. I can't have you making all this noise. It's the middle of the night.'

'*Bor*ing,' he said, but he didn't try to fight me. Simply whumped down on the bed, harrumphed and let me straighten the covers over him. His eyes gleamed in the darkness. 'I won't sleep. I *don't* sleep.'

'Then stay awake. But stay *there*,' I said firmly.

And, to my surprise, he did as he was told. Well, for an hour, at least. I was woken again at 3 a.m. – this time by a different noise, which turned out to be the sound of a tennis ball being thrown repeatedly against his bedroom wall.

He was kneeling on his rug now, his suitcase open at the side of him, throwing the ball and catching it, putting me in mind of that iconic scene in *The Great Escape*. But this was no German camp and he was no prisoner of war.

'Miller, what on earth are you doing?' I asked exasperated, eyeing the case and its spewing contents. What other diversions did he have in his box of tricks, I wondered?

'I *told* you,' he said. "I don't sleep. Not ever. So I have to find stuff to do because I get so *bored*.'

I sat down on the edge of the bed, still fuzzy with sleep myself. He, in contrast, couldn't have looked more wide awake. 'Well, I'm sorry, love,' I said. 'But the rest of us *do* sleep.' I pointed towards the tennis ball, which he was now throwing into the air and catching. 'And you doing that is keeping us all awake. So if you really can't sleep – and I know it's hard when you're in a place you're not used to – then you'll have to find something more quiet to do. How about reading?' I nodded towards the books I'd put on top of the chest of drawers. 'There's some Harry Potter books, and a couple of David Walliams ones too. D'you like David Walliams?'

'Ish,' he said. 'I'm not really fussed about reading. I'd rather watch *Diners, Drive-Ins and Dives*. But I can't get it on that telly,' he added scathingly. 'It needs tuning into the internet. But it's not.'

I looked across at the TV, which couldn't have been more than a year old. What? What did 'tuning the TV into the internet' mean? Every time I thought I was just about up to date with technology, some new thing came along to confound me all over again. I made a mental note to ask Tyler what that meant in the morning.

I stood up then, and plumped his pillows, then beckoned him to get back into bed. 'Well, I'll get Mike to look at it tomorrow,' I said. 'But for now, Miller, I'm afraid it has to be reading or nothing. I need you to be very quiet so that I can get a couple of hours' sleep.'

'Ok-ayyy,' he said, tossing the tennis ball back into the suitcase, and, again, to my surprise, meekly doing as he was told.

And again, at four, when I had to go in and tell him to stop singing 'Bohemian Rhapsody', and then at five, when I heard him fiddling about in the bathroom. 'Told you I don't sleep,' he pointed out as I chivvied him back to bed a fourth time.

But once again, he let me lead him back to bed without arguing and, by six thirty, when the scent of coffee roused me reluctantly from my slumbers he was, of course, sleeping like a baby.

'You should have woken me up,' Mike said, when I regaled him with the extent of my nocturnal activities. 'I'd have gone in to have another word with him.'

I reached for the coffee in much the same way as a drowning man would grab a passing lifebelt. 'I'm not sure

47

it would have done any good, love,' I told him. 'It's almost like his body clock's set to nocturnal. I don't know about Lego Batman – he's like a flipping bat! He wasn't even tired. Not remotely. He was buzzing. So much for the sleeping pills he's been taking.'

'But a challenging day for him, don't forget. Perhaps he was just over-stimulated.'

'I wish I thought that, love, but I don't. I got this impression that last night was pretty much as per. And with him not going to school, you can see how that might happen. And what's the point of him popping pills if they're not helping? It's clearly something we're going to have to address as a matter of urgency. Direct with the GP if need be.'

And his former carers, for that matter. Had this been true for them too? If so, it was a habit that needed breaking, and fast.

For the time being though, I was too tired to start, so once Mike went to work, and Tyler headed off to school, I did some housework, drank coffee and fired off a couple of emails, in the hopes of at least getting some sort of medical history. And all the while, our 'non-sleeping' nocturnal house guest slept on.

I also decided to try and speak to Miller's previous foster carer, Jenny, to get a better sense of his routines and habits. No, he'd not been there long, but, from their point of view, anyway, clearly more than long enough. Was it the lack of sleep that had pushed them to the brink with him?

After flipping through the little paperwork I had, I found her number and punched it into my mobile. If Miller did come downstairs unexpectedly, I could easily take myself off into the back garden. And perhaps take him out there later, too, in an attempt to tire him out.

'Oh, hello!' Jenny said. She sounded happy. Like a woman, it occurred to me, who'd had a decent night's sleep. 'I would have called you but I was going to give it until tomorrow so you weren't inundated with endless calls,' she said. 'I know what it's like when you have a new placement.'

I almost laughed. Did we even work for the same fostering agency, I wondered? When I had kids delivered, all I ever seemed to be inundated with was a big, noisy silence – the parcel, and the problem, passed on. 'I haven't heard from anyone,' I told her. 'That's why I was calling. He's been up half the night. Is he always like this? I was hoping you might have a few tips for me.'

'Ah,' Jenny said. And it was a very telling 'ah'. 'I wish you all the best with that, I really do.'

My heart sank to hear my fears so swiftly confirmed. 'So it's not a one-off, then? I was hoping it might be just a first-night thing.'

'Hmm,' she said. 'Sorry. I wish I could tell you it was but, to be honest, we didn't have an unbroken night the whole time he was with us. It's one of the main reasons we had to let him go. He's hard enough to cope with at the best of times, but when you aren't getting any sleep … And with the hours my husband works … well ...' She sighed. 'Look, I'm sorry to be the bearer of bad news, but the whole thing's been a bit of a nightmare, if I'm honest. No point me sugar-coating it, is there? I'm sure Libby's already

49

told you, bless her. I mean, we've had our fair share of challenging kids, some of them long term, as I'm sure you have. But this one …'

'So it's not *just* the sleeping …'

It was hardly a question, as I already knew the answer.

'No, it wasn't just the sleeping. If it had been …' Another pause. Despite what she'd just said, I could sense she was reluctant to be *too* candid. As would I have been in her shoes, since it was another carer she was talking to – and, in this case, the one to whom the baton had now been passed. 'Well, perhaps we could have coped better if he *had* slept,' she said eventually. 'But the truth is that he's sneaky. Manipulative. And clever. You've probably already noticed that yourself. He's also methodical. And ruthless – knows exactly how to push your buttons. Though did Libby tell you? After all that – after pushing us *way* beyond our limits – he carried on as if leaving us was the end of the world. So much crying and begging and refusing to go. She literally had to drag him away. And only then because we promised he could come back and stay with us on respite from time to time. That was a lie,' she finished, bluntly. 'I'm sorry to tell you that, but it's true. But we didn't know how else to get –' She stopped abruptly. Had she been about to say 'rid of him'?

'Well, thanks for filling me in,' I told her. 'I appreciate your honesty. I'm going in blind here, pretty much, and forewarned is forearmed.'

Though it was worrying, to say the least, that she *had* been so candid. That she was talking about him as if he was a little demon, not a child; an evil force that she was only too glad to have expunged from her life. 'I tell you what,' she said. 'Let me gather my thoughts and set everything down in an email. You know, anything that comes to me that I think you need to know.' Then she laughed – actually laughed. 'So expect a long email! Seriously, and this is strictly between you and me, if you value your sanity don't agree to take on this kid lightly.'

'Oh, don't worry,' I said. And I meant it. 'I won't.'

Miller obviously couldn't know it, but his timing was impeccable. Because it was only moments after I'd rung off that he appeared in the kitchen doorway. He was tousle-haired, sleepy-eyed, barefoot and shyly smiling. And a great wave of guilt mushroomed up in me from nowhere. Because no child was a demon. He was just a child who *had* demons. If I refused to try and help him how could I look myself in the eye?

Chapter 6

Taking on a new child, particularly when that child has multiple issues and challenges, is almost always a bit full-on for the first couple of weeks, and can be intense in a variety of ways. There is invariably a measure of drama, and very often there are floods of tears. There can also be outbreaks of unexpected violence, meaning you sometimes feel more like a zoo-keeper than a carer, trying to fend off, feed and socialise a distressed, out-of-control child.

Miller, however, did not seem to fit any recognisable mould. Here was a lad whose fearsome reputation had arrived before him. A child variously described as a nightmare, as sneaky, as manipulative and ruthless, yet, apart from the outburst when Libby Moran had left him, he'd done nothing to provide evidence that any of that was true. Yes, he'd been chippy about the gaming, and a little petulant about rules, but other than that he'd presented no notable challenges. Yes, he'd push at the boundaries, but once he established they were firm, he didn't kick off – he just meekly accepted them.

So was there a bigger game being played here? Was he sounding us out just as we were doing with him? Apart from the sleep situation, which hadn't yet improved, I was struggling to understand just why he'd been flagged up as such a challenge.

The only pressing problem – and 'pressing' was unquestionably the word for it – was that three days had now passed and I'd not left the house, and the walls felt as if they were closing in on me.

It wouldn't have been quite so bad if I'd at least had some outside input, but no email had arrived yet from Jenny, and I'd not heard anything else from Libby either. The only call I'd received had been from Christine, who'd called the previous afternoon and, when I told her I'd been given nothing further from social services, told me she was going to 'kick some butt', and promptly rang off again.

It was now lunchtime – almost a full twenty-four hours later – and I was still waiting to hear from her. Or anyone, for that matter. In the meantime, we'd fallen into a less than ideal routine of disturbed nights, as I tried in vain to get him to either sleep or read quietly, and him sleeping in till gone eleven.

So it was odds-on that the melatonin wasn't working. Either that, or the dosage or timing was wrong, and, since Miller was on an adult dose, experience told me it was more likely a problem with the timing. As it stood, he was supposed to take them at 7 p.m., the idea being that, at around ten, he would simply 'drift off'. Which he wasn't.

But why the three-hour gap anyway? Would it really take that long to work? Was he simply taking it too early in the evening? I'd looked after a child who'd been prescribed melatonin a few years back, Olivia, and though she'd been younger I had a hunch that the principle held true; she'd take the pill at bedtime and, for the most part, would be asleep fifteen minutes later. Should I hold off giving Miller his three till it was time to go to sleep? Perhaps having it too early made it easier for his body to resist it – something I would need to discuss further with my GP.

For now, though, I decided, it was time to stop the rot. Yes, he was a serial absconder, but I'd managed my fair share of those, and even if taking him out meant risking him doing so, there was no way he could remain shut up in a house indefinitely. I needed to get him out, not least because it wasn't rocket science that, everything else notwithstanding, some physical exercise would obviously aid sleep. He might manage to escape from me – from what I already knew, it was odds-on he would try – but I was reassured by what also I'd read and heard about him *always* coming back again and, in the absence of anyone else stepping in to either sit with him or accompany me, I was going out and he was coming with me, end of.

To that end, I'd already told him it was too late for breakfast, and that, today, we were going to sit down and have lunch together before him getting bathed and dressed, and going into town.

I'd made pasta, which he apparently liked, and set the kitchen table. 'It's almost ready, Miller!' I called up the stairs. 'Come on down, love.'

As I was beginning to realise was his instinctive way, he immediately responded to the request. Not with 'I'm coming', however, but with his own counter-order. Just as he'd done with the games console the first night we'd had him, he seemed incapable of responding to any request for action without adding several minutes before he did it. In this case, apparently, he required three.

This, in itself, wasn't that unusual. Kids who are insecure because of abuse or neglect – and often both – will often attempt to exert control on their surroundings via time, needing to know what's happening, when it's happening, and needing constant reassurance that it actually *will* happen. This seemed different, though. It was almost as if he had a built-in resistance to doing anything without imposing his own timeframe on it. I suspected that if I told him there was a giant Easter egg downstairs waiting for him, he'd practise the same curious delaying tactic before he took it. It seemed almost knee-jerk, and I wondered if this was what Libby meant when she'd commented that he needed control. It didn't matter what was asked of him – clean your teeth, go to bed, brush your hair, or whatever. He would only do it after a further few minutes had passed, the number of which *he* decided.

I'd tried to be wily, saying things like 'breakfast will be ready in three minutes', but, faced with that, it was almost as if he turned into an android, for whom it simply 'did not compute'. He'd either shrug or mumble, or not respond at all. Then duly appear, not in three minutes, but in five.

I wasn't stupid. I knew I had two choices in how to deal with it. I either accepted this oddity, and planned things accordingly, or tried to address it by tackling it head on, which would, of course, lead to endless confrontations, at least in the short term. But this was no easy choice till I knew what I was dealing with. If he genuinely had some kind of timekeeping phobia, then it would do him no good if I bulldozed straight in and created even more disorder in his already insecure world. If, however, it was simply a long-ingrained control thing, honed over years of manipulating various carers, then the sooner I tackled it the better. Quite apart from my own desire to escape the proverbial four walls, I knew, both as a mum and an employee – as a foster carer – that I wouldn't be living up to my responsibilities if I simply allowed him to fester in his room, surfing the web. But without the bigger picture – all those long years of records I could pore over – I didn't yet feel able to make the call. I simply didn't know him well enough.

Today, though, other concerns over his welfare took precedence. We were down to the last of the melatonin Libby had brought for him, so, one way or another, a visit to the doctor had to happen – as well as the necessary phone call to discuss it, so I could pick up a prescription. And with Mike at work, and my reluctance to rope in poor Tyler, that was happening this afternoon, come what may.

Miller shuffled into the kitchen just as I was dishing up two bowls of pasta. 'So, after lunch, love,' I told him as I set them on the table, 'I'd like you to get dressed, as I said earlier, because the two of us are going out. Remember?'

He slid into his seat and picked his fork up, his gaze flickering intermittently towards me. Though it was almost impossible to catch his eye for any length of time and I wondered if there had been discussions about autism in his records. Struggling to make eye contact was common for kids on the spectrum.

'Going where?' he asked. 'It might be somewhere I don't want to go.'

'To pick up a prescription for your pills,' I said. 'And then …' I shrugged. 'Who knows? It's a beautiful day. Perhaps the park?'

'But I feel sick,' he said immediately. The response seemed automatic. And this despite the speed with which he was shovelling pasta into his mouth. 'So I can't go out. It'll make me feel sicker.'

I sat and watched him eat, waiting for him to recognise the absurdity of what he was saying. But he didn't – or didn't appear to. He just polished the lot off. All but licked the bowl out, in fact. '*What*?' he said, as he raised his head finally and caught me smiling at him.

'Enjoy that?' I asked him mildly, nodding my head towards the empty bowl, and inviting him to get the point I was making.

But bright though he obviously was, he didn't. But perhaps that was intentional. I stood up and reached across for his bowl. 'Half an hour.' I told him. 'Then it's bath, dress and out, okay?'

He pushed his chair back, rolled his eyes at me and headed back upstairs. I didn't push it, but I did need to decide how to play it. Stern adult mode? Pleading mode? Negotiation-for-a-reward mode? I had a selection of ways to approach the problem. I just had to decide which one to try.

Because of his many problems – both behavioural and medical – Miller was under a consultant who specialised in sleep disorders, which meant that though I knew my GP would be happy to take him as a patient, he would be unable to prescribe his current medication without the surgery first contacting the doctor in question and him confirming that it was okay to do so. In the longer term I'd doubtless be taking Miller in to see him, but, for the moment, it was more a case of all the boxes being ticked so that I could have a new supply of the apparently precious pills – even though they seemed to be doing precisely nothing.

I'd just finished speaking to the surgery, who'd confirmed the fax had come through okay, when my mobile trilled again. It was Libby Moran.

Finally.

'So, how's the little monkey been, then?' she chirruped, putting the lie to what I'd seen with my own eyes when they'd arrived: that she didn't see him as a little monkey at all.

There was no point in being anything other than frank. 'Well, to be perfectly honest, I'm struggling to work out how best to look after him,' I told her. 'I know so little about him, and nothing else seems to be forthcoming, either. It's like I'm trying to feel my way in the dark. Plus, right now, I can't even get out of the house.'

'I know, I know,' Libby replied in what I imagined was meant to be a soothing tone. 'That's precisely why I'm phoning you. To check how things are going, but also to tell you that I'm about to send you an email with some attachments. It's mostly bits and bobs of things I've managed to get hold of, but I wanted to highlight a couple of things before they land in your inbox, because I feel they need a bit of clarification.'

This was an oddity. Wouldn't the record for Miller speak for itself? Why would his official history need clarification? If it did – and she clearly thought so – why not just amend the record before sending? That said, I could probably answer my own question. Because experience had long taught me that 'facts', taken out of context, could be misread. Perhaps that was the case here; perhaps she'd done some digging and decided time was of the essence. Better to put me in the picture first, and amend the record later.

'What sorts of things?' I asked her.

'Just a couple of things I wanted to flag up, really,' she said. She was obviously in her office. I could hear paper being moved around, the clack and clatter of people typing. Other people. What I wouldn't give for spending time with some right now. 'Firstly,' she went on, 'the report from a particular foster carer, a Mrs Lyndsay Taylor. She tells of an incident – a really horrible incident actually – where Miller has killed a pet rabbit with a rake …'

Oh, great. 'Libby,' I interrupted. 'How old was he when he did this?'

'He was nine,' she said. 'But the thing is, the report just states exactly that, that the poor boy killed a family pet, and how he did it, but after double checking this morning, I found that the full story wasn't there. I tracked Mrs Taylor down and she admitted that Miller had already been bitten twice by the rabbit. And on that particular day, he'd unlatched the cage and it had leapt out, scaring him half to death. He'd snatched the rake up in fear – she's sure on this point – and started to swing it. And unfortunately, he hit the rabbit, and one of the spikey things went into it. And the injury was so severe that they had to put it down.'

Well, that makes it all so much better then, I thought. *Not.* But I also knew how instinctive it could be for damaged kids to lash out first and think later. It was often all they knew. It was exactly how it had been with Tyler, for that matter – pushed to the brink and grabbing the first thing to hand. So it was important not to judge without first establishing context. And a good sign that she'd taken the trouble to find out a little more about it. She was obviously conscientious and that could only be a good thing. 'Right, I'll bear that in mind when I read your email,' I said. 'And the other thing?'

'Just about his past, and how he came into care. There's a lot to read on that, and I really recommend that you do. It's a shocking read – worse than I expected, to be honest – but it's also really illuminating.'

'Thanks,' I said. 'I'll look forward to getting my teeth into that.' Which then struck me as not quite the best way to put it, given what she'd just told me about the rake. 'What about school?' I hurried on. 'Any news there? I just think the sooner we get him back into education the better. The rate we're going, I wouldn't be surprised to go upstairs and find him gone – sucked into one of his flipping computer games.'

She laughed. 'I hear what you're saying. But, tentatively, that's a yes. ELAC have apparently found a provision, and you should be getting a call later to let you know what's been arranged. So that's good news, isn't it?' she finished brightly. She sounded pleased with herself. And she'd a right to. Though I was still feeling a bit unsupported with my 'little monkey', at least we had some progress at last.

I thanked her, and clocking the time – it was fast becoming a habit – headed to the foot of the stairs to do battle. And in the real world as opposed to the virtual. But no sooner had I opened my mouth to give him his three-minute warning, than I heard, 'Shit, shit, shit, SHIT!' from upstairs.

'Miller!' I called up. 'Please don't use that language in this house. And you have three minutes left to play your game, so finish up, okay?'

I waited for a reply but all I could hear was the din from the PlayStation. I tried again, 'Miller! Answer me, please!'

'*God*!' came the reply. 'What is it *now*? I'm busy!'

I took a deep breath. *Start as you mean to go on, Casey.* I pushed my sleeves up, and thundered up the steps to his room and, since the door was wide open, I went in.

He was cross-legged on the floor, in front of the TV screen, with his back to me. 'Miller, I told you. We have to go out. We *are* going out. Now put down the controller and get yourself dressed. Otherwise, I'll have to switch off the internet.'

There was a heartbeat of silence and stillness. Clearly, though he affected not to, he *was* listening to me. And, as a consequence, to my surprise, he didn't bother giving me more lip. Simply threw down the controller, scrabbled to his feet and launched himself at his unmade bed, where he burrowed under the duvet and rolled himself up, Swiss-roll style. Completely, from head to foot. He then started to howl – not like a child would, but like a wolf. 'Ahhhooooooo! Ahhhoooooooooo!'

It was, as Tyler might put it, interesting. Quite unlike anything I'd heard before. I'd heard all kinds of noises coming out of kids' mouths over the years, but this one definitely had an unusual repertoire. And, since he showed no sign of stopping – perhaps he was waiting for a reaction? – I crossed the room and placed a hand on the squirming mound. 'Stop being silly, love,' I told him. 'Just come out from under there and get dressed, please. It's such a lovely day out there, and you need some fresh air.'

He twisted away from me, with another howl. This time one of pure anguish. 'Nope!' he shouted. 'Nope, nope, nope, NOPE!'

He sounded more like a toddler having a tantrum than a twelve-year-old, but while a part of me still felt an almost overwhelming urge to grab one side of the duvet and simply unroll him, I reminded myself that this wasn't a normal twelve-year-old. This was a kid with a whole lorry load of deep-seated problems, most of which I hadn't the first clue about beyond the various prophesies of doom that came with them. And who now appeared to be having a major meltdown. Cursing myself for agreeing to take him without first demanding the tools to enable me to understand him, let alone help him, I took another deep breath and quietly walked out of the room – time out for both of us, while I read Libby's email.

I was halfway down the stairs when I heard the sound of laughter. Then his voice, light and calm, came floating down the stairs.

'Miller, one,' he called out. 'Hah! Casey, nil.'

Ah, I thought. So *that* was how it was going to be.

Chapter 7

Difficult to like. Those had been John's words, and as I headed back downstairs again they nagged at me. I'd fostered many a child who had fitted that description – it sometimes felt as if it went with the territory. Kids who'd been in care for a long time often fell into that category, simply because they so often displayed long-entrenched behaviours that would challenge the patience of a saint. This was almost always because they had profound psychological problems, and sometimes, in addition, because they'd created a mental 'loop' – bad behaviour got them attention, so it was self-reinforcing, and, in addition, because that attention was negative in nature, it then confirmed their highly negative sense of self. This led to more self-loathing, and, even if it was subconscious, it almost invariably led more bad behaviour.

Breaking the cycle, therefore, was, in part, about re-programming a child's ability to control themselves – getting them to realise, through the use of a strict regime of consequences and rewards, that they had choices in how they handled a situation, earning points for good behaviours (obviously geared to their age and relative maturity) and losing privileges when they fell short of what had previously been agreed.

It was the cornerstone of the programme Mike and I had been trained to deliver, and once negotiated and agreed upon, usually as soon as practical at the start of a new placement, it was simply a question of sticking to it, and rigidly. I've said it a million times but it wasn't exactly rocket science. Basically, you did your homework, so you had an idea of what a child liked to do. Then, based on that, you'd decide what rewards were suitable reinforcements to offer in exchange for good behaviour and completed tasks.

A child might want a cinema visit, for example, or a weekly trip to the leisure centre. Or they may enjoy having a particular takeaway meal, or like a certain weekly comic or magazine. In order to get these things they would have to earn points for doing chores, or getting off to school on time, or keeping their rooms clean.

But this all assumed I had an idea of what 'inducements' might work for Miller, and since all I knew for sure was that he liked to park himself in front of a computer game 24/7, it would require a huge upheaval to adopt a new regime where his access to that reward became something he'd need to earn rather than assume was his right. In short, I badly needed to know what I was dealing with, and, ideally, before the pattern set in. Three days was one thing – a period of acclimatisation was obviously necessary – but more than that and we would be making rods for our own backs.

So when I opened my laptop and saw Libby's email had arrived, I decided to leave Miller to bask in his 'one–nil victory' for the moment, and try to find out what else made him tick.

The body of the email told me little. It was really just a bullet-pointed summary of the dozen or so attachments that ran like a blue ribbon along the top of it. But at least there was plenty for me to read. So I plunged straight on in, clicking on and opening the most obvious. The one marked 'Initial Care Plan Reports'.

As the name suggests, this was the first report, logged when he'd entered the system, which, as John had said, had been almost seven years ago. So Miller would have been four or five. Only just school age. Still a baby. And if I knew anything about warming to a 'difficult to like' child, it was that it helped to be mindful of the journey they'd been on, and to remember the child they might have become, had their circumstances, and their life chances, been different.

The report had been written up by the first social worker on the scene – presumably whoever was on call with the emergency duty team. It was a simple Word document, dated, but with no other details in terms of time and location; clearly just the notes they'd written up after attending the scene.

The day that changed one little boy's life forever. I scrolled down and got stuck in. The report began:

Having received numerous phone calls from passing motorists, two police officers drove to where it had been reported that a young boy was playing dangerously close to a railway line. It had also been reported that he was dressed in nothing more than a nappy, and people were obviously very fearful about his welfare.

When the officers arrived, it was to find the child – who'd presumably slipped underneath a fence – was about fifteen metres below them, down an embankment. Initially, though he saw them, he didn't respond to their calls, so, given the danger the child was in, the female officer climbed part of the way down to the embankment, and eventually persuaded the child to climb up and join her. He still didn't speak, answering questions with unintelligible sound and gestures, and appeared to be agitated and afraid.

As the child was reluctant to take the officer's hand, the other PC went down to help, but when the male officer attempted to grab him to pull him up to safety, he began hitting himself repeatedly on the side of the head, and kicking out when they tried to restrain him.

He then ran away along the embankment, managing to evade both officers, to a hole in the fence some way down the line, which led to the rear garden of what appeared to be the only property in what was a mostly rural area: a dilapidated and abandoned-looking detached house. Both officers followed, catching up as the child began banging on a rear door, and were surprised to hear adult voices shouting from within.

Coming up alongside the boy, who was still banging repeatedly on the door, the male officer knocked as well, and the door was then opened by a man who appeared to be in his mid- or late fifties. The man grabbed the child roughly and ordered him inside then demanded to know what the officers wanted.

The police officers explained that they needed to go inside and, despite the male initially trying to shut the door, and then barring the entrance, eventually succeeded in persuading the male that they needed to go into the house.

They described the scene as being 'filthy and chaotic'. It appears the family (a 25-year-old female, a 58-year-old male, and the young boy, called Miller, who was four) were all living in something resembling a large conservatory, at the rear of the property. The house itself was derelict and abandoned. There were faeces covering the floor, dirty clothes lying everywhere, and takeaway cartons littered on every horizontal surface. There were also overflowing ashtrays and alcohol bottles everywhere.

The female officer noticed the child had now disappeared and asked the female where he had gone. She replied with 'to bed' so the officer asked her where, and was led into another area – a former utility room, which also housed a toilet and wash basin. There were no utilities – just a single mattress along the back wall, with various coats, curtains and other clothing items strewn across it. The boy was apparently huddled beneath all of this.

The woman, who seemed inebriated and/or under the influence of drugs, seemed to already understand that the officers would want to remove the child. 'If you come to take him,' she said, 'you'll need a few nappies. The filthy little savage still shits himself.'

She apparently laughed as she said this and then picked up a half-pack of nappies and tried to hand them to the officer. Having established that the adults were the boy's parents, the male officer explained that he was phoning a social worker, as the living conditions were clearly unsuitable for a young child.

'Fuck the social workers, just take him now,' the father told him. 'We're sick of looking after him. Look at him, he's a simpleton. Four years old and he can't even talk.'

The boy had by now emerged from under the pile of coats, looking distressed and afraid. The mother laughed at him. 'Don't you think he looks like an alien?' she asked, pointing at the child. 'You'll have to get the social to buy him some clothes because we can't find his stuff since we moved.'

The boy began to cry then, leading the officers to suspect that, though he'd yet to say anything intelligible himself, he understood exactly what was being discussed.

* * *

I turned my head upwards, as though I might be able to see Miller through the ceiling, and wondered how much of the memory of that day – and those cruel, cruel words – still burned brightly in his head. He'd been four. He was twelve now. I was almost certain he remembered every last awful thing said. Either that, or he had worked hard to try and erase them from his memory; buried them, in other words. Which was not always emotionally healthy.

I returned to my reading. The social worker herself was on the scene twenty minutes later, by which time the female officer had found something for Miller to wear. He'd cried and whimpered continually, but his parents, who she'd also noted seemed under the influence of some sort of drug, apparently took no notice. They just sat passively smoking on the rattan sofa in the conservatory, leaving the female officer to dress him. The report continued:

I arrived at the house, and took in the squalid conditions, as the officers explained where and how they'd found the boy, and such information as they'd been able to establish up to that point. I then explained to the parents that we'd be taking the child into temporary foster care, until a decision was taken by the courts regarding a full-time care order. Neither objected. As had already been conveyed to me by the police officers, they made it clear they didn't want to keep him anyway.

Sobbing convulsively now, Miller allowed me to carry him out to my car, but only after he had rummaged through some rubbish on the floor to pick up a small toy train. It had no wheels, and almost all the paintwork had been chipped away, but it was clearly important to the boy. There seemed to be no suitable footwear for him, bar a pair of adult socks, so carrying him was more necessity than anything. Again, he allowed me to do this, clinging on to my jacket, and once I placed him in the back of my car, alongside the female officer, he continued to sob as we followed the squad car to the station.

Further reports will follow once an emergency placement has been identified.

* * *

I leaned back in the dining chair and put my reading glasses on my head. I was well used to reading such reports because, in one form or other, they came with every child we cared for.

But they never failed to move me, despite the clinical, emotionless way in which they were written. Which, of course, they had to be. They were designed for one purpose only – to record the facts. But the very lack of emotion, or comment, or judgement (and it was important that there weren't any), was precisely what made them so difficult to read, as it brought it home that such tragedies, abhorrent as they were, filled files and folders the length of the land; Miller had at this point become a 'case'. A numbered statistic. And you didn't need to be given to extremes of emotion to know just how much damage had already been done to him. Damage that would almost certainly prove hard to heal. It didn't matter how much money was thrown at the problem (and there was precious little of that around anyway), or how much time and loving care was devoted to trying to help kids like Miller, some of the scars sustained by children such as him would never fully heal.

So it was something of a relief, just as I was about to open to the next report, to hear the front door open and a familiar voice.

'Only me and Dee Dee!' It was Kieron's.

My son and my gorgeous youngest grandchild couldn't have been a more welcome diversion at that moment, so I hurried out into the hall and scooped up my little granddaughter. 'So what's all this about?' I asked her. 'Why aren't you at school? And, more to the point,' I asked Kieron, 'why aren't you at work, love?

'Had to step up to the plate,' he said, shrugging off his jacket. 'Glands are up,' he said, nodding towards Dee Dee, who was busy trying to show me the inside of her mouth.

'And she's been complaining of a sore throat so we thought best to keep her off.'

Though no such concerns about her showering her poor nanna with germs, obviously. But that, of course, was a given.

I smiled. 'And I'm sure you were quick to sacrifice yourself so that Lauren didn't have to, my brave little soldier.'

He grinned at me as he followed us into the kitchen. 'Okay, I admit it, I did fancy a play day. So shoot me.' He glanced at my computer screen. 'You're not too busy for us, are you?'

I lowered the lid. 'Absolutely not,' I said. 'Just catching up with some reading.' I tilted my head upwards. 'Trying to gather a little intelligence to work out a strategy.'

'How are things?' Kieron asked, while I got some crayons and paper out for Dee Dee. 'Any better?'

As always, I'd briefed the children on the latest houseguest – well, as far as possible – because fostering, in reality, is a whole-family enterprise, and their support and involvement was key.

'Not yet,' I admitted. 'I've not even managed to get him out of the house yet, to be honest. And I'm still feeling my way as to how best to approach things. But I've had some stuff through now at least, so I'm hoping that will change. Though he's a complicated kid, no doubt about it.'

'It certainly sounds like he has some issues,' Kieron mused. 'But don't they all? Sounds to me like you should go all Casey on his butt.'

'Oh behave,' I said. 'You sound just like Tyler! Like I'm some scary monster mum or something.'

'Well, fight fire with fire, I say.' I'd told him about the

dinosaur impression. 'Have you forgotten how to do "your look"? Trust me, that will definitely do the trick.'

The door opened at that very moment and the kid in question appeared. I hoped he hadn't been listening outside.

Though he didn't seem to have been. He looked agitated. As if he'd literally just run downstairs. 'Drink,' he announced, 'I need a drink. And something to eat as well. I've got to get these guys banned from the game and take all their coins from their accounts.'

I had absolutely no idea what he was talking about. 'Calm down, Miller,' I said. 'And come in properly and say hello, please. This is my son, Kieron,' I told him. 'And this is Dee Dee, my granddaughter. Dee Dee? This is Miller. Say h—'

'I don't have *time*,' Miller said, not even looking at her, let alone acknowledging her. 'Hurry up! I need to get back upstairs!'

Kieron, who'd just sat down, now stood up again. 'Alright, mate?' he said amiably. 'So what game is it you're playing? And say hi to Dee Dee, will you, mate? She's only little.'

Seemingly stunned to have been spoken to, Miller looked Kieron up and down. Though mostly up. Kieron's tall, like his dad. He then mumbled a 'hi', then something else, which I didn't understand, but which I took to be the name of the war game.

Kieron raised his brows. 'Really? Aren't you a little young to be playing that one?'

I'd been pouring a glass of squash and Miller now reached out to take it from me. 'It's my own. I brought it with me,' he said. 'And my social worker says it's okay, so it's okay.'

I held on to the glass, waiting for a 'please', which wasn't forthcoming. Instead, just, 'And a snack. I *told* you, I need a snack.'

I was just about to remind him that he'd not long eaten lunch, when Kieron said, 'Mate, please don't be rude to my mum. Just ask nicely and say please. That's the way to ask if you want something.'

There was a moment of silence, Miller's gaze darting between us, as if assessing the necessity of bending to our combined will.

Dee Dee broke it. 'We say thank you, we say please,' she sang. 'We say 'scuse me when we sneeze. I learneded that in school,' she added proudly.

'Quite,' Kieron said. And would have said more, no doubt. But Miller, with an almighty '*God!*', had already turned tail and, drink-less and snack-less, left the kitchen.

'Ah,' my son said, 'I see what you mean.'

* * *

After Kieron and Dee Dee left, some forty-five minutes later, I sat once again at my laptop and pondered; did this constitute one–all, or was it two–nil to Miller? Probably the latter.

I then chastised myself for even thinking in such reductive terms. This was a child with a horrendous background, and though I didn't doubt everyone had subsequently done their best for him, his years in the system had only added to his misery, compounding his considerable emotional problems, and hardening the angry shell he had built around himself. The question was, was it too late for me to take him on long term and try to fix him? The tentative answer was that I hadn't yet found a child that I hadn't at least tried to, and, for all that he tried so hard to make himself unlovable, I wasn't about to give up on him without a fight – even if it meant fighting myself in this case, because the temptation to pass him on was still strong. That 'month-by-month basis' John had alluded to at the outset was never far away from my thoughts. It was almost as if I'd been given a free pass should I give up on him. No blame. No shame. Except I would feel shame, wouldn't I? I *would* blame myself.

Even as I was having these thoughts, I was also chastising myself for using the term 'fix'. Social services don't like us to use the word to fit any more, because it's no longer politically correct. In my world, however – the coal face of care – I don't always have time to search for the right socially acceptable expression. I had been told off for putting the word 'liar' in a report once, the correct term now being 'a tendency to create an alternative story'. You can no longer refer to a child having 'stolen' something, either – you have to say 'they take things without asking'.

I know it's progress, and it definitely sounds less accusatory, but, at the same time, it still feels a bit alien to me, because I grew up in a world where a spade was called a spade.

But that's the way things work now, and one thing I can no longer do is try to 'fix' kids. I can only try to help them 'reach their potential'. But given what I already knew, and what I was going to learn over the coming weeks, what kind of potential did Miller even have?

The phrase 'not a lot', though politically incorrect, was, sadly, the first that sprung to mind.

Chapter 8

So. Casey nil. Miller – what must it be now? Around twelve? Because over the next dozen or so days, I had failed to make progress – either on getting him to sleep through the night, on any night, or in getting him out of the house.

Most frustratingly however, the rot was setting in, because, despite throwing everything at the problem, and pretty forcefully, I'd made little inroad in addressing the number-one issue: Miller's obsession with staying in his room, playing computer games all the time. It would have been easy to regret having got him the PlayStation in the first place, but, in truth, without it, I don't know how things would have panned out. Without it – and we rationed it regularly and frequently – he would simply get into bed and roll himself up in his duvet, and no form of inducement or threat of sanctions would winkle him out. We tried offering incentives, such as the purchase of a new game a few days hence, to reward good behaviour, but he seemed incapable of understanding the 'jam tomorrow' concept. Miller was only interested in the here and now. And if we tried sanctions – no getting the controller back until he spent an hour downstairs with us, say, watching TV together, getting to know each other – he would simply assert that he didn't care if he never got it back; he was not 'hanging out' with us, and that was that.

In fact, the only time he seemed able to amuse himself differently was in the small hours of the night, when he'd while away his time playing with the assortment of distractions in his suitcase.

It was obvious that Miller had an addiction to playing computer games – and in that, he was far from alone. But I also had to factor in the control aspect of his make-up; with no one *to* control, because the household was asleep (well, in my case, more often than not, tactically feigning sleep), there was no incentive to exert his considerable will, because it would achieve nothing, manipulate no one.

It was also impossible, without him having a daily spell in formal education, to get him started on our strict behaviour modification programme, as so much of its effectiveness relied on the daily routines around education: getting up at a set time, getting washed, dressed and fed, then, in the evenings, doing any homework he'd been given without making a fuss, and going to bed at a time that had been agreed.

Without these simple daily rhythms – part and parcel of any childhood – we were in limbo, and had been for way too long a time now. It was only half-jokingly that I'd quipped to Mike one night that I half-wished he *would* bloody abscond.

Not that I'd been stuck in every day, all day. The day after Kieron's visit, he'd been on a late shift, and had, to my immense gratitude, come over for the morning so I could have a couple of hours to myself. I'd like to have been able to report to Libby that this had proved a help to Miller, but, on my return it had been to hear that the nearest Kieron and Miller had got to 'bonding' was Miller's grudging acceptance of Kieron sitting in his bedroom, and being 'permitted' to sit and watch him play his game.

'Mum, he's weird,' had been Kieron's considered view after spending a little time with him, echoing Tyler's thoughts. 'His face when he's killing things is plain creepy.'

And it was an impression that hadn't changed for Tyler either. He seemed happiest skirting around Miller wherever possible, and as he was knee-deep in revision for his coming exams, I wasn't about to try and coax him to do more. Not least because I could feel the tension crackle between them whenever they were in the room together; I had this strong sense that Ty, though he'd never actually said so, would much rather his home hadn't been invaded by Miller – our Ty, who, because of his own difficult background, had a huge amount of sympathy for difficult kids as his default. And I really didn't want him to have to deal with any stress; not with his exams coming up.

Ditto Mike, despite him similarly being happy to do his bit. We were supposed to be a team, after all. But of all the kids I'd ever fostered – and this struck me as weird myself – Miller felt very much *my* responsibility. My personal cross to bear.

And my self-inflicted personal *bête noire* as well? It was becoming to seem so. 'Love, just *make* him go out with you,'

A Boy Without Hope

Mike had said, more than once. But no tool in my toolbox seemed up to the job. Short of lassoing him and dragging him bodily to the car, kicking and screaming, I had no means of doing so, did I? Not with a child who knew exactly the way things worked; that physically dragging him anywhere could so easily be 'spun' into an official allegation of assault.

And that was the confounding crux of it all. Most kids, in my experience, at least have some fear of consequences. The bar might be set high with damaged, vulnerable children, but there would usually be some point, even if way beyond normal boundaries, when they'd pull back, frightened about what might happen to them if they tried to go further. Miller, however, displayed no fear at all. Indeed, it often felt as though he pushed us because he *welcomed* the consequences, because they fitted with his world view. Certainly, when he got them – almost exclusively to lose the right to play computer games – he would smile, almost knowingly, as if his hunch had been right: that adults couldn't be trusted; that all they wanted was to make his life difficult.

Still, today was Saturday, which at least meant I had a little company.

Though right now, not of the pleasant kind, it seemed.

I was just easing into another day, sitting sipping my second coffee in the kitchen, when I heard a furious yelling coming from the top of the stairs. Not Miller, but Tyler, who was decidedly unhappy.

'Mum! What the *hell* is going on with this internet?'

I pushed my chair back and pulled my dressing-gown cord a little tighter, then went out into the hall to see what

79

was going on. Though things 'going on' when it came to anything internet-related were about as far from my area of expertise as it was possible to be. I was still at the same 'bash the telly to see if the picture improves' stage I'd been at since about 1973.

He was standing at the top of the stairs, fuming. 'What's up, love?' I asked. 'Has it gone off again?'

Tyler's face was a picture of barely contained anger. 'Yes it has. And if I've lost my assignment I'm going to go *so* mad,' he said. 'It's the third time this morning and it's driving me nuts. I was halfway through some coursework, which I haven't even saved yet, and all the bits of research I had opened have gone!'

'Well you can still save the work you've done, love,' I said, trying to be helpful. 'And Dad'll be home from work before too long, won't he? I'm sure he'll know what to do. But if he doesn't, we'll get on to the internet company and find out what's happening, okay?'

Tyler sighed theatrically, and slapped his hands against his sides. Then glared pointedly towards Miller's closed bedroom door, before stomping off into his own room. I saw his point. It had gone off suddenly a couple of times one night in the week, and we'd already visited the idea that it might been something to do with Miller. But Mike had interrogated, investigated, and run all kinds of checks, and declared it to have been 'just one of those things', reassuring me that while Miller could control lots of things, our entire domestic internet wasn't one of them. Not without us realising, anyway.

A Boy Without Hope

Even so, it now occurred to me that if the internet was off again, then Miller couldn't be playing on the PlayStation, could he? So why wasn't he kicking off as well? He had ants in his pants if he had to wait five minutes to eat a sandwich, if it meant losing some precious game time.

So what was he up to instead? I headed upstairs to find out.

I was surprised to see him sitting quietly on his bed, writing something on a large unlined notepad. It wasn't one I recognised. Perhaps something from his case? I wondered if the little train I'd read about was somewhere in there too. Though now obviously wasn't the time to ask him.

The TV screen was also blank. 'First time I've see that thing off,' I remarked mildly. 'You not playing on your game this morning?'

Miller didn't look up from his writing. He simply shrugged. 'I was. I can't play it right now, though. It's off.'

Again, a completely uncharacteristic lack of concern.

'Because of the internet going off again?' I asked. 'I'm going to try unplugging it and reconnecting it. See if that works. It often does.'

'I wouldn't bother,' Miller said. 'It'll be back on again in ten minutes.'

It would be wrong to say alarm bells rang in my head. They didn't need to.

'And how exactly would *you* know that?' I asked him, perching on the bed.

Silence. 'Miller, answer me, please. How do you *know* that?'

The pen left his hand and whistled across the bedroom. 'Oh my *God*,' he said, as it clattered against the opposite wall and fell to the floor. 'You moan when I'm on my game and now you're moaning when I'm not! It's fine. Everything is *fine*. We've just been hacked, that's all.' *Hacked?* 'But it's only for half an hour and then he'll put us back on. So there's no need to go off on one. It's *fine*.'

'Hacked?' I spluttered. 'What on earth do you mean, "We've been hacked"? Miller, what on earth have you done?'

'*God*. There you go. Straight away blaming me. I told you. It *wasn't* me. It was a hacker!'

There were so many levels on which this whole exchange was wrong – in fact, on *every* level – that I hardly knew where to begin. With the pen that had narrowly missed me? With the cheek and disrespect? Or with the fact that he'd just told me our home computer network had been hacked? Probably that one, for starters, though there was one important point. I didn't really have the first clue what he was talking about. 'Hacked' was one of those terms that just pushed all the buttons. Like 'scammer', or 'identity theft', or 'virus'.

'So you just said,' I went on. 'But what I don't understand is why a hacker would suddenly want to interrupt our internet service.' I paused. 'But something tells me you do, Miller.'

Miller threw the pad down as well now, and I could see what he'd been writing. Or, rather, couldn't. It just looked like rows of weird hieroglyphics. Then he sighed and scratched his head, then rolled his eyes, as if despairing. Of the situation, or of my ability to understand anything he might say?

'Look, I just chucked the wrong guys out of a game and stole their money. And because the moderator of the game knew my IP address, he hacked into our system and got us chucked off to pay me back. But he's putting us back on again. It's no biggie.'

I still didn't have a proper grasp of what he was saying, but one thing I *did* know was that he didn't have access to my laptop – anyone's laptop for that matter – so how did he know that? 'How the heck did this guy know our IP address?' I demanded. 'Even I don't know that, Miller. How do *you*?'

'Because *I* gave it to him!' I turned to see Tyler standing in the doorway. 'God, Miller, you little *shit*!'

He turned to me then. 'Sorry, Mum, but he really is! You told me you needed it to reset the PlayStation!' he said, jabbing a finger in Miller's direction. 'God, *why* didn't I think of that? Listen, you've got to stop whatever it is you're doing, get out of that game and change your player ID, and pronto. Because this won't stop, Mum.' He turned back to me. 'Trust me, it won't. Not unless he stops messing around with other players. And he knows it.' Another jab of the finger.

I had even less idea what was going on now, and absolutely no idea what Tyler was talking about, but Miller clearly did. He looked suddenly nervous. Even slightly afraid. Tyler wasn't a particularly big lad for sixteen, but a few years make a world of difference at that age. So, for all that he'd take us on over every tiny thing, sheer physicality still held sway over Miller, clearly. I put a hand on Tyler's arm. Felt the anger in him. 'So at least you know what's going on round here, then. *Good*. So, Miller,' I went on. 'You need to sort this out, now. And if we have any more of it, I will disconnect the internet, full stop. No more online gaming, period. Are we clear?'

In answer, Miller picked up his control pad, flicked a switch, and his TV sputtered back into life again. 'It's all back on now anyway,' he said, pointing to the PlayStation. 'Drama over.'

'No, mate, it's not,' Tyler said, 'and I *mean* it. You need to stop hacking and just play like everyone else does. It's not fair and it's causing big problems for everyone. I *mean* it. You knock it off. You hear me? I'm sick of your nonsense!'

'Fine!' Miller huffed at him. 'Whatever!'

* * *

'You really need to get some schooling sorted out for him, Mum,' Tyler said as I followed him back across the landing to his own room. 'He's a menace, he really is. And too clever by half. And he doesn't know the half of what he's dealing with, trust me. And why the hell is he still hanging around here all the time anyway? *Why* isn't he in school? It's not like he's special needs or anything, is it? Or did he just get excluded from everywhere?'

'Something like that,' I told him.

'But they shouldn't *put* all this on us. It's not *fair*.'

'I know, love,' I said. 'And I'll be on to Libby pronto.' Much good that would do, I thought but didn't say. 'Look, you get back to your revision, eh? I'll have Dad have some stern words with him later.' I grinned. 'No point me doing it when I don't know what half of them mean, is it?'

His shoulders lowered slightly. 'True dat,' he said. 'But Dad really needs to give him hell.'

'And he will,' I said. 'Promise.'

So, crisis over. At least I hoped so.

Except perhaps not. Or, at least, another one brewing. 'Tyler,' I said, 'did you see the stuff he was writing? You know, on that pad? What's that when it's at home?'

'Oh, that'll be code. Code from the dark web, most probably. He's in some sort of hacker group from when he had his own laptop. I think he's trying to get back in but he can't till he gets it back from his previous foster family. Seriously, Mum, he's up to all sorts. Or would be, I'll bet, given half a chance.'

I still only understood about one word in six, but if Tyler thought Miller was up to 'all sorts' then he probably was. And though I didn't know exactly what made that mad, bad or dangerous, I *had* heard of the dark web, and didn't like the sound of it – and I definitely didn't want it entering our house. Wasn't the dark web what terrorists used to plan attacks, and paedophiles to organise their evil gangs?

I went downstairs and called Jenny, Miller's previous foster carer, to find out about the laptop I hadn't heard about.

'Ah, yes,' she said immediately. 'And I'm loath to give it back. Though I suppose I must. I'll drop it round to Libby for you, shall I?'

'But why do you still have it? I'd have thought it would be welded to his side, day and night.'

'Because we confiscated it,' she told me. 'When he smashed the screen on ours.'

'Ah,' I said. 'Why?'

'Bit of a long story,' Jenny said. 'From back at the start, when he would actually leave the house with us. But the short version is that he'd been watching a movie on his own laptop and the power went. We were camping at the time and didn't have access to anywhere to plug it in, so we allowed him to continue watching it on ours. We were outside the tents with some friends who had met up with us, at the time – Miller, of course, had stayed inside. And when I went to check on him, I saw that he was actually looking at bloody porn! Can you believe it? Anyway, when I tried to drag it away from him, he got angry and threw it across the tent, smashing it into a gas bottle.'

I was happy she'd only told me the short version as I don't think I could have taken all the gory details just at that moment, but I did make a mental note to check the search history on my own and Tyler's computers.

And to redouble my efforts to get a commitment to provide us with more support. With all the budget cuts, I knew I'd have a fight on my hands, but I was in the mood to fire off a few stern emails. And sterner than usual, given what I'd just found out. People needed reminding just how much I was out on a limb, and, given how Miller preferred to spend his time – and with whom – on the internet, how pressing was the need to get him back into education. And if they couldn't offer any education in its normal setting, then I needed, *badly* needed, an alternative. Something that would get Miller out of the house for a couple of hours every day. Something to inspire him to get up and get dressed.

Something more concrete than Libby's empty promises – certainly of more substance than her 'Yes, ELAC have something sorted' had turned out to be. Which, as far as I could tell, was nothing more than the promise of a possibility to get Miller into a 'new project' they'd bought into – whatever that meant – and which so far had amounted to nothing. Well, bar what seemed like the social service term of the moment – the oft-repeated 'just give us a few days'.

I was just trying to put all that into 'acceptable' wording, when the door opened and the means of my salvation came in. Not in the form of an email, but my husband.

Mike didn't mince words. One of the reasons I loved him. 'Go on, Case,' he said, 'get your coat and your car keys, and have a few hours shopping, or whatever it is you do in town.'

I could have kissed him, and probably would have, but for a meek little Miller-shaped voice from behind me. 'Would it be alright if I come to town with you, Casey?'

We both gaped. I didn't know whether to be pleased or frustrated. On the one hand I felt like I had just been given the keys to my jail cell, but on the other, I couldn't shake the feeling that taking Miller with me just might help me with the key to *him*. If he didn't do a runner on me, that was.

Because that was obviously a clear and present danger. Miller's long history of absconding might not have been an issue up to now (quite the opposite – he was stuck to home

87

like glue) but perhaps he'd been operating a watch and wait policy. Who knew what went through his mind? I certainly didn't. But if, for whatever reason, he'd decided to make today his bid for freedom, there would be little chance of me stopping him once we were out and about. And if he did decide to scarper, precious little I could do about it either. Just the grim prospect of calling up the cavalry and all the hassle that would ensue. Reporting it to the police, to the emergency duty team, becoming part of the search party, and all the resources and time and energy that would involve.

None of which I relished, but it was a chance I'd have to take. After all, I wasn't, and couldn't be, his jailor – either legally or emotionally. Plus I wanted to get to know him – something I felt I'd hardly done at all, despite us spending so much time cooped up together. It was as if we were just co-existing; separated by an invisible film. One that crackled with resistance every time I tried to push past it with a friendly greeting or an affectionate gesture.

'Course you can, love,' I trilled, to Mike's obvious surprise. 'That would be *lovely*. Go comb your hair and grab your hoodie. Five minutes, okay?'

He shook his head. 'No, I need eight,' he corrected, before turning around and running back upstairs.

Another crackle. And, to my shame, I was tempted to mutter 'six'. As in 'six of the best'. The traditional teacher's threat. One that, back in my day, invariably worked. I held my tongue, though. Definitely *not* in today's protocol.

Chapter 9

What's that story about the little Dutch boy with his finger in the dam? Knowing that if he pulls it out there will be a torrent and then a flood? I don't know what had happened, exactly – was it the action of leaving the house? Or getting in the car? I had no idea which, but one thing was clear. It was almost as if a switch had flipped inside Miller, and turned him into a completely different child.

'Do you think Donald Trump is a good president, Casey? Do they have a phone shop in your town? And have they got a game shop? Or are we just going to do boring things when we get there? I hate shopping. I like phone shopping and game shopping, but I hate shopping-shopping. Just so you know.'

This just in the few seconds it took to reverse off the drive. More words that I'd heard him say at one time in a long while. And on it went. Was there a climbing wall, like in the last place he'd gone to? How long would the journey take? Would he be allowed any sweets? 'And, as well,' he continued, 'do you know what horse power this engine has? It's important, for, like, when you are loading it up with passengers and suitcases and everything. And, as well, did you know that the size of your feet when you're a baby determines how tall you're going to be as an adult? Casey? Answer me. Did you? Did you *know* that?'

It was such a torrent of words that I even checked the rear-view mirror, just in case Miller had run off and persuaded a completely different child to take his place.

I managed to meet his eye, even if only briefly. 'Goodness me,' I said. 'One question at a time, please, Miller. And maybe it should wait till we get into town, eh? There are lots of new road works and I don't want to end up in the wrong lane or something. Okay? And could you stop yanking my seat back while you're talking, please?'

'Okay,' he said. But it did nothing to stem the astonishing tide. This was more unsolicited conversation than I'd heard from him since he'd been with us, in fact, and I was truly stumped by what had brought it about. 'What do you think about that North Korean leader?' he asked brightly. 'I reckon Trump will off him. His followers all have the same haircuts, you know. Shall I tell you the history of the Korean divide? Casey, *do* they have a game shop in town? I bet they do. Towns always do. I bet they have lots of phone shops as well. Which do you think is best, the Galaxy or the iPhone?'

By the time I'd wound my tortuous way through the road works and into the town-centre car park, I felt almost like my head was exploding. And before long, with no sign of his non-stop chatter abating, I began to wonder if there wasn't more to this uncharacteristic animation than I'd first supposed. Yes, it was great that he was chatting to me, but was that all there was to it? He seemed to leap from one bizarre train of thought to another, and though my professional head wondered if this, too, was a sign of autism, my instinct, increasingly, was that I was being wound up. That he was babbling on at me with the express intention of irritating me. To the point, given I was trying to negotiate Saturday afternoon town-centre traffic, that I would tell him to shut up?

It was an effort of will (why did this kid keep bringing out the worst in me?) to stick to the former. 'Right!' I said cheerfully, once we were safely in our parking space and I'd opened the door to let him out. 'Shoot. Ask me anything you want.'

Miller yanked his hoodie down over his skinny hips. He seemed all out of questions. 'Donald Trump, was it?' I prompted, as I shut and locked the car.

Silence. I pointed towards the pedestrian exit and he stomped along beside me. 'Are we going to the phone shop first?' he finally asked.

'The phone shop? No, love. We're not. I don't need to go to the phone shop.'

'The game shop, then? The game shop and then the phone shop.'

I stopped by the fire door. 'Miller, I've come into town to pick up a few bits that *I* need. Then maybe to get a coffee – and you can have an ice cream, if you like – and only then, *if* there's time, we *might* go in the game shop. Whether that happens or not will very much depend on you.'

He stood and pouted, his gaze darting around me rather than at me. 'Not going, then. Not till you promise about the game shop.'

'That's not a promise I'm prepared to make, Miller. That's not how it works. You asked to come, and I've brought you, but I'm here to do *my* shopping. So your choice is to accompany me without moaning and groaning, in which case, there will definitely be an ice cream in the mix, and, if there's time, we *will* go to the game shop. Alternatively' – at this point I pulled my phone out of my handbag – 'I can ring Mike and have him come and pick you up now instead. Your call, love. I'm easy. But I have been cooped up for days now, and I *am* doing my shopping. Whether you stay with me or get taken home is entirely up to you.'

'Fine!' he huffed, pushing open the door to the stair-well. 'I'll *do* all the boring stuff. But it best not take all day!'

Had I levelled up Miller's imaginary scorecard? I hoped so. Though it nagged at me anyway, that sense of not quite being in control; of having to pit my wits against him to try and 'win battles'. We were not supposed to be point scoring, like kids in a playground. I was his carer, and he was supposed to be *earning* points. Or would be, had we been able to sit down and create the chart to put them on together. Still, early days, I decided, as we emerged into the shopping mall. This was new territory – we were out, and that was something in itself. And in this new landscape – both in terms of the physical and the mental – all I could really do was go with the flow.

Though 'flow' was a long way from being achieved. 'What exactly are you going to buy in here?' he asked, as we went into my favourite clothes shop. 'Do you know? Because if you know what you want, it won't take very long, will it. And then we'll have time for the game shop.'

I almost cracked a smile at the thought that those would be Mike's thoughts and words exactly – well, if he dared voice them. Which, of course, he wouldn't. One of the reasons our marriage endured was that, unless it was for some big manly electrical item, Mike didn't come shopping with me any more. As far as he was concerned shopping was a chore, not a hobby. So I did have a smidge of sympathy for Miller. Or would have, had he not finished with, 'Well?'

'Miller, please!' I said. 'We had a deal, remember? And if you want me to keep my end of the bargain, then you have to be patient, and not badger me, okay? We will get to the game shop when, *and if*, we get there.'

I was obviously long used to expecting the unexpected when fostering, but even I was astounded at what Miller did next. Which was to drop to the floor, lie down on his back and start cycling his legs madly, as if an enthusiastic participant at a legs, bums and tums class. Round they went, as if piston-powered, while his arms did their own thing – mostly flapping up and down as if miming a doggy paddle, right in the aisle between the jeans and dresses. Not so much 'downward-facing dog' as 'stricken beetle'.

I wasn't stunned for long, despite his accompanying shrieking. For this was clearly no tantrum. Just a ploy to deflect me. Designed to ensure maximum embarrassment, and so ensure we beat a hasty retreat.

So, rather than doing so, I ignored him, just as I would with a toddler, and began riffling through a pile of pastel jeans. Then, having selected a pair, I walked around him to a nearby mirror, where I held them against me, deciding whether they'd suit me.

'Excuse me, madam.' Another person appeared beside my reflection. 'Is that young man over there' – she gestured backwards – 'with you?'

It was obviously important that I brazen this one out. 'He is,' I confirmed, *sotto voce*. 'He's just amusing himself while I finish my shopping. He's not bothering anyone, is he? He'll be done soon.'

'Um,' the shop assistant said. And would doubtless have said more. Except Miller, red in the face, had scrambled to his feet, and now did his T-Rex impression for her. Then, having roared at her, he bolted from the store.

I passed her the jeans. 'See?' I said. 'Sorry. I have to go.'

* * *

Perhaps oddly, I felt calm. And, to some extent, pleased. Finally, out in the world, we were getting somewhere. At least in as much as I was now able to start building a picture, and interacting with him in a way that might help open him up; help the precious process of my getting to understand him better.

Given what I already knew about him, I wasn't worried about him disappearing on me. Not least because there's a big difference between twelve and, say, seven. But mostly because it was something he'd never before done.

Coming back was his thing, every time. So it needed no play-acting to emerge slowly and nonchalantly from the shop, and cast around as if I didn't much care either way. And there he was, across the street, leaning, apparently indifferently, against a bin. But I wasn't fooled. He'd had his eyes trained on the shop front since he'd left it; I knew because, by virtue of my (lack of) height and the throng of people all around me, I'd spotted him before he'd spotted me.

He straightened up, yanked the hoodie down again and glowered across the road at me. 'Ha!' he shouted. 'You're an *idiot*! Get me a game or I'm not coming back in the car!'

I crossed the road, but as I did so he sprinted a few yards down the street.

'New game or I'm gone,' he said.

I walked towards him. Again, he sprinted off a few yards.

I carried on walking. 'We didn't say anything about buying a game, Miller,' I told him. 'And do you really think that this kind of behaviour will get you anything?'

'Well, I'll stop if you say you'll get me one.'

'That's not how it works, Miller. You've made sure that I can't do what I needed to do now, so, I'm sorry, love, but that means no trip to the game shop today. And no game either – you're going to have to make up for this behaviour before I consider buying you a treat now.'

'Bitch,' came the response, as he ran further up the street.

'And all the while you keep doing this, you're just making it worse,' I called out.

'Don't care!' he yelled back. And off he went again.

And again. And again. And again. And mindful of whichever American politician coined the 'three strikes and
you're out' rule, I stopped following Miller down the high
street, got my phone out and called Mike. 'What kept you?'
he asked, chuckling, when he answered the phone. 'You
need me to come get him for you?'

Yes, indeed I did. But since it was going to be at least a
fifteen- or twenty-minute wait, I followed my hunch that
Miller (unsure how to play it now, clearly) would go
precisely nowhere, and popped into the big bookshop
outside which I'd told Mike to meet me.

And I'd been right. When I emerged with a couple of
greetings cards ten minutes later, he was exactly where I'd
left him, leaning disconsolately against the chemist's window
and, though he was quick to turn away when he noticed I'd
spotted him, he had clearly been waiting for me to come out.

I experienced a moment of clarity. And sadness. How did
it feel to be twelve, and so alone in the world that you were
reduced to spending your Saturday afternoon playing 'catch
me if you can' with a middle-aged virtual stranger? Because
that was what was happening, wasn't it? That was what this
amounted to. He was like a stuck record, going round and
round and round, and heading nowhere. I was just the latest
in a long line of well-meaning strangers into whose lives –
and I'm sure he'd have put it this way – he'd been uncere-
moniously dumped. I smiled. 'Coming home?' I called.

'Fuck *off*!'

Which, give or take the odd expletive, was exactly what
I did, as soon as Mike pulled up and told me he'd take over.

'Go and do your shopping, love,' he said. 'Just head back when you're ready. I'll round up me laddo, and we'll see you at home.'

But I didn't shop, not in the end. I tried for a bit, but my heart was no longer in it. For all that Mike was confident he'd be able to coax Miller back eventually, it was hard to concentrate on summer tops when I knew what was happening. After all, a little voice told me as I renegotiated the road works, there was always a first time, for everything. He might well have run off. He might have refused to get in Mike's car. And I didn't know, because Mike had insisted I leave him to it – one less person to provide an audience for his current game. So instead, I went home, to find neither of them there. So what merry dance was he now leading Mike?

But there was no point in phoning him, because he'd probably be driving, so I made myself a coffee, and took a sandwich up to Tyler, then, having regaled him with the shenanigans I'd 'enjoyed' on our little outing, left him to it, and went back downstairs to wait for them both.

And wait … It was more than an hour and a half later before Mike arrived home. But *without* Miller. By which time, having gone through a range of emotions, I'd already had a serious crisis of professional confidence. And this confirmed it. I'd called it all wrong.

'Oh, lord – where is he?' I said, contemplating the call to the emergency duty team, and the inevitable debacle that would follow. 'Don't tell me you lost him?'

'I bloody wish!' he growled.

He shut the front door, and went into the living room, where he threw his car keys down onto the coffee table. Then he went across to the window and looked out.

The penny dropped. 'So he *is* here?' I felt a stab of relief.

'Oh, he's somewhere out there, certainly. And I've a good mind to leave him out there, as well! And hope for rain. Wipe the smile off his bloody face. Can you imagine what it's like? I must have looked like a kerb crawler or something.'

'You mean he's *walked* all the way home from town?'

Apparently so. Because there hadn't been a great deal Mike could do. Miller wouldn't get in the car, and Mike couldn't – wouldn't – make him. And I sympathised; a man bundling a screeching, kicking twelve-year-old into a vehicle, in the middle of the town centre? It didn't take much of a leap of imagination to work out how *that* might pan out.

But there was no way Miller could walk home on his own, and he knew it. Bright though he was, he'd never even spent time in our part of the county. He'd never have found his way home on his own. Which left Mike with one option. To play leapfrog with Miller. Driving ahead of him, then waiting for him to saunter past him, then, when faced with a junction, driving ahead once again, so Miller knew the way and could follow him. Then a saunter past, and a drive, and a stop at another junction, while waiting for him to catch up again.

'I must have asked him twenty times to get in, but he wouldn't, of course. Just kept sticking two fingers up at me and laughing. 'So he can stay out there for a bit. No way am I going out to beg him to come in. And I don't think you should either.'

I could understand how angry Mike was, and I agreed that perhaps we should wait and see how this played out for a bit. Would Miller come in under his own steam or wouldn't he? Just how long was he prepared to keep this up?

We agreed half an hour, and were just contemplating our next move in the kitchen when we heard a loud shout from above. Tyler was up in his bedroom, still engrossed in revision. Well, had been. Because it was his voice we could hear, booming out across the front lawn.

'You've got two minutes to get in before I come down there!'

We both went to the window, to see Miller transfixed on the pavement. And it hit me that there was one person he couldn't manipulate. Couldn't push to the brink, because *he* wasn't hidebound by all the rules. A peer. And an older one. A bigger, and possibly badder, one. Someone who was genuinely scary.

'I mean it!' Tyler barked. 'If I have to come down there …'

Upon which, as if electrified, or jerked by an invisible string, Miller scuttled up the path and exploded into the hall, then thundered up the stairs to his room before we could get to him.

I went to follow but Mike placed a hand on my arm. 'Leave it be,' he said. 'I reckon Tyler's got this one, don't you?'

Upon which, the hero of the moment came ambling down the stairs. 'No need to thank me,' he said, grinning.

Food for thought, I thought. Definitely food for thought. Perhaps Tyler would turn out to be our secret weapon.

Chapter 10

I needed help. And had resolved to start the ball rolling on Monday. To where, I wasn't sure, but at least I had a plan. I'd gone through such notes as I'd had and one thing seemed clear. Miller had been in several foster homes but up until now, as far as I could tell, he'd been the only child in them. Just him and whichever pesky, interfering adults had been given the task of looking after him – and, where, up to now, he'd been able to call the shots.

He was, therefore, increasingly used to ruling the roost. Playing the system to set the system up to his liking. Which might be what he thought he wanted but also the last thing he needed. We weren't a pack of dogs, but some things were, and should be, set in stone even so. That as a dependent child he understood his place in the pack.

So I resolved to make lots of phone calls, send lots of emails and generally make it clear to everyone involved that I needed help with Miller, and needed it fast.

A Boy Without Hope

And when I woke up on Sunday morning, to greet a stunning spring day, there was no doubt where my motivation lay either. I wanted to help Miller (how could I not, knowing what he'd been through?) and I knew the absolute first priority, to enable me to do so, was to get help for *me*. It was something I hated to admit, even to myself, but I knew being cooped up all the time was bad for my own health, and, in tandem with the sleepless nights – well, let's just say there's a reason new parents walk around like zombies half the time – it was increasingly leading to compassion fatigue. Despite my head's constant mantra – that inside the exasperating little dictator was a frightened, lonely child – my heart wasn't in it nearly as much as it needed to be. It wasn't helped by the constant feeling that I might have made a bad call in agreeing to take him on in the first place. That I should have heeded John Fulshaw's warning. That I also should have listened to the little voice that had whispered since day one. That I was burnt out, at least for now, and should have said no.

It also wasn't helped by John being out of the picture. I had no reason to, not really, but I couldn't shake the feeling that I was no longer as well supported as I was used to being. Just that sense that if things did become unmanageable with Miller, I could pick up the phone and pour my heart out to a *friend*. Who might not actually be able to do much – we were all victims of the same lack of resources, after all – but who'd listen, and sympathise, and do whatever he could. Who *valued* me and Mike – that was the crux of it.

There was also the basic truth that we all need time out. That no one – not even the most conscientious and loving

parent – can be in a state of enmity and stress and confrontation all the time. We all need spaces in our lives where we
can kick back and simply *be*, with time to do all the everyday
things that we take for granted – 'everyday' till we're denied
them, that is. Things like shopping – that still rankled – or
going round to Riley's for a natter. Playing with the grandkids. Having a quiet sit on a park bench in the April sunshine.
Simply going for a stroll round the block would recharge my
batteries. Just having time to stand and stare and smell the
roses. So if I could just manage that – just some regular
'escape' time – I was sure I could shake off the nagging nega-
tivity, stop feeling so sorry for myself and concentrate on
finding the inner Miller.

For now though, it being Sunday, I'd have to settle for
the sunshine, which, as I lay in bed musing on how much
sleep I'd now been deprived of, was creeping across the
floor and sliding up onto the duvet – almost as if command-
ing me to get up and seize the day. A new day. And, hopefully, a better one.

It needed to be. We'd done little more than muddle
through the rest of Saturday. After Tyler had left the house
to meet up with his friend Denver, a sense of defeat had
settled over me. Mike had suggested I head back to town
and resume shopping – there had still been an hour or so
left for me to do so – but I couldn't face it. Not the road-
works, not the crowds, not even – unbelievable, this one –
the actual shopping, so I ended up on the sofa, watching
rubbish on telly, still stewing about our irascible little visitor upstairs, and how thoroughly he'd managed to rile me.

Mike did try – he went up twice to suggest a kick-about, or a bike ride – but though Miller was at least chastened enough not to give him any backchat, all his answers had been mumbled, grunting versions of 'no', and on one occasion he'd even been back in his duvet cocoon, despite the warmth of the afternoon, too apathetic even to fire up the telly. (The PlayStation, naturally, was now off limits.)

Yes, he'd come down for food, but it was joyless and mostly silent, all of us, I decided, too busy inhabiting our own private universes of disgruntlement.

This would not do, I decided. A new day, and a sunny one, demanded positivity. So once the sun had engulfed me, I slipped quietly from beneath the covers (so as not to wake Mike), threw on my dressing gown and went down to make some breakfast.

Forget smelling the roses, at least for the moment. It was my experience and my theory, and I'd yet to be proven wrong on this, that the smell of frying bacon was a universal panacea, and that a decent fry-up – the whole family, sat together round the table – could set the tone for the rest of the day. I started pulling out pots and pans with conviction.

Activity too is a great lifter of moods, and, with everything apart from the eggs warming in the grill, the coffee pot simmering, and the table all set with toast, jams and juices, I went out to call Mike down in a much better frame of mind – just in time to meet him coming down.

'I thought I could smell something delicious,' he said, grinning. 'Shall I rouse his nibs?'

'You go and pop yourself an egg in,' I said. 'I'll go and get the boys up.'

Mike gave me a quick peck on the lips. 'Aye-aye, captain,' he said as he leaned down to pick up the morning paper. 'Though Ty's up already. Nose like a beagle, that one. He's just in the bathroom. Tell him his egg's going on, too. No signs of life from his lordship's room as yet, though. With the amount of banging around he was doing last night, I imagine he's still dead to the world. Still, if you open his door and waft it back and forth a bit, I'm sure he'll come too. There surely isn't a kid alive that can resist the smell of your bacon!'

Cheered by Mike's jaunty tone, I went up and crossed the landing, and knocked softly on Miller's bedroom door. I couldn't hear any sounds of life, though, so I knocked a second time, only louder. 'Miller?' I called. 'You awake, love?'

Still nothing. So, wondering if he was sulking after the previous day's debacle – or perhaps sitting up in bed, writing dark-web code on that pad of his, ignoring me – I pushed down the handle and went on in.

The room was pitch dark, as it was intended to be. Because we'd had numerous foster children who found it difficult to sleep, we'd invested in decent blackout curtains a couple of years ago. So it took a few moments for my eyes to adjust, even with the door open.

'Miller, love,' I called softly as I walked over to his bed. 'Time to come down for breakfast. I've made – let me see now – bacon, eggs, beans, mushrooms, sausages and pancakes. And lots of other delicious stuff too.'

I leaned down to pat the warm comma shape of his body under the duvet. 'Come on, sleepy head. Let's put yesterday behind us. All done and dusted now, okay? Today's a new day, and it's a lovely one, too.'

There was a stirring beneath my hand, as he rolled onto his back. In the semi-darkness, a pair of sleepy eyes half opened. He had indeed been fast asleep, then. Still wasn't quite awake. And in that moment, I felt a knee-jerk rush of affection and sympathy. Half-asleep children have that power – always have had for me, at any rate. In their not-quite-conscious state, it's like the mask slips away. What I saw, as he blinked, was the sweet boy he should have been, with his fuzzy hair, the indentation of the wrinkled sheet on his cheek and the soft scent of freshly washed pyjamas eddying around him.

His eyes fluttered closed again, and I studied him in silence. And for a long moment, because I wanted to hold on to the image. And it turned out to be the best decision I'd made since he'd come to us, because in that long moment, I spied something I hadn't seen before. Half buried under the muddle of covers was a small photograph frame. One he'd obviously taken to bed with him.

I slipped it out carefully and, so I could see it, padded back to the bedroom doorway. It was a cheap painted frame, with much of the paint chipped off – so it was obviously old and well travelled. It was a photo of couple, taken in what looked like a park, with a child in between them – very obviously Miller. He was in a football strip, one I didn't immediately recognise, and clutched in his hand, only just visible, was what appeared at first to be a Dinky car, but closer inspection revealed to be a toy train.

I felt a shiver run through me. Could this be the same train the social worker had alluded to in her initial report? No way of knowing without asking, and perhaps it was a long shot, but something about the way he held it – the very fact that he held it – told me there was a fair to middling chance it might be. He was also smiling shyly, squinting against the sunshine from beneath a long fringe. And the adults, both dressed for summer – him in shorts, her in a strappy maxi dress – were also smiling, a hand apiece on Miller's skinny shoulders. He looked about six – perhaps seven, given how small he was for his age – and, for all the world as if *his* world was a happy one. At least then.

It felt as if I'd been gifted something precious in seeing this. Almost as if destiny had decreed that it find its way into my hands. I wasn't normally so fanciful, but given the train of my thoughts the previous evening, I had a sense of it whispering to me – a new voice, to drown out the others – saying, 'See, Casey. See? Now commit this to memory. *This* is the child you are trying to do your best for. So *do* try. Don't give up on him now.'

I heard Miller yawn then, and braced for the inevitable explosion. His privacy was sacrosanct, and he guarded it obsessively. Though the suitcase this had presumably come from was often open when he was in there, when he wasn't it was locked and safely stashed against the wall, under his bed. I had no idea where he hid the key to the tiny padlock – only that I doubted I'd ever find it with turning his room upside down. And, most importantly, we both knew I wouldn't dream of looking in it without permission in any case.

I turned around to see him shuffling up to a sitting position, yawning and rubbing his eyes with the heels of his hands. How would he react to seeing the picture in mine?

Here goes nothing, I thought, I had nothing to lose, after all. But, to my surprise, when I crossed the room and pulled back one of the curtains, he said nothing – even though I saw him clock it.

'Who's this?' I asked, sitting down on the edge of the bed again. 'They look nice.'

He held a hand out for the picture. 'That's Neen and Rob,' he said, taking it. I noticed how gently he moved a thumb across the face of it.

'Neen and Rob?' They weren't his parents. They couldn't be, could they? Though I was still to get my hands on a complete timeline of his history in care, I was pretty sure there had been little contact with them since they surrendered him. Besides, I just knew they weren't – not just from the body language, or the names. But because I knew his birth father had been a man of fifty-eight. This was a young couple. A foster couple? I imagined so.

He nodded, still sleepy, still not quite fully Miller. 'My foster mum and dad,' he said.

His only ones? The most important ones, obviously. 'They look nice,' I said again. 'When was this taken?'

'On holidays.'

'At the seaside?' I ventured, hardly daring to believe this might continue. It felt like an opening, but a slim one.

Unstable. One wrong move, one wrong tone, and it could so easily slam shut.

He shook his head, his gaze still fixed on the photograph. 'No, in the country. In a caravan. In a holiday park. We went twice,' he carried on. 'This was the second time. I was in a football tournament.'

'Hence the strip,' I said. 'Did you win?'

He shook his head. 'We came second. I was in a team with a bunch of retards. But I scored a goal in the final. They gave me man of the match.'

I hardly dared speak now, for fear that something would break the spell. But since he didn't continue – lost in precious memories of that special moment? – I ventured a finger towards the photograph.

'And what's that in your hand? Was it something you won?'

'Nah, that's just my train,' he said, placing the picture down on the duvet. 'I got a trophy, but I forgot to take it with me when I left.'

'Left?'

'For the home.'

My mind was whirring now. 'For the home?'

'After they said I had to leave there.'

'Why was that, love?'

Now a sigh. The first stirrings of impatience. 'Because the social *made* them. Like they always do. Else I'd still be with them, wouldn't I?'

I had a powerful urge to hug him, but I doubted he'd allow that. 'That's sad,' I said instead. 'How long were you with them?'

'Dunno,' he said, stamping the duvet back with his feet. 'A long time. They should've let me stay with them. But they wouldn't let them.'

'So you couldn't ...' I groped for words. Groped for the *best* words to keep this going. Finally settling on, 'That must make you feel very sad. But it's a comfort to have things we can see and touch that remind us of happier times, isn't it?'

He shrugged then. And twisting round, lay the photo on the bedside table. Face down, I noted. Then he scrambled out of bed.

I stood up, too, yanked at my dressing-gown belt, opened the other curtain. Sunlight flooded in, and I remembered something Kieron once said. One of his sometimes interminable summaries of favourite films. In this case, some time-travelling movie or other, and the complexities of escaping through some temporary portal, crucially, before the portal was shut. It seemed this one was.

But I was wrong.

I turned around to see Miller rootling beneath the head-board, behind his pillow. He pulled his hand out. 'I've got my train still. And see? Rob repainted it for me.'

And there it was. In his hand. 'That must be precious then,' I told him.

He nodded and placed it back, pushing it deep down behind the mattress. ''Tis,' he said. 'So what's for breakfast? I'm starving.'

*   *   *

In a perfect world, my brief glimpse into Miller's past would have marked a sea of change. The moment of connection. The point at which we moved on to a more productive stage with him. But this was not a perfect world, so I didn't hold my breath. Breakfast done – and, true to his word, he *had* been starving – it was almost as if our moment of tender reflection hadn't happened, because straight afterwards it was as if the Miller we knew and loved had been restored to us – approximately half a second after Mike, on hearing his impassioned representations, decreed that, no, there would be no resumption of PlayStation privileges till at least tomorrow, and that obviously dependent on his behaviour today.

So it kicked off. And though, to be fair to Mike, I'd not had an opportunity to share what had happened with him, I felt the route to the precious portal now fading away. No, he didn't want to kick a ball about. No, he didn't want to go to the park. He just wanted, Greta Garbo-style, to be 'LEFT ALONE!', his words hammered home by the thump of his feet on the stairs.

Mike rolled his eyes, obviously, and Tyler wearily shook his head. But the voice in my head reminded me that, nevertheless, we had made progress. That the exchange in the bedroom proved further progress *was* possible. I just had to keep chipping away.

* * *

It was my new link worker, Christine Bolton, who was first on my hit list on Monday morning. Much as I was loath to be critical, Libby had been less than helpful on all of my previous calls, and I was sorely tempted to ring her manager directly. First though, I would see what Christine had to say.

Well, only after I'd said some things to her. Like how I was feeling. Like how Miller was behaving. Like when I could expect to have a fuller, more useful picture. Like when I could expect to get some *help*. 'I really do need some support, Christine, like *yesterday*,' I told her firmly. 'I can't put our programme into practice without some structure outside of the house, and he clearly needs it. Urgently. Before the rot sets in. And quite apart from that – and I'm sorry to labour the point – but I feel like both a jailor and a prisoner. There's no way I'm going to make progress with him until we have some *structure*. Some sort of *plan* put in place.'

To my surprise, I thought I heard my link worker snort before she answered. 'Oh, Casey,' she said, 'I know nothing about this is funny, but John was right. You certainly do call a spade a spade, don't you?' Then a tinkling laugh. Which amused me not a jot.

But then she went on to wax lyrical about my passion and commitment, and though she didn't exactly get round me, I did at least get an inkling, and it was a positive inkling, that Christine called a spade a spade as well. 'Look,' she said. 'I'm feeling *exactly* the same as you are about all of this. It's terrible. There's no way the boy should be left out on a limb like this and it's the social care team's job to do something about it. Leave it with me for half an hour and I promise you, I'll be back with an answer.'

'You mean a resolution?' I asked hopefully. 'Because Libby's already been giving me answers, none of which so far have been helpful.'

'You're right, Casey,' Christine said. 'I promise you, I am on to this. I will have a resolution of some sort. I'll speak to you very soon.'

'And his history,' I said, before she had a chance to escape. 'He has a photo. Of a couple who fostered him early on. Neen and Rob. If you can find anything out about them, or his time with them, that would be a great help. They were obviously very important to him. Still are.'

She promised she would, and I passed the time waiting for the promised call back by writing up some reports about the weekend. As a foster carer, you get used to keeping such records. It's so important to get down all the details, good and bad, as it helps with reflection, both when writing them – the immediate thoughts and reactions – and also later, when you look back and read them again; I'd often then be better able to identify triggers for behaviours, and reflect on which strategies worked and which didn't. It was simple good practice, and I'd learned not to censor myself.

So out it all came – all the anger I'd felt on Saturday, and the frustration, as well as the sadness and empathy that the events of Sunday morning had elicited. And it was always cathartic, so by the time Christine called back, I was in a much more amenable place.

'Good news!' she told me straight away. 'Great news in fact. The outside agency you've been told about are called Helping Hands. They're a project that send outreach workers in regularly to take a child off your hands for a few hours, a few times per week, while they are not in formal education. The idea is that they take a child on activity-based outings, such as rock climbing, bicycle riding, seaside trips, etc., and the time is spent' – I could sense she was reading from a crib sheet – 'both in learning and in openly talking about the past, the present and the future.'

'Sounds a bit hippy dippy,' I said. 'I haven't heard of Helping Hands. Do they have a proven track record of success with this programme?'

Christine laughed. 'Well, it's quite new at the moment, Casey, but my thinking is that anything is better than nothing right now, isn't it? And I have more news. We've an appointment arranged for next week at a school for you. It's a very exclusive school for boys with behavioural problems – and I do mean exclusive – and the entry criteria is really strict, so we've done extremely well to even get that much. So keep your fingers crossed. I'll email you the name of the head, the address and the time, okay? In the meantime, someone called Sheila from Helping Hands will call you later today to arrange to come and take Miller out tomorrow for you.'

Tomorrow? 'Really?' I said. 'Blimey, that's quick work.'

She laughed. 'Well, you did want a resolution, didn't you? Oh, and by the way, that couple you wanted to know about? Janine and Robert Cresswell? You were right, they were his foster carers. From about three months after he came into the system till he was almost seven. So a little shy of two years.'

'And what happened? Why was he moved?'

'Because they could no longer keep him. She fell pregnant with twins. And you know what it's like. Not the easiest decision to make, I'm sure. But with the prospect of two babies … and given the challenges he posed … Sad, but there you go. Such is life, eh? So he was shunted off to a children's home while another family were found for him. And I imagine it all must have gone downhill again from there.'

Christine carried on then, explaining that she'd spoken to Libby's manager, and that fuller records should be emailed to me by the end of the day. But all I could think about was the word she used. 'Shunted.' Shunted on like his little red train.

I thanked her for the 'Helping Hand', for which I was really extremely grateful, but my mind was mostly on the couple who'd made the decision to let him go, and how, somehow, they'd been able to manage the process so that, in Miller's mind, at least, it had been a decision foisted on them, rather than made by themselves, however regretfully.

I was ambivalent about it, to be honest. On the one hand, it meant less of the pain of rejection, which had to be a good thing for Miller's psyche. If he truly believed he'd been taken from them rather than discarded (a hard word, but, if he *had* known, it would surely have been his one) he could retain bright, happy memories of his time there, rather than hating them for 'shunting' him on. But, on the flip side, all that pain was then directed at others – in this case at the powerful people in social services who, for their own inexplicable cruel, callous reasons, had decided he'd be 'better off' in a children's home.

Would it have been better for them to be honest with him? We'd never know. But what I did know was that this, surely, must have been the start – or if not the start, at least a hardening and deepening – of his mistrust and hatred of the adults who 'ruled' his whole life.

I thought about 'Neen', Miller's foster mum, and the day she had found out she was pregnant. With the child she had longed for for a very long time? I imagined so. Perhaps that had been why they'd taken up fostering in the first place – because they thought they couldn't have children of their own? And to then find out it was twins. The delight. The shock. The re-calibration for the foreseeable future. And the big, difficult conversations that must than have ensued. The mental contortions they must have gone through, weighing life as it was with Miller, and life as it might be with two new babies *and* Miller – who, given his developmental stage, and the neglect and abuse he'd suffered, must have been a challenging prospect even then. And the decision they had reached – and for which I would never judge them, because it wasn't as if they'd adopted him – to give Miller up and begin new and different lives. God, that must have been a hard one.

That one day, that sent his childhood in a whole new direction. A direction which Christine had already described as 'downhill'. One day he had been a damaged child who was making steady progress. The next, the brakes were off, and he was hurling downhill. A runaway train that no one had yet been able to stop.

One thing was for sure. No wonder Miller had control issues.

Chapter 11

They say be thankful for small mercies and, in my job, I knew exactly what that meant. More often than not, it meant grabbing hold of the little things that went well, in the hope that, sooner or later, the more frequent big things – the things that *didn't* go so well – would eventually be outweighed.

And today my luck was in, because two came my way.

The first took the shape of a call from my GP. We had a new one these days, a Dr Patterson. He was young enough to be full of energy and up-to-date medical knowledge, and old enough to have acquired lots of experience and wisdom. He was also very much on the ball in terms of social care situations, which meant he understood the specific needs foster carers routinely had.

'So I've had word back from Miller's consultant,' he said, once he'd explained why he was calling, which was to confirm he'd received Miller's medical records and made contact with his sleep doctor. 'And we're both of the opin-ion that since Miller's been using melatonin for so long, it wouldn't hurt – since it's clearly not having the desired effect – to replace them with a placebo and see how that goes; try and get him back to a more natural sleep pattern.'

My first thought was 'here we go', because it meant another bout of tinkering, with me at the sharp end, as the dispenser. But I quickly realised that it could hardly be any worse, could it? And perhaps it would help. After all, no one knew what his usual sleep patterns were, did they?

'Okay, great,' I said. 'Thank you. So for how long?'

'Oh, a couple of months or so, I think,' he said. 'We can review things from there. And if there's no deterioration, or an improvement, then we'll obviously take him off them. Anyway, I've made up a prescription for you. Pick it up whenever you can.'

'Well, funnily enough,' I said, 'I'm escaping for a couple of hours this morning.'

He laughed. 'Bit like that is it?'

'A *lot* like,' I said.

And the other small mercy was in the shape of a small blonde woman called Sheila, who arrived at my doorstep ten minutes later. She wore a black leather jacket atop an oversized linen top, and faded, fashionably ripped-at-the-knee jeans. Teamed with her black ankle boots and her big cross-body handbag, she looked very trendy. And definitely ready for business.

And she'd clearly just finished a cigarette, as she was also accessorised by a waft of eddying tobacco smoke; something I'd become surprisingly attuned to since giving up my own habit. In a spirit of solidarity – no one likes an evangelist, after all – I tried not to wrinkle my nose. I guessed her to be in her late fifties.

'So,' I said when she'd followed me inside, 'Miller's quite excited to be going out with you today, which is a plus. He's currently upstairs getting his trainers on, so he'll be down in a minute. In the meantime, come on in and take a seat. You can tell me all about the all-singing, all-dancing Helping Hands. My link worker didn't seem to know much about it.'

I grinned so she would know I was only teasing, and she laughed out loud. 'God, not much chance of that,' she said. 'I only started there two weeks back. Your Miller is actually my first outreach kid, so I'm really still fumbling my way through. I mean, don't worry, or anything. I do know what I'm *supposed* to do. Take him off for a bit, and try to find out about his interests. Any ideas? Any thoughts on what he might enjoy?'

I shook my head. 'To be honest, I'm as much in the dark as you are and he's been with us almost three weeks now. Aside from his computer games, and pretending to be a dinosaur, he hasn't really given us any indication of what he likes. Though there is one thing,' I added, the little red train, and his attachment to it, still very much on my mind. 'I'm not sure how it would tie in with what you do, but I think he likes trains, or at least he used to. He has a toy one in his room which he's had since he was little. It's very special to him.'

'That's it, then,' Sheila said, slapping her hands down on her thighs. She really did seem very no-nonsense. Very capable. 'Most towns have a train station, right? We can have a drive to one today and go for ice cream or something in their café. I'm sure they'll have one. Then we take it from there. See how it pans out. You never know, it could lead to a bit of a cross-country trip over his sessions – you know, to visit different areas and different trains.'

Two things occurred to me. One being, why hadn't I thought of that? And the second being the circumstances of him coming into care in the first place. Was a fascination with trains the reason he'd been playing by the railway? Why hadn't I thought of that either?

Probably because I'd been too busy hacking my way through the trees to see the whole wood. In any event, this seemed a grand plan, and when Miller arrived in the living room, I was grinning like the proverbial Cheshire cat.

'Oh, I think you're going to have *great* fun,' I told him after introducing Sheila. 'And while you're out on your adventure I'll go and do all the boring stuff like shopping, going to the doctor's for your pill prescription and paying all the bills.' I checked the time. 'So half twelve then?' I asked, calculating the two and a half hours I'd been allotted. 'I'll make sure I'm back by then.'

'And don't worry about us,' Sheila reassured me, even though, in reality, I wasn't. She looked more than capable of doing her job. 'Me and Miller are going to have a ball, aren't we? So you get out and have a bit of a break and we'll see you soon. Come on, kiddo,' she said as she stood up and motioned for Miller to follow. And he did exactly that. All meek and mild, as if butter wouldn't melt in his mouth. I almost gaped as I watched them go. A. Maze. Ing.

'I'm freeeee!' I squealed down the phone to Riley, the minute I'd seen Sheila's car drive off. 'I've just got to pop in and pick up Miller's prescription, then I'm on my way. Are you ready to hit the shops?'

Riley laughed. 'Calm down, Mum! We're only going to the flipping supermarket.'

'Might have time for coffee and cake too,' I said, 'so long as you're ready to be picked up in fifteen minutes.'

She was. With the kids all off in school now, and David at work, Riley also had some welcome free time on her hands. She and her partner David were still doing a bit of fostering – short-term emergency care or respite – but these days she was studying, so had taken 'respite' herself. She wasn't exactly sure what she wanted to do yet, but had recently completed a course on counselling, done some training in outreach support work and was now one year into a child psychology qualification.

'I actually feel like we're bunking off,' Riley giggled as, prescription procured, we pulled into the car park of the large hypermarket that had recently been built on the outskirts of town.

'Me, too, and I've been dying to sample the delights of this place,' I said. 'It says in the paper that there are thirteen different places to eat in here. Can you imagine?'

'Flipping heck, Mum,' Riley said as she drove into a space. 'You sound like you fell asleep in the seventies and have just woken up!'

* * *

We spent the next hour and a half browsing and picking up essentials, both enjoying the simple pleasures of laughing and catching up. Though it would take a full day to take advantage of the multitude of shops here. No wonder Riley had laughed when I'd suggested we use our scrap of time to come here to shop. Because all too soon, it was time to get back into the car, and it shocked me to realise that a dark cloud had started to descend over my shoulders. I tried to shake the unwelcome and unfamiliar feeling.

'I know what you mean,' Riley said when I tried to explain it. 'Remember when Jackson had that bad bout of chickenpox and I was stuck in the house for a week with him? That one day when David took over so I could escape? I honestly didn't want it to end – I didn't want to go home. And this was Jackson!'

I nodded, but wasn't sure that was exactly the problem. Yes, I'd been stir crazy, but it was more than that. More like a sense of impending doom. Because, in truth, despite that glimmer of hope I'd experienced on Sunday morning, it was as if *that* child – the child I was desperate to reach again – had been spirited away, never to return.

I told myself I was just being silly and over-dramatic, and by the time I dropped Riley home, I was in a much more positive mood. Yet as soon as I reached my own street, the gloom once again descended. For no good reason – because I had none. Sheila had looked so on-the-ball and unflappable. She *was* that. *Stop flapping*, I told myself sternly. *All will be well.*

I was surprised, however, as I pulled up to our house, to see Sheila's car already parked up outside. I checked the clock on my dashboard. I was a good fifteen minutes early. And no one was in the car. So where were they?

Perhaps they'd got back early, I decided, and gone for a walk to pass the time. Which at least gave me time to get my provisions inside.

I struggled through the front door, juggling my car keys, door keys and three carrier bags, wondering how the train station trip had gone, and whether Miller had been happy about his adventure. Remembering how lovingly he had looked at his own little train, my bet was that he'd have been thrilled. But passing the living-room door, slightly ajar, I almost jumped out of my skin.

'This is not *funny*!' came a shrill voice. 'Let me out of here right *now*!'

I stopped. How the *hell* did they get into my house? I dropped the bags in the hall and ran through into the kitchen. Where I was gobsmacked to be greeted with the sight of Sheila, who was hopping mad – literally – behind the glass door that led into my conservatory.

The key was in the lock on my side, so, still completely at a loss as to how she got there, I unlocked the door and went in.

'What on earth is going on?' I asked. Though as I spoke, I already had my answer. Miller was outside in the back garden, in the middle of the lawn, doing some kind of weird dance and laughing hysterically. 'Sheila?' I asked, ignoring him (the response was now automatic). 'What happened? Why on earth are you in *here*?'

'I'm locked in here, that's what,' she said. She sounded almost on the edge of tears. 'And I have been for the last bloody hour!'

A Boy Without Hope

I still couldn't understand it. And Miller was still dancing. Dancing even more manically now he could see I was in there as well. He was also now jiggling a pair of keys at me. Obviously those to the outside conservatory doors. How the hell did he get them? I asked Sheila if she knew.

'He had them with him,' she said. 'Was more than happy to tell me, too. Said he crept down in the night and took them. Then spent the rest of the night plotting how to trap me in here.'

No wonder he'd looked so cheerful when they'd left. I cursed my stupidity. My inexcusable naivety. As much as I was angry, I could see how that could have happened. The inner door was always kept locked so I would have had no reason to unlock it, just to check on the keys in the conservatory door.

And it wasn't like he couldn't creep around the house in the small hours. Once I was asleep – and no way could I keep awake all night – there was nothing to stop him doing so, either. Why hadn't that occurred to me? Because it hadn't, that was why. Because as long as he was quiet in his bedroom, that was enough. Or *apparently* in his bedroom. God, so stupid!

But why? With the prospect of doing something fun? Again, it was painfully easy to answer my own question. Because this wasn't about fun, was it? This was about being in control. And I'd been so fixated on that precious two hours with my daughter that I'd failed to consider that this was exactly the sort of control tactic he would employ.

I went and got my spare key and unlocked the back door. 'Miller get inside please,' I said, keeping my tone even. 'I really can't believe you've done this. You need to come inside and apologise to Sheila.'

To my surprise, Miller strolled in, smiled sweetly, handed the keys to me and apologised. He then said he was going upstairs to change, as his trainers had been hurting his feet. I shook my head in disbelief as he walked by us.

'I'm *so* sorry,' I said to Sheila, but then picked up on something else. 'An hour, you said? Did I get the time wrong?'

Sheila shook her head. She looked slightly uncomfortable. 'It was probably longer than an hour,' she said. 'We'd only just left the town really. Miller asked if we could stop at the big McDonald's drive-through for a breakfast burger and a milkshake. I'd planned to buy lunch anyway, so I didn't object, but when we parked up for our food he said he needed the loo, and when he came out he was acting all shocked' – she frowned and pointed – 'and waving those very keys at me. He said he'd taken the dog out first thing and must have put the keys in his pocket by mistake, and that we needed to get back to give them to you or you wouldn't be able to leave the house.' She frowned again. 'I *know*. Born yesterday, or what? And, of course, when we got back here he asked me to go in with him as he was scared. Never even occurred to me to point out that your car wasn't on the drive any more. So of course I went with him – round the back, into the garden and through the doors there – and he immediately ran back out and locked me in here. I feel such an idiot,' she finished.

'But we don't even have a dog.' Hadn't she noticed?

'I know that *now*,' she said. 'God, I'm such a fool. Oh, and another thing,' she said, picking up her huge handbag. 'I don't know when he did it, but I'm pretty sure he must have. There was a full pack of cigarettes in my bag when I arrived this morning, and now there isn't.' Which, of course, she would have checked because, boy, she must have wanted one. 'Look, I have to go, Casey,' she said, slinging the bag over her shoulder. 'I have another child to pick up, and I don't want to be late.' She smiled a grim smile. 'Let's hope the day doesn't get any worse, eh? But I'll give you a ring in a couple of days to arrange the next visit, okay?'

'Of course,' I said, wondering if she actually would, after today's fiasco. 'And, look, don't worry about it. You might not have discovered any new interests, but at least you know what you're dealing with. And how!'

'All grist to the mill!' she said, as I showed her out. I watched her go. And pondered the metaphysical as I watched her drive off. No wonder I'd had the sense of foreboding.

And now I had a number of new things to deal with. Stealing the cigarettes – was he smoking? And the not insignificant matter of him taking our keys. I also needed to think about how on earth we could enforce him staying in his bedroom during the night. I shut the front door, and before tackling the subject of my dark thoughts (he could stew for a while yet) I picked my bags up and put the shopping away.

It didn't take a detective, I mused, as I banged cupboard doors shut, to work out the scores on Miller's virtual board right now. I was definitely on the losing team, and the victor was winning. By a mile.

Chapter 12

A few days after the incident with the perhaps erroneously named Helping Hands, Miller's social worker was standing on my doorstep. She was wearing a large straw sun hat, huge rainbow-coloured disc earrings, and a long, floaty yellow and lime green dress. She also wore the same pair of Dr. Martens boots (in this heat!) and an extra-large grin.

She was summer personified, which was perhaps why I felt so irritable. Because, despite the sunshine that had obviously inspired her clothing choices this morning, I felt as if I was living beneath a perpetual black rain cloud.

'Hi, Libby,' I said with as much enthusiasm as I could muster. 'Do come in. Though I'm afraid Miller isn't up yet. I have tried but he's ignoring me at the moment.'

'What a little lazybones,' Libby said, as she wafted down the hall behind me. 'But no matter. I can always go up to have my chat with him if need be.'

This was a statutory visit – one which all social workers are required to make at least every six weeks. Though, admittedly, it hadn't been quite that long yet, it still felt like a lifetime since I'd last seen her. I led her through to the kitchen diner, and ushered her to a chair. 'Would you like a drink of something?' I asked her, reaching for the kettle.

'Oh, just something cold for me,' she said, fanning herself with one of my coasters. 'Water or juice, or something? I'm roasting.'

Chance would be a fine thing, I thought, glancing wistfully at the bright blue outdoors. Yes, I could sit in the garden, but there was only so much of that you could do without aching for a chance to actually venture *out*. Which, apart from a lingering trip to the supermarket after Mike got home from work a couple days earlier, I hadn't had since the debacle with Sheila from Helping Hands. Whose silence, incidentally, was beginning to speak volumes.

As was Miller's.

I'd read the riot act to him after the Sheila business, albeit in a necessarily restrained fashion, and pointed out that I'd have to report the incident to both mine and his social workers, and that it would be written up on his record. 'You really don't do yourself any favours,' I'd told him, 'having things like this available for others to read. These incidents follow you around, Miller, as I'm sure you realise.'

He'd simply shrugged. 'I don't care,' he said. 'Why should I? You'll get rid of me, like they all do, and they're going to run out of places to send me to soon. And then I'll have my own way, won't I?'

What? I felt totally exasperated. 'Is that what you want, then?' I asked him. 'To leave here and be sent somewhere else?'

The pause was lengthy. And I let it extend. Did he really want to leave us? He'd had at least two opportunities to do so, and had taken neither of them. Or was running away, under his own steam, and fetching up at, say, a police station, not good enough, not dramatic enough, for him? Was it that important that he orchestrate things so he was forcibly removed, rather than leaving – and removed with as much upset and recrimination as possible? Increasingly, it seemed so. And I felt at a loss to understand it. To understand *him*. But perhaps I was asking too much even to try to. Even Miller didn't seem to know what Miller wanted.

He continued to sit and scowl at the floor, arms crossed tightly across his chest. 'You know what, Miller,' I said eventually. 'You're right. At least half-right. There are only so many foster carers out there, as you say. But there are *alternatives* to foster care, and they won't run out of those. And if you –'

'I *don't care*!' he screeched, leaping up and running from the room.

Which was precisely why it was so clear that he *did*.

* * *

Later, when Mike had come home from work, we'd had a debrief over coffee. Most frustrating of all the current crop of frustrations was that I was so powerless to do anything about the missing cigarettes and lighter. Miller had naturally denied that he'd taken them and equally naturally – assuming he had, which I was sure of – wasn't going to leave them anywhere I could easily find them. Which meant the only way to do so would be to properly search his room; something I was categorically not allowed to do without his consent.

And, for the most part, this is a very important safeguard for children – they have a right to their privacy, and that needs to be respected. So the only way I was going to be able to conduct a proper search of his bedroom would be to wait until he next left the house without me – a pretty long wait, I suspected. The only other way would be if I made a formal complaint of theft to the police and social services, which would mean an equally long wait until they had the time to come over and help me to do an official search. Which left me a bit stuck, because I obviously didn't want to waste precious resources, so I decided I'd have to take my chances and wait for the opportunity to take a proper look myself.

And just at the point when I was explaining my frustration, Miller had appeared in the kitchen doorway with the PlayStation in his hands.

He'd held it out to Mike. 'Save you the bother of coming up to take it off me,' he'd said. 'Just let me know when I can have it back.'

* * *

I looked now at Miller's sunny social worker, who was fanning her face with her hand at my table. Where did I start? Libby's language of 'little lazybones' was about as far off the mark as it was possible to be.

I poured two glasses of apple juice and sat down at the table opposite her. 'Well, we might as well make the most of Miller's refusal to join us for a bit, mightn't we? It'll give us a chance to talk freely.' (Where, in 'us', I meant 'me'.)

Libby sighed. 'I have read all the emails and reports you've been sending in, Casey,' she said – slightly defensively, I thought. 'And I really do feel for you. I honestly thought we would have him in education by now.' She sighed. 'If only he wasn't such a little monkey.'

I swear, that if I heard that expression one more time, I might have to shake her. Well, not really, obviously, but it really did make me want to scream. 'Little monkey' was what you might call an errant toddler, or a naughty puppy. Not a boy entering his teens with multiple, complicated, deep-seated behavioural and emotional problems, and a massive god complex, to boot. I took a breath and forced a smile out.

'We need something as soon as possible,' I said firmly. 'And I'm conscious that there is very little time left now until schools break up for the summer, so if we don't get something sorted asap, we're looking at schools closing down, and no chance to make progress till September. Not a thought I'm exactly relishing, as I'm sure you can imagine, Libby. So there is a great deal riding on this.'

She beamed me a mega-watt smile. 'I have some good news in that regard,' she said. 'Though also a bit of bad news. I'm afraid the Helping Hands project have withdrawn their offer of support. They feel that Miller is too much of a risk to be out and about in the community, what with his running off, and his refusal to co-operate. The good news, however,' she added quickly, 'is that we have an appointment arranged for Miller at a special school tomorrow. One that deals particularly with the kind of behavioural problems Miller presents with.'

A Boy Without Hope

I was still digesting the bad news, which rankled. No, it wasn't surprising that Sheila wouldn't be coming back – being locked in a conservatory for over an hour whilst being taunted from outside the door must have been a traumatic experience for her – but really? The entire project withdrawing their support? That did surprise me. Surely they had a team of resilient, dedicated, up-for-a-challenge staff? Couldn't they have at least tried someone else before giving up?

Clearly not. So not the all-singing, all-dancing answer I had been sold, then. But there was no point brooding on it. I had to focus on the good news.

'Well, it's certainly good news about the school,' I said. 'Christine Bolton did already mention it, actually.'

'Ah, of course,' Libby added. 'And I believe she's going to email you all the gen on the school itself – which sounds as if it couldn't be more ideal.'

She already had in fact. Though there was obviously no point in mentioning it. 'And you think there's a good chance they'll take him?'

She waggled her hand up and down. 'Let's hope so,' she said. 'Much will depend on how things go tomorrow, I imagine. Have you given any thought as to how you're going to coax him there, by the way? Because the school's out of town, over beyond where I live, so there doesn't seem much sense in me driving all the way here just to turn around and go back on myself, so I was going to suggest I meet you there, if it's okay with you?'

She looked at me hopefully, clearly well aware that this first hurdle was likely to be a high one. How exactly *was* I going to coax him to the interview if he decided he didn't want to go? From everything I'd read, Miller was fully aware that he had to be in education, by law, and once in a school, did actually manage to get some work done. The problem, as ever, seemed to be rooted in control. Without close super- vision, one-on-one, he couldn't resist trying to get it, despite knowing the probable consequences, through long experi- ence. He'd also managed to establish – again by experience – that if he refused to get into transport to get him *to* school, then no one could physically force him. I don't think I'd ever had to deal with a child for whom the expression 'cutting off your nose to spite your face' felt so painfully apt.

One thing was for sure. I *had* to find a way to get him there, because the prospect of him attending school felt as if someone had just presented me with a free all-expenses- paid holiday, without any small print or bolt-on compul- sory attendance at timeshare presentations.

'Leave that to me,' I said. 'I'll get him there. By hook or by crook. What time do we have to be there, and who else is going?'

'Just me,' she said. 'And I know it's a long old round trip for you, but if and when he starts attending, we'll obviously organise transport for him.' The smile now became a frown. 'Hmm. That's quite a point too, isn't it? We'll need to be able to actually get him *into* the transport, won't we? And to stay put once he's in there.'

My mood grew a little fractious again, because I'd never known pennies to drop so painfully slowly. Of *course* that was likely to present problems.

A Boy Without Hope

First things first, I told myself. 'Let's cross that bridge when we get to it,' I told Libby. 'The most important thing initially is to get him to that meeting and try to get him a starting date, isn't it?'

Libby downed her juice. 'Exactly,' she said. 'And fingers crossed we'll be all set for September.'

'September? If they offer him a place, why can't he start now? Is the place not available yet?'

She looked surprised. 'Not that they've said, but I think September will be the better option anyway, surely? I'm not sure he's in the best emotional place to be thrown in at the deep end. What with all the upheaval he's already been through.'

I was tempted to point out that he was already in the deep end. And the small matter that I felt like I was drowning in it. 'Libby, he needs to be in *school*,' I said. 'As soon as possible. Trust me. All this holing up in his room is only making things more difficult.'

'But a period of adjustment ...'

Count to ten, Casey. She *really* wasn't getting it. 'Seriously, Libby, I really think –'

'And I've also got a couple of trips for him half-planned over the next couple of weeks. One of our play-workers I've been liaising with is –'

'Which is *great* but, as I say, I think the priority is *school*.'

I could see I was getting nowhere, so I gave up even trying. No point arguing over something that was still only hypothetical, after all. But if he *did* get a place, then I'd be ready. With six long weeks of school holidays looming over me – coming ever closer – two weeks of Miller in a school, as in out

133

of my sight, was beginning to feel like the only way I could even consider the future without mentally screaming.

So I would be more than ready. I would be an unstoppable flipping force. 'Well, we'll cross that bridge when we come to it,' I said brightly. 'In the meantime –'

'I should pop up and say hello to the little monkey, shouldn't I? Unless you want to try and coax him down? Though if he knows I'm here, he's unlikely to want to, is he? So maybe best if I just slip upstairs and surprise him. What do you think? He must be bored out of his mind stuck indoors all day, day after day, mustn't he?' *Count to ten, Casey.* 'So at least if I'm the bearer of good news about some trips and a possible school place, I've got the tactical advantage, haven't I?'

'Indeed you have,' I agreed, marvelling at how she could refer to him so benignly then talk in terms of a war campaign all in the same thought process. But perhaps that was the central conundrum in dealing with a boy like Miller, right there. 'Yes, of course,' I added. 'Go on up.'

Libby did so, and, glancing at the time, I decided I'd use a bit of it in deciding what to have for lunch – something else which was still a major headache. Though I still felt in the dark about lots of aspects of Miller's behaviour – there had sadly been no re-run of his unguarded moment about the toy train – I was now an expert on the vagaries of his eating peccadillos. Even if I didn't yet know what they meant.

For starters, if he came down too late for what he considered to be the right time for breakfast, he would refuse to eat anything till lunchtime. Literally nothing I could say would convince him that it was okay to have toast or cereal or a bacon sandwich at, say, ten o'clock. He would simply frown – even look upset – and decline any offer of food, preferring to go hungry, and eat 'lunch' food at what he considered to be lunchtime. And, even if he was ravenous, not a single moment earlier.

A lot of kids had food fads. I knew this from experience. And that some of them were often seemingly inexplicable in their regulations. A former foster child, Georgie, for instance, would only eat what he considered 'white' foods, such as rice, white bread, white-coloured sauces and pasta. And would freak if offered anything else. But then Georgie had been quite profoundly autistic, and set in that context his obsession with colour rather than taste did make some sense.

Similarly, our first foster child, Justin, had food issues. He too was obsessed with timings – specifically what time his next meal was going to be served. Until he had this confirmed – in writing, on a chart on the fridge door – he couldn't relax, and woe betide us if we subsequently ate late. But, again, Justin had been neglected to the point of being half-starved, so fear of going hungry was a very real emotion for him.

Miller's rules around food, though, still foxed me. Though I was beginning to realise that it wasn't just about controlling *us* – it was about exerting control over himself. It was almost as if he was punishing his own body. If he was awake at eight, and I called up to coax him down for breakfast, he'd call back 'eight-oh-three' and all would be well. But if he had decided the night before that he would get up at eight and *didn't* – slept in till nine, say – then it was no good me trying to make him eat anything. No 'nine o'clock, three minutes past nine' rule applied. Having had his own body clock fool him, he'd refuse to eat at all.

And, of course, my suggestion that perhaps I should wake him at a set time every morning – such as he'd have to adhere to, of course, when back in school – was greeted with predicable haughty disdain. Because that, of course, was ceding control.

Oh, he was a puzzle, and no mistake, as my mum might have said.

* * *

Libby was back down within ten minutes. 'Oh dear,' she said, the bright sunny smile having packed its bags now. 'He really does hate me. It's as simple as that. He only spoke one word the whole time I was up there, and that was 'nope'. He was rolled up in his duvet, and all I could do was ramble on, trying to get him to say something – *anything*.'

'And how about the school visit?' I pressed. 'How did he react to that?'

'Like I just told you. That was all he said. "Nope." He really is a little ...'

'... boy with a bit of a god complex,' I interrupted. I really didn't have the stomach to hear her favourite term for him again. 'Leave it with me, Libby,' I said, for a second time. 'We shall have him at that school appointment tomorrow, one way or another. Don't worry. I'll sort it. I'll see you there at ten.'

The smile returned. 'Well, if anyone can, you can,' she said.

A Boy Without Hope

And that's because, I thought, *I have never wanted anything quite so badly.*

* * *

I saw Libby out and went back into the kitchen, and stared up at the ceiling, almost as if, at least if I looked hard enough, I might be able to see into Miller's room. Into his *head*. How *should* I play this? Softly, softly, or a no-nonsense, tough-talk approach?

But I was interrupted in my reveries by the very antithesis of 'softly, softly' as Tyler bounded in through the front door. 'Woo hoo!' he yelled, throwing his backpack dramatically across the kitchen floor before doing a victory dance. Or something like that, at any rate. 'I did it, Mum – I actually did it! I finished my last exam!' He then punched one arm into the air, leaned his head back dramatically and, in a voice vaguely resembling that of Mel Gibson as William Wallace, yelled, 'Freeeeeeedom!'

I couldn't help but laugh at his theatrics. 'Oh, well *done*,' I said, hugging him. 'I'm *so* proud of you, sweetheart. And so's your dad. We should plan something to celebrate.'

'Steady on, Ma,' he laughed. 'I don't get my results for six weeks yet. Doing them's one thing, but passing them is another thing altogether.'

'Give over,' I scoffed. 'You've worked so hard, love. I just *know* you'll have done well. So. What should we do? Go out for a meal or something?'

Now it was Tyler's turn to tilt his head up to the ceiling. 'Aren't you forgetting something, Mum?' he said. 'Like

Mister "I-don't-want-to-do-anything" up there? Nah, I thought I might just do something with Denver and a few other guys tonight, if that's okay.' He grinned his cheeky grin. The one that had always melted me. 'And maybe you could celebrate by giving me some, um, money?'

I went to punch his arm, even while knowing that we'd do exactly that, but then another thought stopped me in my tracks. Now that Tyler had finished school, perhaps tomorrow's school visit for Miller might not be so difficult after all. Much as I hated the thought of using Tyler to my own ends, I was already having a eureka moment. And not just for my own ends, either. Perhaps roping Tyler in with helping me with Miller might just change the dynamic between the two of them. Perhaps it would give Tyler a stronger sense that he was in the driving seat a little more, and diffuse some of the tension that had built up between them. Responsibility was empowering for kids; I knew that from my days running the Behaviour Unit in school. Plus it might help make Miller see that we were a united team – *all* of us. It certainly couldn't do any harm.

'Oh, of course we'll pay for whatever it is you want to do, love,' I reassured him. 'And yes, it does make much more sense for you and your friends to do something fun tonight. We'll just go out for a nice family meal down the line. But, Ty, I might need a little favour from you tomorrow. Which would mean you getting up early. Are you up for that?'

Tyler held out his hand. 'Deal,' he said, as we shook. 'And I'm guessing it involves looking after Miller?'

'Not quite,' I said, winking. 'Come on, let's get a sandwich and I'll fill you in on my cunning plan ...'

Chapter 13

The next day, as I'd asked him to, Mike woke me up early. 'I'm ready to set off to work, lovey,' he whispered, placing a mug of coffee on the bedside table, 'but are you absolutely sure you wouldn't like me to phone in and take the morning off?'

When we'd discussed it the previous evening, he'd been more than happy to do so; he knew full well how important it was that we managed to get Miller into some sort of school. And if we didn't manage to pull it off today, it was almost a given that our next shot at doing so wouldn't be happening till September. We were just too close to the summer holidays now.

The school summer holidays ... all six long weeks of them. I couldn't even begin to *think* about that. But at the same time, I felt confident that we could do it.

'No, no,' I said, shuffling to a sitting position and reaching for my coffee. 'You go off to work, love. And don't worry. Me and Tyler have this, I promise.'

Mike frowned. 'To be honest, I'm still not sure we should be getting Tyler involved with it all, Case. Not just because it's getting him to do our dirty work, either. It just feels a bit too much like we're admitting defeat.'

I tutted at him. 'Oh, don't say that, Mike! You make it sound like I'm forcing him to do something horrible. Which I'm not. Well, apart from dragging him out of bed early, which hardly counts as child abuse, does it? I'm simply using him as an incentive, to encourage Miller to attend the visit, and with his full agreement, I might add.'

'I get that,' Mike conceded. 'I know he's as keen to get him out of the house as we are. But I heard him on the phone to Denver last night after you'd gone to bed, and I'm not sure he's quite on message in terms of the word "encouragement". The way he seems to see it is as "by any means necessary". So I've told him in no uncertain terms that under no circumstances is he to get in a scuffle with the lad. Seriously, love, it's not muscle we need here. If it ends up coming to that then we're on a hiding to nothing.'

I couldn't help but smile as I gave him his goodbye kiss. 'As if it even would!' I said. 'Honestly, Mike, I'm not bloody Ma Baker!'

Nevertheless, I did still feel a little guilty. Truth be known, Mike was right. I shouldn't have been enlisting Tyler's help in the first place. And though I didn't anticipate a scene, because our plan was a subtle one, I wasn't naïve enough to assume that just because Tyler was involved, Miller would miraculously find the whole idea thrilling.

Still, it was decided now, and Tyler had already done his 'homework', so all I could do was cross my fingers.

With both my coffee and ruminations finished, I got up and showered before going downstairs to sort out some breakfast, then, as per the plan, went into the hall and shouted up the stairs. 'Tyler! Time to get up, love! We don't want to be late. Can you make sure Miller gets up too please?'

'Already up, Mum!' Tyler yelled back. 'I'll be down as soon as I've got Miller up and ready!'

I then waited patiently at the bottom of the steps to listen to what might follow. If a bad tone was set, it could set in for the day. I heard Tyler calling Miller's name as he went into his room, and a few moments later heard, 'Come on, mate, don't ignore me'. Then some unclear mutterings before Tyler appeared at the top of the landing, with a grin on his face, and his thumbs in the air. 'He's getting dressed,' Ty called down – loudly enough so that Miller could hear him. 'I've explained how I've been wanting to take a look at this school for ages, so I could see the huge motorbike track they have there.'

This threw me into confusion. 'You shouldn't have said that!' I scolded as Tyler followed me into the kitchen. 'He's going to go mad when he realises you've made that up.'

Tyler rolled his eyes. 'Mum, I *haven't*. Did you even bother checking out their website? They *do* have a bike track. The whole place looks amazing. More like a holiday camp than a school, if you ask me.'

'Really?' I asked. 'Motorbikes? Wow! I bet he'll be impressed with that and, for your information, mister clever clogs, I did look at the website. I just didn't have a chance to go through every single page. Any other delights we could point out to him?'

'Oh, loads,' Tyler said, grabbing his cereal box from the cupboard. 'You'll see. There's all sorts of amazing extra-curricular stuff that you don't get at normal schools.'

'Oh, please don't say "normal" schools, Ty,' I said, as I passed the milk. 'I get into enough trouble as it is for not being politically correct. It's just a *different* school – focusing on behaviour, that's all. We shouldn't really start making comparisons.'

Whatever remark Tyler was about to make died on his lips, as Miller walked into the kitchen and scraped a chair out from under the table. He put his head into his hands and banged his elbows as he slumped forwards, clearly not willing to engage in any morning chatter.

'Morning, love,' I said brightly. 'Cereal? Toast? Or would you like something else for breakfast? We've got a long drive ahead so best to eat something.'

I waited for him to respond but he just shook his head. 'Not hungry yet?' I asked. 'Well, no worries, in that case. I'll put a few bits on the table and if you fancy trying anything, just help yourself. If not, it's not a problem. I'm sure it won't kill you to wait for lunch.'

Again, no response. I also noticed that Miller had not put on any of the clothes I had washed, ironed and neatly laid out for him the night before. Instead he was wearing a pair of trackie bottoms he'd arrived with – ones that were clearly too small and showed around four inches of his socks. Mismatched socks, moreover – one fluorescent orange and one blue. He also sported a crumpled T-shirt, a similarly creased hoodie and a pair of ancient trainers with holes in the toes.

In short, he looked like he'd got dressed at a church-hall jumble sale. With the lights off. 'What was wrong with the clothes I sorted out for you, Miller?' I asked mildly. 'The ones you've chosen look too small for you, love. Do you want to go get changed again? Choose something different?' I carefully avoided making mention of making a good impression, but the unspoken hint was, of course, there anyway.

'No!' Miller snapped, finally raising his head and glaring. 'I *chose* these. I *like* these. I am going to wear *these* clothes. I should be allowed to *choose* my *own* clothes at my age.'

He was spoiling for a row. Nothing new there. But he wasn't going to get one. There was no point in having one over something so trifling. I would surely have some time alone with the school staff to explain that I hadn't selected his attire and that it was probably his intention to dress to un-impress. Instead, I dug out a yoghurt, plus some grapes, strawberries and blueberries, and placed them on a plate along with a glass of milk and a cereal bar. 'There you go, love,' I said, as I put the plate on the table. 'Help yourself, and you are right, of course, you are most definitely old enough to choose what to wear.'

'Charming!' Tyler called out, his mouth filled with muesli. 'Miller gets all that lot and I get a bowl of rabbit food.'

I knew Tyler was only teasing; trying to lighten the mood, and perhaps diffuse his own irritation, but Miller clearly wasn't having any of it.

'You can fucking have it!' he growled, his face pinched and contorted. 'I don't eat that shit.' He pushed the plate away, causing the glass of milk to topple and spill all over the table.

Tyler jumped up to avoid the white stream falling onto his jeans. 'What the hell?' he shouted. 'Go get a cloth and sort this mess out, Miller. What the hell do you think you're doing?'

Gr-eat. 'Tyler, leave it, love,' I said, as I hastily reached for a tea towel. 'Miller, I'm not having this behaviour in this house, do you hear me? Now go sit in the living room until we're ready to leave, please.'

As if he'd been waiting for this exact situation to come about, Miller smirked as he stood up and pushed the chair away from him. 'I'll have "a little think about my behaviour" while I'm there as well, shall I?' He put the words in finger quote marks. 'I'm not fucking *five*!'

I could almost feel the waves of anger emanating now from Tyler. 'Get out of here,' he said, his voice even but loaded. 'And don't you *dare* speak to my mum like that. Ever. You really don't want to test me, mate. Got that? Because I mean it. You're lucky it's me here just now – not Riley or Kieron. Now do as my mum says and *get in that room!*'

Grrrr-eat, I thought again. This was going *really* well.

Miller marched away as instructed, but in a ridiculously comic manner, lifting each leg almost up to his chin before taking every step, putting me in mind of Mr Bean. It would have been funny if it wasn't so bloody infuriating. 'And what will *they* do?' he yelled, as he slammed the door behind him. 'I'm a foster kid, remember. They can't touch me!'

I placed my arm round Tyler's shoulders. I could feel that he was shaking. 'Calm down, love,' I said. 'He's just trying to push our buttons. And we can pull this back again if we refuse to let him. I know you're angry – I am too – but if either of us lose control too, we're playing right into his hands. Because that's what it's all about – him trying to control a situation that's *out* of his control, and in the only way he knows how. He doesn't want to go to that school – he doesn't want to go to *any* school – and he knows from experience that if he creates a huge drama, then there's a good chance any plans will go out of the window. Which means he gets to stay put. Which is the last thing he needs. Or really wants, for that matter. Not deep down. So we *have* to try show him a different way somehow. At least show him that his tantrums – his attempts to manipulate us – won't work.'

'Mum, I know that,' Tyler said. 'I understand what you're saying. But how the hell do you manage not to throttle him when he speaks to you like that? Honestly, I could swing for the little … God, he's just so … *Grrr*!'

'I know,' I said. 'And I feel the same as you do. But I'm not sure I'm allowed to throttle young children in my care. Though I'll double check the manual if you like, just to be sure. You never know – they might have updated it, mightn't they?'

Tyler at least managed a grim smile. 'I know that as well, Mum. It's just, *God*, he's so desperate to *get* that reaction. And the nicer you are to him the more he pushes you, every single time. How do you *deal* with that?'

Hmm, I thought. As of this moment? Hand on heart? Total truth? Pretty badly.

* * *

But it seemed my strategy – to leave Miller to stew while I counselled Tyler and tidied the kitchen – was going to bear fruit. When I put my head round the living room door twenty minutes later, and told him it was now time to leave, I didn't get so much as a peep of protest in response. No, he didn't exactly leap up in a state of excited anticipation, but he did, thank goodness, follow the pair of us out to the car. Indeed, his only protest was a silent one, in that he wouldn't properly put on his trainers; just slopped out with them untied and squashed down at the back, under his heels. Okay, I thought. Leave it. Let him score that small point. Because actually getting him into the car – and with the child lock deployed – was by far the biggest, most important one.

As per our plan, though Tyler would normally sit up front with me, he dutifully climbed into the back with a surprised Miller, all the better to enthuse, one-on-one, about the coming school visit.

Though, almost from the off, he had a hard time getting a word in. As had happened before, there was something about being in a car that seemed to set Miller off on his endless rambling chain of random questions. Though, today, it was more a monologue, and there was a definite 'disaster' theme. Floods, train wrecks, fires, earthquakes, bombs and plane crashes – in fact anything that was likely to produce casualties.

He was also animated to a point that was extreme, even for him, claiming among other things that if you paused your computer and enlarged the screen you could actually see the different shades of blood on dead or maimed people, and if you looked at mass shootings in war-torn areas you could often spot limbs that had been blown off by bombs. The chatter was endless, one subject rolling straight into another, almost as though he were reading it from a script or report. And with barely a breath in between.

With a sat nav to follow to an unknown destination, I managed, of necessity as much as anything, to tune out from time to time. Poor Tyler, on the other hand, had no such respite, and, not for the first time since Mike had gone to work that morning, I was all too aware of his concerns – should I really be roping Tyler into all this?

Not that Miller was much interested in having a two-way conversation. Yes, there was the odd 'do you see?', or 'don't you think?', but, for the most part, he preferred to answer his own questions, and when Tyler did try to inter-ject, he simply carried on talking over him. I remembered a snippet I'd seen in his file – that more than one set of foster carers had reported the same thing. That, owing to the danger his constant chattering and seat-yanking presented, several taxi drivers had refused to be his driver.

In one case, the council had even paid for an escort, for the driver's safety. Not to mention his sanity, I suspected.

It was, therefore, a very long, tiresome journey. So I don't think I'd ever been so pleased to hear the sat nav lady announce that 'you have arrived at your destination'. And I'm pretty sure Tyler felt the same. Far from having an opportunity to enthuse to Miller about the school, he'd had a masterclass in the finer points of battlefield trauma, extreme first aid and lower-limb amputation.

Happily, though, the school needed no bigging up. Because it looked not so much a school as a huge stately home. And as we swept up to the enormous gates – 'swept' being the only word to choose – we had an eye-popping view of a jaw-dropping place. And though Miller couldn't bring himself to show any interest, Tyler and I went 'Woweeee!' in unison.

Because it really was a magical-looking place. Beyond the gates, the school itself was at the end of a lengthy drive flanked by emerald grass, but as we drove up it there was so much else to see as well. I spotted huge flower beds, rows of trees, a pond, then another, larger pond. I could see areas that were fenced off and where it looked like they grew fruit and vegetables, and, adjacent to those, even chickens!

What thrilled me even more, though, was an area I spotted in the distance, where a large stand of trees, like a forest in miniature, was accessorised by ropes, swings and climbing frames – even treehouses. Surely this was every child's dream?

Forget our carefully planned programme of Tyler acting all excited – he was genuinely gobsmacked by what he was seeing.

'Oh, my God, Miller, *look*!' he was saying, pointing out each new wonder as we passed it. 'Oh my God, just how lucky are *you*? God, I'd have given *anything* to go to a school like this. *Seriously*.'

Miller, however, was now, finally, silent. Was he as awed by what he was seeing as we were? As I pulled into the visitors' parking area, my wheels crunching on the pale gravel, I took the opportunity to check on his reaction. And what I saw there was plain. It was terror.

I don't mind admitting that it caught me off balance. And it shouldn't have. Of course he'd be scared. But it was so at odds with the way he'd been both before and on the journey, that, at least for a moment, it caught me off-guard.

But it was only for a moment. Of *course* he was fearful. What, for Tyler and I, was a Hogwarts-style palace of adventures was, for him, the first sighting of a step into the unknown. Potentially, the start of another nightmare. So of course he would be afraid. He'd been shunted around from place to place all his life, never knowing why, never knowing when, never knowing where. Never having the chance to get settled in anywhere, before being moved on again, chucked out, or (I didn't doubt) shunned by the other kids. And I suspected that his principal thought at that moment was how he could control things to ensure it would soon all be over. That he could get back to his small world, his safe world – the one *he* controlled. With his computer games, and solitude, and routines, and certainty. With no one telling him what to do, where to go, *what* to be.

Because that was surely the most important thing about Miller. That even *he* didn't know what that should be.

But here, right in front of us, was a real shot at helping him do that. A school that, from what I'd heard and read, could offer him the opportunity of becoming the best Miller he could be. Well, only if he'd open up and let them help him. I leaned into the back and squeezed his arm. And, to my astonishment, he let me. 'Don't worry, kiddo,' I said. 'I'm going to be with you all the way. Everything will be okay, I promise.'

Because it *had* to be. There were precious few shots left.

Chapter 14

After security had taken us through a small reception area, we emerged into a grand hall. It was oak-panelled, and in the centre was an enormous chandelier; it had several rooms leading off it. The man who greeted us (no less imposing – so very obviously the headmaster) introduced himself as Mark Hammond.

He smiled and shook my hand. Then Tyler's. Then Miller's. 'Welcome to our humble abode,' he boomed as he led us to a room off to the right. 'I've been head here for just over ten years now,' he added conversationally, 'and by the time you've seen the whole place I hope you'll understand just why I'm so proud of this school. And, of course, who wouldn't want to work in these beautiful surroundings?'

He swept his arm around the room we were currently entering. 'This is the library,' he said as I took it all in; luxurious leather Chesterfields, set on deep patterned rugs and surrounded by walls of towering book cases. 'The boys here enjoy a minimum of an hour a day in here, reading –'

He grinned at Tyler. 'Obviously quietly. Though it's so relaxing and peaceful here that they often stay longer. Which we don't mind at all,' he added. 'Indeed, it's a matter of some pride that many parents feed back to us that being here has resulted in their boys reading the first entire book of their lives. Do you read, Miller?' he then asked.

'A bit,' Miller mumbled.

Mr Hammond placed a hand on his shoulder, as if knighting him. 'Well, then, I'll consider it my personal mission to change that to "a lot". Anyway, come along, everyone. Let's get on with the tour.'

And tour it was. Mr Hammond marched us along a dizzying array of corridors, up staircases, down stairwells, along various landings. You could get lost here, I thought. And not be found for days. I hoped that wouldn't end up being the case with Miller.

But I knew I mustn't get ahead of myself – he didn't even have a place yet. For all Mr Hammond's bonhomie, and regular use of the term 'when you', rather than 'if you', I knew this wasn't a done deal quite yet.

Oh, but, if he did get a place, *what* a place for him to be. Every wall was adorned with huge framed historical pictures, each of which (we were told, via the ongoing commentary) had been crafted by both alumni and local artists, many of them going back generations. And it did feel as if we'd stepped back in time; reliving a golden age in this magnificent building, which seemed more like a grand museum than a school. In fact, the only thing that gave the game away that this was a place of education were the many, many photographs of smartly dressed boys, singly and in groups, receiving various awards. For sporting achievements, or for work in the community, or for making outstanding contributions to this subject or that subject. The very quantity of them was incredible in itself. My old inner-city comp this was definitely not.

I kept glancing at Miller, to make sure he wasn't too overwhelmed, and was pleased to see Tyler, who was walking alongside him, pointing out various noticeboards, and photographs, and art works, and rolls of honour, and once again appearing to be genuinely awed by the majesty and history of the place.

Even the day's menu for the school canteen was a curlicued poster set in a golden frame.

'Breakfast, lunch, dinner *and* supper!' Tyler declared. 'As if! Have you read it, Mum? It's like a menu in a fancy restaurant.'

Mr Hammond, just ahead of us, turned and nodded towards it. 'Ah, you've seen the menu, have you? Yes, the boys all eat well here. Tell you what, perhaps we'll take a detour through the dining room, so I can show Master Green where he'll be taking his meals.'

Master Green? I think we all gaped at that.

The dining area was, of course, just as impressive as the rest of the school. Forget the usual school stereotype of rows and rows of Formica tables and chairs. No sir-ee, this was like stepping into a Georgian tea room. Here were half a dozen circular tables, all of them covered by snowy table cloths – tablecloths! – and each was encircled by eight high-backed, burgundy velvet-covered chairs. They were already set for lunch – fancy glassware, polished cutlery – and would have looked just as at home at a wedding reception. Now it was me who was gobsmacked. This was a school for boys. Boys with *behavioural* problems. Who dined here daily, as if undergraduates at Oxbridge. How on earth did *that* work? I was floored, and on all sorts of levels.

And on we went – from the dining room, via two sets of stairs and another thickly carpeted corridor, to arrive eventually at a sizeable panelled wooden door.

Mr Hammond opened it. 'Do come in,' he said, 'and, ah, good, you're already here, Tom.' At which, a lad of around sixteen or seventeen, who'd been sitting by an enormous desk (*not* behind it), stood up – almost to attention – and smoothed down his hair.

'All ready to go, sir,' he said.

'Good,' said Mr Hammond. 'So, Tyler, I'm going to leave you in Tom's capable hands now, if that's okay?'

The boy grinned. 'And you drew the short straw, I'm afraid. You get to help me go out and feed the horses.'

Tyler obviously wasn't allowed to sit in on our meeting – nor, indeed, was Miller, not for this bit – and I'd envisaged both boys being shepherded off somewhere quiet to wait – perhaps the cavernous library we'd started off in. But, once again, this school had surprised me. As short straws went, this was possibly even contravening the trade descriptions act. Was there anything not to love about this place?

'Cool,' Tyler said. 'I love horses.'

Tom stuck a thumb up. 'And how d'you feel about chickens?' he asked. 'Because we're feeding them as well.' I heard Tyler chuckle, and I smiled – I don't think either of us would have been surprised if they were going to feed the school unicorns as well.

With Tyler gone, though, Miller's angst seemed to notch up a level. He'd been quietly taking everything in as we'd wandered round the building, but I could now see the same unfocussed agitation on his face that had been evident when he very first came to us; as if he was retreating into a fug of anxiety, presumably wondering what was now in store for him too. He was looking so agitated, in fact, that I began to worry that he might go the whole hog and unleash his dinosaur impression.

I sensed Mr Hammond had seen his agitation too. 'And you, sir,' he told Miller, 'are having your own personal tour now. And with your own personal tour guide, as well. So you can explore the place properly while we go through all the boring stuff. Then you can rejoin us to tie everything up. Does that sound okay to you?'

Miller's expression while being addressed had been one of darting-eyed discomfort. But there must have been something special in the headmaster's tone, because Miller looked him in the eye now – and did I imagine it, or did he also straighten a little? – and said, 'Yes. Sounds okay,' and then, even, 'Thank you.'

Yes, I thought. There is definitely something good happening here.

'Excellent,' said Mr Hammond. 'Good man. Ah,' he added, glancing behind Miller, 'Rory, are you out there? Come along in and meet Miller.'

There was a knock at the door then, which was already ajar, and a small boy, another pupil, came in. He was impeccably dressed; smart grey suit, black and red tie, polished shoes. He was also tiny – tinier than Miller – looking around ten or eleven, so I was surprised when Mr Hammond told us that he had just turned thirteen and had been at the school for a year and a half. 'And making excellent progress, too. Isn't that right, Rory?' The boy nodded. 'Which is why Rory's been selected to show you round today, Miller. He'll be taking you around all the classrooms so you can meet some of the teachers, as well as giving you the proper lowdown on all the things pupils get to do here when *not* in class. Which I'm sure will be the thing you're most keen to find out, eh? Right, young man,' he said, turning once again to Miller's diminutive escort, 'off you both go, and no calling into cook's room to beg a biscuit, okay?'

The little boy smiled. And I suspected that the exchange I'd just heard was code for *do* go into cook's room, and *do* blag a biscuit. Things couldn't get any better than this, surely? It was as if our hour's drive hadn't so much taken us into the country – it was as if we'd landed in another country altogether. No, more than that. In a parallel universe.

Because it seemed incredible, at least to me, that such a place even existed. Yes, I'd had dealings with special schools before. Had had a couple of the children we'd fostered attending them as well – in one case, a child who fitted into one so well that he was the first to suggest he move in and live out his childhood there, lock, stock and barrel. But I'd

never seen anywhere like this. I knew that it had been originally been founded by a very wealthy individual; a traditional philanthropist. Someone who'd either inherited or
made a fortune and wanted to do something worthwhile
with it. Which was amazing in itself, but even more amazing to my mind was that it was now being funded partly by
the public purse. And at thousands of pounds per week, per
child, it needed to be an extremely big one.

I generally tried to avoid getting involved in politics,
particularly where the allocation of public money was
concerned – partly because I didn't feel qualified to discuss
such complicated matters and partly because dabbling in
amateur philosophy wasn't a hobby of mine anyway. I
preferred to stick to my own little sphere of influence. To
deal in the here and now of the individual children in
Mike's and my care and leave the 'bigger picture' stuff to
those whose job it was to debate it.

But it didn't take a maths degree to look past the cost of
this kind of facility to the cost – financial and social – of
another profoundly damaged child ending up as an equally
damaged adult. Because damaged adults not only had the
capacity to damage themselves further, in terms of poor
relationship choices, drug and alcohol abuse, pretty crime
and so on – they also had the power to damage those
around them. Not least the next generation. How many of
the children we had fostered been born to and parented by
people who'd come from similar disadvantaged circumstances? In one way or another, almost all of them. The
ripples in such situations spread widely. So, actually, the

potential benefits of such interventions far outweighed the immediate costs. And given the way Miller was going, after years 'in the system', it had never seemed truer.

The boys gone, Mr Hammond set about pouring me a coffee, from the little refreshments tray that someone had obviously already brought in.

'What a lovely young boy,' I said. 'And such nice manners too.'

Mr Hammond passed me bone china cup and saucer. No mugs around here. My mother's 'best' was the norm, clearly.

'Indeed,' he said. 'If you'd seen him even a year ago, you would never know it was the same lad. He was almost feral when he joined us. And, yes, I do mean that in the most literal sense. He couldn't sit still for more than a few minutes at a time, spat and lashed out at anyone he felt intimidated by – and that, sadly, was almost everyone – and he spent the first two months doing his school work under a refectory table.' Mr Hammond laughed then. 'Something of a challenge in itself, as you can imagine, none of our staff being Lilliputians. There were a number of creaking backs, I can tell you!'

As someone who'd worked for a long time with the most challenging pupils in a comprehensive school, I could readily picture the scene. Sometimes, rather than 'battle against', you 'went with' – a luxury most mainstream teachers, with their responsibility to teach and nurture upwards of thirty pupils, just didn't have.

I was lucky. Running my small behaviour unit I had the freedom and the time to 'go with', too. But this was 'going with' on a whole other level. 'Unbelievable,' I said, even though I suspected it really wasn't – it was just time, care and wisdom; behavioural cause and effect. Oh, if only all of those things could be available to *all* kids. 'Are you allowed to tell me what brought him here?'

'Well, I think I can tell you without breaking any confidences that he was actually found abandoned; he'd been living on the streets for a number of months. Apparently his father, who was a drug dealer, had been sent to prison, and his mother – a heroin addict; night follows day, eh? – chucked him out soon after.

'He went to a foster family but, as you can imagine, he was a difficult boy to deal with, and as they were new to the game they were struggling to cope. We took him as a boarder from the off – luckily, we had a vacancy – and, well, you've had a glimpse at the results.'

I wondered how things might have panned out had the young Miller been transported straight from Neen and Rob's to here. Very differently, I suspected. And if they'd been given the opportunity to board him somewhere like this so that they could have managed to keep caring from him despite having their twins? Again that sense of life turning on a sixpence was strong.

'And *wow* – what results,' I said. 'That really is incredible.'

'Indeed it is,' he said, 'though I don't want you running away with the idea that we are able to perform miracles. It's just that some boys – we only take boys, as you know – respond particularly well to the clear, unchanging structure we are able to provide. Which is not to say we lack emotion, of course. Just that boundaries are absolute – something else that can be achieved without the usual close-quarters human tendency to fallibility. Though it's also holistic. Rory returns home to his foster family every weekend and, of course, during the school holidays. It's working well. It usually does. I imagine you aspire to something similar yourself?'

'Of course,' I said. And I said it automatically, because wasn't that exactly what I did want to see? I gazed out of the window onto the picturesque landscape, and I wondered at the miracles being performed here. Because they did seem like minor miracles to me, whatever Mr Hammond said. Rory had certainly been granted one. Could I picture Miller getting one too? Could it really be that this school, this regime, was going to be the answer? Was I so close to being able to witness everything changing so dramatically for our boy?

And, if that were so, would I feel able to keep him, to commit to caring for him, indefinitely? That was the biggest question. And one to which, as yet, I still had no answer.

* * *

I'd already been told that two staff members would be joining us to discuss Miller. And, of course, Libby Moran, whose progress across the gravelled entrance area below I was now able to follow.

She looked the part too. Plucked straight out of a historical romance, seeming to float into the building in her green and yellow maxi dress – all that was missing from the tableau was a bonnet. She swept into the room moments later.

'Oh, isn't this just wonderful!' she enthused, as she accepted a glass of water from Mr Hammond. 'What a lucky little lad he is, to have a chance of getting a place here!'

'Well, on the face of it, he certainly seems to fit the criteria,' Mr Hammond said, looking ever so slightly tickled by the vision before him. 'Please,' he added, pointing, 'do have a seat, Miss Moran. Let me introduce everyone so we can get under way.'

The two other staff were the school admissions and special educational needs co-ordinator, a Mrs Grant, and a teacher called Miss Davies, who would be Miller's head of year. *Might*, I mentally corrected myself. *Not a done deal as yet*. Both seemed lovely, and just as I'd seen with Mr Hammond, a sense pride in their school seemed to emanate from their pores – which, as any educator knows, makes a massive difference.

Mr Hammond first explained how the school operated, day-to-day, plus the aspects of the national curriculum it covered, and the results they'd achieved with students over the years. On the face of it, an excellent record.

He then explained something that was further music to my ears. 'At this school,' he said, 'there are no exclusions. Ever. Once we've agreed to take a boy, we take them, warts and all. So you will never get a phone call asking you to collect your child from us, no matter how bad or serious the situation. I'm in the fortunate position of having a highly trained staff' – a glance and smile at the two staff members present – 'which gives us the expertise to deal with everything internally.'

This was an even more incredible revelation. I'd been on both sides of that particularly distressing equation, so I knew from experience just how much such a policy meant. I felt like Charlie's granddad must have felt when he was handed the golden ticket to Willy Wonka's Chocolate Factory, and even more so when Mrs Grant passed me a folder to read once home. 'It tells you all about the school hours, the uniform code and so on, as well as listing all the extra-curricular activities we have on offer, all of which are, obviously, free of charge.'

I couldn't help take a sneak peek as coffees were refreshed. And the first thing I saw jumped right out at me.

A specialist taxi will collect your child at 7.30 a.m., Monday to Friday, and, depending on location, you should expect them back at around 8.30 p.m.. Your child will have all his meals provided, including breakfast and supper, the cost of which is covered by the local authority.

'Is this right?' I asked. 'That Miller will be at school until the evening?'

Mr Hammond nodded. 'Yes,' he said, 'That's right. For day pupils, we run on an extended days model – it's our alternative to a boarding place here.'

'Would Miller be eligible for a boarding place at some point?' I asked. 'Assuming he's offered a place, that is,' I added hopefully.

'Well, hypothetically, yes,' Mr Hammond said. 'Though they are, of course, limited. Once boys become boarders they tend to stay with us till they're at least sixteen. But don't be disheartened.' Was it that obvious? 'We find the extended days option, which roughly half our pupils are on currently, works extremely well too. As well as giving parents and carers a well-deserved break, obviously, it gets the children into a strict routine right from the start, and gives them the very best chance of settling into our regime.'

A routine. A regime. *Control*. Would this work for Miller, or would he rail against such discipline from the outset? This was as much a removal of individual freedom as signing up to join the army in the First World War. In *any* war. He would lose all control. On the other hand, I thought, it might just turn everything on its head. With no way out – no exclusions, Mr Hammond had said, *ever* – might he give up the fight and embrace this new reality? Might this 'bubble' in the countryside prove to be exactly what he wanted – a safe space, well way from the real world? I had no idea. That would take a psychologist to unravel. But, God, I really hoped the latter might be true.

Libby Moran looked as awed as I felt. 'Wow!' she said. 'Casey, this sounds fabulous, doesn't it? Of course, there *is* the small matter of getting the little monkey to actually *come* here.' She looked at Mr Hammond. 'He has a tendency to not get into transport, I'm afraid. It's been a key issue for all his previous carers.'

Mr Hammond nodded. 'I hear you. But you don't need to worry. It's a problem we're well used to, and we have a strategy for dealing with it, too.' He paused. 'I.e. *me*. There have been many boys who've presented the same challenges as does Miller. And when they do, I simply collect them myself. Believe me, they all get fed up of the battle long before I do.'

Was this guy, as Tyler might say, for *real?* 'That's immensely reassuring,' I said.

He smiled. 'All part of the service,' he said. 'And, having read Miller's file, and assuming everyone here is of like mind' – he scanned the room – 'then I'm happy to tell you there is a place for him here. Only an extended days place for now,' he said, 'as we are completely full up with boarders. Though, actually it might be that days will be all he needs. We shall see, won't we?'

A place for him here. I could have kissed him.

And could have hugged him as well, just for the look on Miller's face, when he returned minutes later, with Rory.

He was beaming. I'd never seen such an expression on his face. The smirk I knew well. The scowl even better. The contorted-with-anger mask all *too* well. This was new. This was almost as if a window had opened, and another little boy – the one he might have become, might still become – was peeking excitedly out.

And clearly liking what he was seeing. 'Casey, they have an actual *swimming* pool!' he gushed. 'And a motorbike track. And they go diving, and surfing –'

'And a hundred other activities, too,' Mr Hammond told him. 'Though, as I'm sure Rory here will have explained to you, they don't come for free. First you have to earn them. You earn the points, you get the prizes. It's really that simple.'

He turned back to me and Libby, then. 'And those prizes are on offer every day, every single day, from 2.30 p.m. onwards.'

Behaviour modification again, then. At its simplest. And also – with the small detail of massive financial investment in young minds and spirits – at it best. Rory nodded his head solemnly, arms held behind his back like a little soldier, 'I did, sir. I explained it all, dead clear.'

Mr Hammond patted the boy gently on his shoulder. 'Good lad. I knew I could count on you. Now back to class, and no messing around in Chemistry today, okay?'

'You got it, sir,' Rory said. Then he turned to us all and actually performed a little bow. 'A pleasure to meet you,' he said, then turned to Miller. 'And you. Might see you in my class in a few days.'

He then turned and left, leaving me almost open-mouthed. Yes, it seemed a bit Dickensian, but perhaps that was the key to it. If Rory was illustrative of the way things panned out here, it was clearly having the desired effect.

Mr Hammond watched him go. 'So,' he said, all his attention on Miller, 'I gather you like what you've seen today?'

Again, that small straightening of the back. That slight standing to attention. It was almost as if Miller was under some sort of spell. He nodded. 'Yes, I do,' he said.

'Excellent,' Mr Hammond said. 'So, in that case, transport permitting, I shall expect to be seeing you next Monday, Miller. Mrs Watson can take you to the stores before you leave, have you measured up and collect a uniform for you.'

'Monday?' Libby asked. 'Isn't that a little close to the summer holidays? Wouldn't it be more practical for him to begin here at the start of the autumn term? I'm thinking it's a lot for him to cope with, what with already having moved carers. And I've already made some plans for Miller over the next couple of weeks, so …'

What was she *saying*? I could have happily slapped her, but luckily Mr Hammond was the firm voice of reason.

'No,' he said immediately. 'If Miller's keen, which he seems to be, we'd prefer him to start immediately. Round here, we're great believers in momentum. It will also give Miller a chance to get to know his peers, and when he returns in September, he'll already know his way around. Be on the same start-line as everyone else.'

'Oh,' Libby said. What was *wrong* with the woman? Ah, perhaps the fact that she didn't have to live with Miller, day in, day out … 'Well, yes, that's fine, then. Well, as long as you're okay with that, Miller?'

Miller rolled his eyes. 'I just *said* I was, didn't I?'

Some things didn't change then. At least not immediately. But as Libby was irritating me too at that point, I just raised a discreet warning eyebrow. Then caught Mr Hammond's eye. There was a half-smile on his lips. We were obviously already singing from the same hymn sheet.

And long may that state of affairs continue, I thought, as we said our goodbyes and trooped off to fetch an over-excited Tyler, and collect the various components of Miller's new uniform. Because it wasn't only Miller who was currently in a bubble.

I was, too. And, however grand and big and rainbow-hued this one was, I also knew how easily bubbles could burst.

Chapter 15

I was right to be anxious about that bubble of mine. Because it didn't take long – not even twenty-four hours, in fact – for its fragile walls to start quivering under the strain of it all.

We'd returned in high spirits, even if mine were necessarily tempered by my determination not to count too many chickens, Tyler-fed or otherwise. There was even a little normal family conversation over dinner, when Mike had enquired about how the visit went and Miller had answered his questions with what looked like genuine enthusiasm.

'Glimmer of hope?' he'd asked at bedtime. I'd really hoped so.

But here we were, the next morning, which was a wonderful summer morning, and Miller had yet to emerge from his room.

Tyler had been up early again, because he had a college open morning – he was off to enrol on a course for September. And it had obviously gone well, because when he returned home just before noon, he was full of it.

'So I chose the sports management course in the end. You know, the same one that Kieron did? It looks ace. And there's even a work placement you go on as part of the course. Like, at an actual proper football club. How cool is that?'

I agreed that it was very cool. And also his assertion that, once he'd finished, he might even have a realistic hope of a career as a professional football coach. 'Or even a football *manager*,' he said, with predictable reverence. Just like his dad, he was football obsessed. And, seeing his face, and his enthusiasm, and his motivation to succeed, it was the kind of obsession I very much approved of.

'So where's Miller?' he asked. 'I thought he might like a kick-about.'

'Three guesses,' I answered.

'God, what's he like?' he said, pinching a cherry tomato from the salad bowl I was busy assembling.

'Like a boy who very much needs to be in school again,' I told him. 'As in "now wouldn't be soon enough",' I added wryly.

'You know, I was wondering,' Tyler said. 'You know, if he was telling the truth yesterday.'

'About what?'

'About the bath thing.'

I was lost now. 'What bath thing?'

'You know, the bath thing he was talking about.'

'When?'

'Mum, in the car yesterday? You know. When we were on our way to the school. Remember?' I confessed I didn't. 'Yeah, you do,' Tyler said. 'When he was talking about the best ways to commit suicide and make it look like it was murder.'

I scooped up slices of cucumber and threw them into the salad bowl. 'You have completely lost me, love,' I said. 'In the car? I don't remember.'

'Weren't you listening?'

'I must have zoned out, sorry. What was he saying?'

'It was when he was saying how you might want to kill yourself and blame someone else for it. You know that thing where he breaks off and starts talking about something else entirely?' All too well, I thought. We all did. *And, as well … And, as well …* 'It was when he was talking about how if you're right handed you should use your left hand to slash yourself, so the coroner would think someone else kills you. He was suddenly, like, "and, as well …" You know that way he always says that? And he started saying about how – this was back when he was a baby – his dad held him under the bathwater till he passed out. He said he did it lots of times. D'you reckon he really did? I mean people don't remember things that happened to them as babies, do they?'

How did I miss something that might be so significant? 'Not generally,' I agreed, feeling guilty now. 'Did you ask him?'

'Yeah, course. He said he knew because he heard his dad and granny laughing about having done it. D'you think he might be telling the truth?'

Granny. I'd not heard about a granny before. I was sure of it. 'He might well be,' I said. 'Did he say anything else?

Tyler pinched another tomato. 'No. That was it. He was off then about Kim Jong-un again, and what a clever bloke he is. I just wondered, because I was talking to Denver about it this morning. And we were wondering if that might have made him brain damaged, or something.'

There was a long list of potential things that might have damaged Miller's brain. If not physically, at least psychologically. But this was new. New and horrible. And though Miller's flights of conversational fancy were often exactly that – flights – this definitely held a kernel of authenticity. 'Might be something, I guess,' I said. 'The notes are all a bit vague about his very early life, but I'll try talking to him about it next time he appears to be in an opening-up mood. Thanks, love. Speaking of which, lunch will be ready soon, so why don't you see if you can winkle him out for me?'

'Leave it to me, Mum,' he said as he picked up a pile of paperwork from the table. 'I need to go up and make a start on all this anyway. It's all the stuff from college I have to fill in, and it has to be returned by Friday. I'm going round to Kieron's in a bit so he can help me with it.'

'Aww, that's nice, love,' I said, because it was. It was lovely to know Tyler had asked Kieron for help and advice, and I knew he'd have been really chuffed, but it was also a joy to me that their brotherly bond was growing so strong. In hindsight, perhaps it was always going to – they definitely had a lot in common. But fostering's complicated; such relationships with your own children are never a given. And should definitely not be taken for granted. That it's a whole family enterprise is always taken as read, obviously. No one with children goes into fostering without considering the impact it will have on them – and if they do, they are quickly educated in the reality that it will change the dynamic of the entire family. And we'd been lucky in that regard, because Riley and Kieron had always been supportive of my passion for taking in all the waifs and strays we had down the years. And it had often been in desperate and urgent circumstances, to boot, turning their day-to-day lives upside down in the process.

But what we'd never done was expect them to make befriending these kids a duty. That wouldn't be fair, and, in some cases, it wouldn't even be advisable, particularly given the specialist nature of what we did, and the profoundly damaged and unstable nature of some of those children.

This might well have been true of Tyler, given what he'd been through before he'd come to us, but some kind of alchemy had happened – not just to Mike and me, but to the rest of the family too. So perhaps, in hindsight, it would always be a given that we'd all gel. But it still made my heart sing with joy and gratitude every time I saw evidence of that closeness.

I smiled to myself as Tyler bounded up the stairs now. Increasingly he reminded me more and more of Kieron, too; no, he didn't have Kieron's Asperger's but they were both gentle souls. They both had an almost child-like innocence (a big leap, in Tyler's case, given the horrors that had been visited on him), the same lust for life, the same trusting nature, the same generosity of spirit. It was a comparison that often set me thinking about the nature versus nurture debate. Back when he'd first come to us, as a traumatised eleven-year-old, Tyler had been nothing like my own children, obviously. Yet, five years later, it was as almost as though he'd been brought up in exactly the same way. The longer I fostered, the more evident it became – at least in my experience – that nurture probably played the bigger part in shaping a child. Yet, looking at some kids – for instance, Miller – the ongoing challenges seemed to suggest that nature might be the more persistent, overriding influence. Still a conundrum, then. Perhaps it always would be.

I was cutting some bread when Miller came into the kitchen. Despite the warm sunshine streaming in through the windows, he was wrapped up like he'd just stepped out of his tent in the Arctic. Fleece pyjamas, a hoodie and a heavy fleece dressing gown, the hoods on both of the latter firmly up.

'Good grief, Miller,' I said. 'You must be boiling in all those clothes, love. Why don't you take a layer or two off? I thought we'd have lunch in the garden today. I've made a lovely salad and we've got some of that crusty bread you like.'

Miller pulled his 'd'oh' face. 'I haven't had breakfast yet,' he pointed out. Then sat down at the table, head hung into his open palms as per usual, all trace of yesterday's child long extinguished.

As ever, I stood and looked at him and wondered how to play it. Why couldn't I just seem to 'be' with this child? Was it him, or was it me? All these weeks along and there still seemed no natural connection between us. Not even a smidge of one. Every single day he felt like a new puzzle – like I was being handed a new Rubik's cube to solve every morning, with its endless permutations. And, as ever, at least lately, I thought how fed up I was becoming with having to play out each potential scenario in my head before I could decide which would be the least-worst option.

This was, of course, the stock-in-trade for people dealing with challenging behaviours, but with Miller, because I'd yet to identify a trigger, a thread, a pattern, it was, as a consequence, magnified to the nth degree.

I did it now. I could either do what he wanted and offer him a selection of breakfast items, in which case, depending on his mood, which was unknowable, he would either accept what I offered, or scoff at my suggestions. Alternatively, I could ignore his manipulation attempts, and simply lay out some salad and bread on a plate for him. If I did that, the chances were that he'd either snigger contemptuously, or simply stand up and walk way, saying 'Fine, I'll just starve then, as usual'.

I plastered a smile on my face and went for the middle ground.

'That's right, love,' I said. 'I forgot you didn't come down for breakfast. Oh well, It's up to you, sweetie. Whatever. I'll take my bits out to the garden and leave you to decide. You know where all the breakfast things are, and I'll just leave out the lunch things.'

I then grabbed my own plate, and left him to it.

'What?' I heard him huff, as I went out to embrace the sunshine. 'Why don't you just *make* me something? You're supposed to be my *carer*!'

I went out into the garden where the birds were all twittering – twittering on much like I seemed to be doing a lot just lately. It's fine, love. Whatever, love. That's okay, love. Do what you like, love … Empty words – white noise, like you'd use to soothing a fretful baby. And all the while, it was like there was a finger being scraped down a blackboard, because in reality, my nerves were constantly jangling. Why did this child, this particular child, more than any other child (or so it seemed currently), have this ability to make me feel so uneasy, so on edge all the time?

Pull yourself together, Casey, I told myself. What on earth is *wrong* with you? I really didn't know. I couldn't remember having felt this wired around a child before, and it was getting to me. It wasn't as if I were threatened by Miller, was it? I knew he'd threatened violence to previous carers but not, so far, towards me. So was it just feeling so cooped up? So trapped? So unsupported – that old chestnut again – and frustrated that nothing was being done? He'd been with us all this time now, and not a sniff of a strategy on the horizon.

Yes, I knew funds were tight, I knew Libby probably had a punishing workload, I knew CAMHS (Child and Adolescent Mental Health Services) and ELAC were overrun with other children urgently needing help. But that old phrase 'out of sight out of mind' kept coming back to me. Miller had been placed with us, and there was a note on his file that said 'sorted for the moment'. No, of course there wasn't, but that was certainly how it felt. Until such time as I kicked up sufficient stick to make anyone hear me, 'sorted for the moment', in official eyes, was exactly what he was.

What was worse, though, was that I was even ruminating on it in the first place. This wasn't me. I was 'sleeves up and get on with it' personified. Or at least had been. Perhaps my anxieties about taking another child had been well founded. Much as I hated to use the term, perhaps I *was* getting burned out. It was a term I'd heard countless times, especially about long-term foster carers. But a term that I never thought would apply to me.

In an effort to banish my irritability I turned to my iPad, and lost myself for a bit on social media. I knew Riley and Kieron would have laughed if they could see me (how many times had I ticked them off for wasting their time on social media?) but scrolling through inspirational mantras, amusing kittens and pictures of other people's trips to the seaside was, sometimes, food for the soul. As were online debates, and the robust back and forth of local politics; all good, if argumentative, clean fun. I was just posting my sixpence-worth of thoughts about the new council recycling arrangements, in fact, when the conservatory door banged open and my peace was shattered.

Tyler blocked out the sun as he stormed into the garden. 'Mum, seriously, you have to sort him out. *Now!*'

'What's happened, love?' I asked, looking up into his furious face. 'He's a little liar and my stuff better appear on my bed in the next five minutes or I'm taking his control pad. I *mean* it.'

Before I had the chance to answer, Miller himself appeared. 'I've *told* him, I don't know what he's on about,' he said calmly, 'I haven't even been in his room.'

I put down my iPad. 'Okay, so what's going on here?' I asked. 'Tyler, you first.'

'I came down for food and when I went back up, it was gone. All the paperwork I need for college. It was on my bed and now it isn't. And *he* was the only one upstairs.' He was shaking with anger.

I turned to Miller. 'Okay, where is it, love? What have you done with it?'

'Nothing!'

'Come on. Just give it back, please, like Tyler's asked.'

'Oh my *God*!' Miller said, splaying his hands dramatically. 'I was only two minutes in front of him, that's all. Two minutes! And I never went in his room. And why would I want his paperwork?' He flapped his arms down against his sides again. 'Why do I get the blame for *everything*?'

'Because you were the only person up there, dumb arse!' Tyler barked.

'Tyler!' I said. 'There's no need for that. Now are you sure you haven't put them in a drawer, or left them in the bathroom, or anything?'

Tyler looked as if he could kill someone. Miller, most likely. 'Mum, I *know* where I left them, trust me. Grrrrr!'

I could see him clenching and unclenching his fists, and felt a rush of anxiety. This could escalate fast. He then jabbed a finger in Miller's direction, which literally made Miller jump.

'You are so *for* it!' he yelled. Then, to my horror, he turned the hand into a fist, and began drawing his arm back. Tyler was boiling with rage now, and for one awful moment I really, really though he was going to thump Miller. I leapt from my seat, galvanised. And, thankfully, it was enough.

Tyler wound himself in again, turned on his heel and, with a final scowl at Miller, stomped back inside again.

I then heard a door slam. Though I didn't know which one.

I rounded on Miller again. 'Look, Miller,' I said. 'Please just do yourself a favour here. Did you take them? For a joke? To wind Tyler up? Because if you did, now is your best chance – perhaps your *only* chance – to make things right with him. So I suggest you come clean before this gets any worse for you.'

Even as I was saying it I was all too aware of its point-lessness. This was what he wanted. To make trouble. To wind everyone up. And even though I thought I saw a trace of something when I pointed out that Tyler had been extremely kind to him, he was holding firm, just like a whipped politician, sticking to the party line no matter what.

Shaken, yes – there was absolutely no doubt about that – but still not sufficiently stirred. He just glared back at me, his eyes darkening, his gaze fully focused. 'I. Never. Took. Them.' he said evenly. 'I. Didn't. Go. In. His. *Room*.'

I shook my head in frustration. 'Miller, like Ty said, there is no one else in the house, so if they're gone, then you most certainly *did* take them.' I held his gaze. 'And now is your opportunity to tell me the truth. So stop this right now and just tell me where they are.'

He turned away from me, and for a moment I felt an urge to yank him physically back to face me. It wasn't only Tyler he had managed to goad into the thought of physical violence. 'I hate this house,' he said, as he too stomped back towards the house. 'I can't wait to start school so I can *get out of here!*'

Every cloud, I thought. At least that one thing. Every cloud … But there was no point calling after him, as he'd already gone. I picked up my plate, looking miserably at my half-finished lunch. Feeling so exasperated that I didn't know quite what to do with myself. How could anyone hope to manage, much less make any progress with, a child who so actively sought conflict? Who, in response to 'you are for it', was constantly saying 'bring it on'?

There was nothing for it, then, except to help Tyler search for the papers, and, if necessary, to turn Miller's room upside down. Turn the whole house upside down if needed be. So be it, I thought grimly, as I went back inside.

But it wasn't just the papers that had disappeared into thin air. It seemed Tyler had too.

Chapter 16

'Mum, it's me. Panic over. Tyler's here with us.'

It was now almost six and it was Kieron on the phone, after what had turned into an increasingly fractious afternoon. And not just because I'd got nowhere with finding Tyler's college papers (wherever Miller had hidden his spoils, he'd made sure I wouldn't – I was sure of it), but because Tyler had run off, and I had no idea where he'd gone.

To be fair, he was sixteen, so I wasn't fearing for his safety. And he'd been seriously angry, so I could well see why he'd disappeared. And it wasn't even as if I didn't know he was alright. He was a good boy and when I'd texted to ask him if he was okay, he'd replied immediately. *I'm alright Mum. Just need some distance.* But no word on where he was.

And that was fine too. If he needed to cool off, then okay. But my guilt gnawed and gnawed at me. As did Mike's warning. I had no business expecting Tyler to have to cope with Miller's antics. Yes, ignoring his protestations of innocence, I'd removed Miller's TV and PlayStation. But, yet again, it was a 'stable door and bolted horse' situation. I should have made sure Tyler didn't have the grief in the first place.

So, yes, I was angry with Miller. Very angry. But I was much, much more angry with myself.

'Oh, thank *God*,' I said. 'Is he okay?'

'Yes, he's fine, Mum. He just doesn't want to come back till he can trust himself around Miller. I've suggested he stays here tonight. I'm going to take him to the gym with me.' He chuckled. 'Take his anger out on some inanimate machinery instead. In the meantime, any luck with his enrolment pack?'

I was forced to tell him no. 'God only knows what Miller's done with it.'

'Well, no matter,' he replied. 'I'll drop him down to college in the morning so he can pick up a new one. It's no big deal, Mum. Easily sorted. So don't stress, okay?'

Oh, if only. Because I knew that this wouldn't be the last of it. Casey nil. Miller now in double digits.

* * *

The bedside clock read 3.00 a.m. when I woke. Groggy and confused, I didn't know what had woken me exactly; Mike was fast asleep beside me, and as I lay in the dark, the silence was absolute.

Miller, then. Always Miller. On one of his night ops, no doubt. And I was just heaving the duvet off so I could go and chastise him when it hit me. It hadn't been a noise, but a smell.

Alert now, I suddenly knew exactly what it was, too. As an ex-smoker I could instantly recognise the smell of tobacco, and that was definitely what I was smelling now.

I could have slapped myself. Those bloody cigarettes. That missing lighter. Why hadn't I search Miller's bedroom more thoroughly? Me, of all people. Me, who didn't mind bending the rules? Yet in this case I hadn't. Why on earth hadn't I just *done* it?

I leapt out of bed and padded out onto the landing, where the smell was immediately stronger. I didn't bother to knock – just went straight in, to what first appeared to be an empty room. Till I realised that, silhouetted against the clear night sky, was Miller, sitting astride the windowsill.

He actually grinned when he saw me. He had a cigarette in his mouth, a lighter in one hand, and in the other – that hand that was outside the wide-open window – dangled a burning piece of paper.

'What the *hell* are you doing?' I asked, my anger bubbling up under the surface. 'Get down from there right now, and put that bloody cigarette out immediately!'

Miller continued to grin as he dropped the page he was burning, presumably to float down into the back garden below. He then sucked on the cigarette before taking it from his mouth, and blowing a series of smoke rings – bloody smoke rings! – back into the room.

I marched straight across to him, snatched the cigarette from his hand, and threw it out of the open window into the garden as well. I then grabbed his arm and pulled him in from the ledge.

'I don't know who the hell you think you are, or what kind of person you think I am,' I said, my face close to his own, my hand still clamped around his wrist, 'but I promise you right now, Miller, you can push and push as much as you like, but *nothing* about this placement will change because you want to make it so. Do you understand?'

Miller, for the first time, looked a little taken aback. Afraid even. As he had a right to be. I'd never been so in-your-face angry with him, or as threateningly close to him before. 'No, I don't understand,' he said, pulling away from me and moving towards his bed.

'Well, in that case, let me make it clearer, shall I? I stayed where I was as he scuttled under his duvet. 'I know how you've ended your past placements, Miller. I also know that you think it's an easy thing to do. To push carers to their limits – to make them so angry that they can't stand any more of it, and you get to move on. Well, you ought to know that Mike and me, we're different. We are specialist carers and our job is to look after children who have never been able to settle down elsewhere, and part of our job is to *never give up*. You get that? You understand that? We never give up. No matter what is thrown at us, we will *never give up*. So, I'm telling you this because you're old enough and intelligent enough to hear it. You push as much as you like, kiddo, but nothing changes unless *I'm* ready to change it. Do you understand?'

Miller nodded a meek yes; pulled the duvet up to his chin. He looked exactly what he was beneath the brittle carapace he'd fashioned. A little boy. The little monkey of Libby's fond imaginings. And, for a moment, I *saw* him. He sighed theatrically. Too theatrically. The moment was lost. 'Oh, well, then,' he drawled. 'I suppose you're going to ground me now, then, are you?'

I heard myself laugh. '*Ground* you? You never leave the bloody house, Miller. So what would be the point? No, I'm not going to ground you.'

Then the penny fully dropped. He was playing me. Using classic misdirection. Keeping my focus on him – now across the room, trite, tucked into bed – to keep me from looking elsewhere. To the lighter and pack of cigarettes that were still on the windowsill. Not to mention the pile of remaining unburnt papers that were outside the window, neatly stacked on the window ledge, out of sight behind the curtains.

So *that's* where he'd hidden them. Cursing myself for not thinking hard enough, I grabbed them all. 'Tyler's college things, I presume?' I asked, holding them up. I also crushed up the pack of cigarettes so he could see they were ruined. Then, as my grand finale, I picked up both the remote control for the TV and the control pad for his console. Even though we had been here (and been here, and been here, and been here) these were still the only two things he truly coveted. To leave them would be a dereliction of duty. 'I will let you know when I decide you can have these back,' I told him. 'Now stay in that bed, and, so help me God, if I hear you out of it, it will be months before you get to play those games again.'

'I don't want to play them *anyway!*' he shot back, in what he presumably decided would make for an impressive parting shot.

I couldn't let it go. I was so angry that I simply couldn't walk away and let it go.

'Don't play *any* more games, Miller,' I said. 'Seriously, don't bother. No point playing games that you're never going to win.' I pulled the door to. Not shut. 'And, trust me on this, okay? You *won't* win.'

Chapter 17

I woke up the next morning with a taste in my mouth. Not of cigarettes, though after dispatching Miller's stolen ones, the smell had definitely lingered. No, it was the taste of failure. Of having lost it. Of having handled things badly.

Of course, I'd told Mike as soon as he'd woken up about the early hours disruption, and he was obviously as angry as I'd been. But even as I outlined the furious exchanges I'd had with Miller in the wee hours, I could see his expression begin to change.

'Casey, you're missing the point here entirely.'

'What?' I said, shocked by his slightly exasperated tone. 'I am finally *at* the point, Mike. The point where I've flipping well had enough of it. This game-playing. This manipulation. This –'

'Love, listen to yourself. You've just *proved* it. You are entirely missing the point. Don't you get it? Don't you understand that had you *not* woken up, he could have burned the whole bloody house down? I mean seriously, *think* about it. Just one stray bit of burning paper, and the whole room could have gone up. And the rest of the house – with all of us *in* it – for that matter!'

'Yes, Mike, of *course* I know that,' I said. But as soon as I'd said it, I knew it for the untruth it was. *God.* He was right, I had entirely missed the point. I'd been so busy being furious that I'd forgotten to be scared. Hadn't given a single thought, not in the heat of the moment, to the terrifying 'what if' of what was so clearly a highly danger-ous situation. Had I become so habituated to the actions of this deeply disturbed child that his potentially setting the house ablaze was only a secondary consideration? Had my 'normal' barometer got that badly out of kilter?

'Of *course* I know that,' I said again, more to convince myself than anything. 'And I made it very clear to him, believe me.'

But had I? Had I really? I had not. Not at all. I'd been so wrapped up in rescuing Tyler's precious papers, and in outmanoeuvring Miller in his power-plays, that the words 'burn the house down' hadn't even crossed my mind. Let alone passed my lips.

'Seriously,' I said again. 'And I'll be phoning Christine Bolton as soon as you've left for work, and his social worker. And I've removed his TV remote and his controller. But other than all of that, what else can I do?'

Mike got out of bed and headed for the shower. 'I'm not sure, Case,' he said, 'but we need to do *something*. Just imagine if one of the grandkids had been sleeping over – Christ, it doesn't bear thinking about. For a start, you'll have to search every inch of that room to make sure there's no other lighters or matches in there, then we really need to think about the risks of having Miller with us, full stop. I mean, honestly.' He turned around and locked eyes with me. 'Is it worth carrying on with this? *Really*?'

And that was the million-dollar question. The same question that countless other foster carers had faced before us. The same question that came up for foster carers everywhere. I already knew the answer they had come up with in Miller's case. They had taken the decision to take back their normality, and Miller, as a consequence, had been discarded. Moved on.

And Miller himself had no doubt worked very hard to achieve that. Must have pushed and pushed and pushed before finally getting his marching orders. That was what he did. Started every new placement like a project – like an undercover mission he'd accepted from some evil overlord – already, as soon as he set foot in a place, furiously working out how he could end it.

That, I realised, *was* the handle, was the still unbroken thread. As he'd already worked out that no one would ever want him, there was no point in acting any differently than he did. In his mind, it was simply a new variant – a new level – on the game he'd been playing, and winning, for years.

How did it go with Pandora, and that box she had opened? That in doing so, all the evils of the world had been released. And all that had remained in there was hope.

Not so with Miller. He'd left the box open, and that too had flown. And if you didn't have hope – that things might

Casey Watson

one day turn around for you – then what did you have left to run with? Nothing. Just the satisfaction of achieving that clichéd self-fulfilling prophecy. He truly was a boy without hope.

* * *

Once Mike had left for work, I did as I'd promised him I would. I emailed reports to everyone I needed to, then phoned Libby and Christine to follow them up.

Libby, as I expected, made all the right (and usual) noises; Miller was *such* a little monkey, and of course she understood the challenges we faced. And then reassured me that all would be well after the weekend, when he started at his new school, and, 'You'll be able to get your life back again. At least you'll have all those hours of peace every day, won't you?' she trilled. 'And without the added worry that you might get the dreaded phone call from them, to say he's been excluded and you have to go get him. What a bonus that is, eh? That they have that sort of policy? You can plan shopping trips, days out, whatever you like.'

So, I thought, Libby's solution to my dilemma was to adopt an 'out of sight, out of mind' attitude. Brilliant. What Libby didn't dwell on was that even if this was an acceptable answer – which it wasn't – then I only had two weeks of this sort of respite, then it was the school summer holidays. Six whole weeks stretching ahead of us. What then?

It was Christine Bolton I posed that question to, not Libby.

'God, I absolutely agree with you, Casey,' she said, in her soft lilt. 'And his social worker really needs to be doing

188

something about it – planning for it *now*, so that it's already in place for when you need it. Never mind the Helping Hands project or whatever they were called, she needs to access every resource out there, and we both know they *are* out there, and those summer holidays need to be structured and organised right from the off. This child will not leave the house with you without a fight, he's causing chaos in the home, and he's leaving you with no alternative but to take away the only things he has to *do* in the house. So what's left? Not a whole lot, that's what. And it's neither your responsibility nor your fault.'

Quite a speech from Christine, I thought. Yes, it still needed making to Libby, as opposed to just me. But, as I'd listened, I'd felt something that I hadn't up to now. And it was confidence. Early days, but it was definitely confidence – that she was onside, on my wavelength – that she had my back. That there was a chance that, in time, we would reach the sort of professional relationship I'd enjoyed with my much-missed John Fulshaw. Even friendship. Please let it be so.

And she was also spot on. Which gave me hope that she genuinely understood our daily battles, and the many frustrations involved. She also agreed with Mike that a full strip search of Miller's room was officially now in order (*finally*) and also offered to arrange a visit from a fire officer, to have a stern word with Miller about the danger he'd put us all in. 'They show them some quite horrendous videos of house fires,' she said, 'and in my experience, it usually does the trick. In fact, the kids are quite often traumatised after seeing some of the images, but that's far better than them getting excited about playing around with fire.'

I thought that was a brilliant idea, and asked her to, yes, please, arrange it, and we also scheduled a catch-up between ourselves on the Monday morning, the first day Miller would be at school.

Well, hopefully.

* * *

I'd only just got off the phone when I heard the front door opening. It was still only 9.30 a.m. by this time – I'd packed a lot in – so I was surprised to see Tyler walk in. I braced myself to explain about what had happened to his college papers, and I did manage most of it, but before I could get to the fire safety visit I'd organised, he held up a hand and said, 'Mum, listen.'

It hit me then that he'd been waiting patiently all along, to be allowed to speak. 'What love? What's up?' I asked.

'Nothing's up. Not exactly. It's just – look, please don't be angry with me, Mum – but I've asked Kieron and Lauren if I can stay with them for a bit. Whoah ... don't look like that. Just for a couple of weeks or so, okay? Just till ... well, just till things are sorted out a bit more with Miller. I mean ... well ... it's not working as things are, is it? I'm just, well, constantly wound up and it's just getting worse. It's like ... well, I know you'll think it sounds mad, and I know lots of the kids you take in are just challenging ...' He smiled. '*Me*, for instance. But he's different. He seems to have a thing about me, seriously. It's almost like he's doing everything

190

he can to make me go for him. Like he's got a plan on. Like he *wants* me to hit him.'

Even if he didn't know it, the truth of his words hit me like a sledgehammer. But what hit home the most painfully was the other thing he'd said. That he was leaving. He was going to stay with Kieron and Lauren. That, because of Miller, who I'd just told in no uncertain terms that I was not giving up on, my own son, my beloved son, didn't want to be here any more. I felt tears spring to my eyes and begin to cloud my vision. And a whump of empathy for every foster carer who'd been here before me. Who the hell did I think I was, thinking I could succeed where they'd failed? This was exactly the sort of reason why every foster carer who 'failed' failed. Basic love and priorities stuff. And stultifying guilt.

'But, sweetheart, this is your *home*,' I said. 'I don't want you to leave. I really don't, Ty. Please don't. We'll work it out. We've got the school sorted, and I've been giving them *hell* down at social services, and –'

Tyler shut me up by wrapping his long, strong arms around me. 'Mum, don't be so wet. I'm *not leaving home*.' He laughed then. 'Kieron told me you'd think that. But honestly, I'm *not*. It's just for a little bit. An extended sleepover. This will *always* be my home. I just think that, right now, you and Dad need to concentrate on Miller without having to worry about how I'll react, and to be honest, it'll be better for him, me not being here, because honestly, yesterday, I did nearly hit him and that's just not me. Is it? I just need a bit of time away from him, that's all.'

I looked at this boy who had lived within our home and our hearts for five years now. Who saw us as his parents, because we were now. And my heart swelled with pride. He was such a thoughtful young man, and I loved him so much. I also, despite my tears, understood.

'I'm so sorry, darling,' I said, as I reached up and kissed his forehead. 'Of course you can stay with Kieron for a bit, but I feel so bad that you feel you have to. You know there absolutely wouldn't be a choice, don't you? That we would end this placement now – right this minute – if it meant breaking up our family.'

Tyler kissed my cheek and grinned. 'Gawd, Mum, listen to yourself. You're not in an episode of one of your flipping soap operas. Nothing's "breaking up", as you put it. I'm just going to spend a couple of weeks round Kieron and Lauren's – who are *very* happy to have a babysitter on tap, trust me – so that you can make sure you see this one through. If I don't, I'll end up thumping him, then all hell will break loose, and then he'll have won, won't he? And you'll let him go, and feel terrible. Like you've failed him. Even though you won't have. Now stop your blubbing and help me sort some clothes out so I can go back down to Kieron's before the not-so-clever pyrotechnician gets up. I'll probably be back as soon as all my clothes are dirty anyway.'

I managed a laugh then and replaced my loving hug with a punch. 'You probably will too,' I said. And he probably would too. Which made me feel a bit better. 'Okay, you take the bedroom and I'll check the ironing pile, and fetch that little suitcase down from under your bed.'

'Thanks for understanding, Mum,' Tyler said, as he headed for the stairs, 'and don't worry, I'll be quiet. I won't wake Miller up.'

I didn't really want to dwell on the fact just yet. It hurt like hell that Tyler was moving out, no matter how temporary it might be. It just didn't bear thinking about. And I had to stop myself doing so. For the moment, I had to concentrate on the here and now. The immediate future. The future which, since Miller came to us, I was measuring in hours, rather than days. Days, rather than weeks. I couldn't do anything else, because the longer term was too complicated to contemplate. All I could do was hope for the best for Monday, hope something changed for the better as a result of him attending this frankly almost-too-good-to-believe school, and that Tyler deemed it safe to come back to us. I wasn't some air-headed believer in fairy godmothers, but if Mr Hammond donned a twinkly frock I thought he'd make a good one. I bloody hoped so. The thought made me smile at least.

It was almost lunchtime before I decided I would tackle Miller. Well, not so much Miller as Miller's bedroom. And I would be true to my word. I'd promised Mike I'd give it the full CSI treatment, and I intended to. With or without Miller's co-operation.

Assuming he even woke up, after the extent of his night-time fun and games. Tyler by now had long gone – and heartbreakingly, too, with his case in his hand and his guitar slung across his back, like he was off on some road trip across America. Much as Mike and I ribbed him about it, the house would feel so silent without his endless twanging, and I grew tearful all over again just thinking about it.

Christine Bolton – spit spot! – had also phoned back to say the fire service would be sending a man round tomorrow afternoon, to impart some fire-related home truths to Miller. But of Miller himself, there had been no sight or sound.

Nevertheless, as I marched upstairs – extra loud, to herald my imminent arrival – there was still this sense of being braced for a difficult confrontation, Confrontation with a diminutive twelve-year-old-boy – honestly!

Get your act together, girl! I told myself as I reached the landing, prepared for argument, prepared for attitude, prepared to be resolute and determined in my attitude, prepared for anything apart from what I found.

Which was a seemingly empty room. And within it, a perfectly made-up bed, as if it hadn't been slept in at all. And, to my shock, absolutely no sign of Miller.

My heart began thumping in my chest then, my mind quickly tossing around various possibilities. Could he be in the bathroom? No. I'd seen the door wide open as I came up. Could he have made his bed and gone out early for a walk or something? No, don't be ridiculous, Casey – he didn't do any of those things, ever. Could he have run away from home? That was the question I didn't want to ask myself. Because, given his history, that was the only question with a likely correct answer. And it all fitted. I'd called him out, and he'd scarpered. I tried to steady my breathing as I sat down on the edge of the bed. *Think, Casey, think.* Think like *he* might.

So I sat and thought, and it wasn't long before I noticed something strange. That the old wooden wardrobe – a family heirloom that had been in service for years now – had a small chunk missing from one of the doors, about four inches from the bottom. I craned my neck forwards to look more closely at it. I had no idea when or how, but a hole had been neatly carved out of it. Almost like a spy hole for a giant mouse. My first instinct was annoyance. Had he been destroying our property too?

I got up and moved towards it, bending down to inspect it. And almost jumped out of my skin.

'Stop!'

It was whisper, but a very loaded whisper.

What the …? '*Miller?* Is that you in there?'

'Yes,' he said. 'Please do not open the door.'

What the hell was this all about? I retreated and sat back on the bed again. I knew he could see me through the newly carved hole, but what on earth was he doing in there? Was this some kind of childish response to being castigated? Sort of 'if I stay in here long enough it'll all go away'?

'Miller, please come out and talk to me. What are you doing in the wardrobe?'

'I like it in here,' he said. 'I want to stay here for a bit. 'Can you leave me now,' he added. Then, 'Please?'

Curiouser and curiouser. 'No, love,' I said, 'I can't. I need to know you're okay. And I also need to have a proper look around your bedroom. I'm sorry. I know it's not nice to have your room searched, but after what happened last night, I need to make sure you don't have any other lighters or matches.'

'I am okay.'

'So will you please come out?'

'No. Just go on and do it. Look anywhere you like. I don't have any more lighters or matches or anything. But you can look, and then when I'm allowed out of here you can look inside here as well.'

'What on earth do you mean, "When you're allowed out of there"? You can come out of there right away, love. No one is stopping you. And if this is you punishing yourself, then that's silly. We just need to talk about it, that's all. Come on. Come out, Miller. Please.'

No response.

So I decided I'd start searching anyway. Whatever he was up to – whatever reason he had for squirrelling himself away from me – perhaps once I started searching he'd change his mind. I got up off the bed to begin a systematic investigation.

Miller's case was locked, as I'd expected, unable to give up its secrets unless I broke it. But, in the circumstances, with Miller behaving as he was, that felt too dramatic and potentially disruptive an act. I didn't know what was going on here, but I was keen not to derail it. It might, after all, prove to be illuminating.

But that didn't mean there wouldn't be things to find elsewhere, and he'd told me to go ahead, hadn't he? So I started looking in all the places kids who'd stayed with us had stashed things over the years: inside pillowcases and under them (the little toy train was still in place), inside board games, behind books, under mattresses, above cupboards, beneath the laundry bin and, on more than one occasion down the years, taped to the slats in the bed base. I was on all fours, in fact, peering up under his bed when he began speaking again.

'And, as well, I counted one hundred and fifty times one hundred and fifty, and he didn't come back. He didn't come back. I saw three darks and three lights. And nobody came. And, as well, all the custard creams had gone after the first dark, and I had nothing to eat at all, and I was hungry. I could see him kissing her on the couch and they were drunk, and sometimes laughing, and I had to be quiet. I had to be mouse-quiet. Or else. And, as well, there *was* a mouse and it scared me and I wet my pants, and had to take them off and cover myself with a big coat ...'

I stopped searching and sat back on my heels. Miller was so obviously relating something that had happened to him when he was little. And he knew I was still in there. He could see me through his spy hole. Which meant he wasn't just talking – he was talking *to* me.

God, I thought. Car, I thought. *Back* of the car, I thought. It was a bit of leap – strike me down, professional psychologists – but it didn't take a genius to reach the conclusion that Miller found it almost impossible to speak about his demons unless he didn't have to make eye contact when he was doing it. He struggled to make eye contact in lots of situations. Lots of kids did when it came to personal matters. Which was why I'd often used car journeys to encourage children to open up – not least my own too. Had

I become so fixated on Miller's distracting, sometimes dangerous in-car behaviour (well documented in his files, of course) to lose sight of the fact that they could be a tool I could use to try to get to know him better?

I thought back to the garbled bath stuff he'd apparently disclosed to Tyler. Had he been trying to let me know about his early childhood then too? I went back to sitting on the bed, and thought about what to say.

'Miller, sweetie, was this when you were little? Did you get closed in a cupboard? Was it when you lived with your parents?'

Silence.

'It's okay, love, I won't speak, then. I'll just sit here for a bit. It's okay for you to talk by yourself.'

Another short silence, then off he went again. 'And, as well, I got a big coat to pee on because it soaked it up. I had to, because one time he saw some leak out onto the floor in the hall, and he pulled me out, and he hit me and he spat on me. Mummy threw me a nappy in after two darks, but no more custard creams. And as well, and as *well*, all those babies in that earthquake. Those that are dead, they're the lucky ones. No one likes babies. No one wants the babies. There's too many in the world already, so they don't need no more. Those dead ones are the happy ones. They're the lucky ones.'

Silence fell again. I stayed sitting where I was for five minutes. Apart from the bit about the earthquake – which had recently been on all of the news channels after a terrible disaster in the Middle East – the rest seemed so obviously his own, raw, experience.

'You there, love?' I ventured finally.

More silence. Then off he went again, his voice soft and urgent. 'When you're a runt, you should *die*. Granny said so. You should be drowned. Because you're no use to anyone if you're the runt of the litter. And, as well, some animals kill and eat the runts of their litters. And if you're a runt, you should be taken to a field and left to die there. Granny said so. And, as well, without your clothes on. So the birds can come down and pick your skin off when you're dead. And then the worms can eat the rest. Till you're bones. Just the bones.'

Granny said so. Granny said so …

A picture formed in my mind, to sit alongside that social worker's long ago report. Damage breeds damage, I thought. This had clearly passed down a familial line.

I waited, my breath held, wanting more. But none came. Miller had obviously done talking for the time being.

The silence lengthened, and knowing he could see me as well as hear me, I stood up again and smoothed down my dress. 'I'm going downstairs now, love, okay? But please don't stay in there too long. You just come down when you want to, okay? And I'll make you something to eat. And don't worry, okay? We do have to have a chat about us all keeping safe in the house, but it's nothing to worry about. And we don't have to talk about this if you don't want to,'

I left the room, and hovered silently on the landing for a little while, hoping that now I'd left him, I'd hear the wardrobe door click open. But I didn't. Just more of the same silence. A silence more deafening than any amount of ranting he might have done.

Decided then, I went back downstairs. More emails to write, to Christine and Libby (I cc'ed the latter to her supervisor for good measure) while things were still fresh in my mind. Not that I kidded myself that anything would happen because of them – not immediately, anyway – but they would at least help paint a picture for any professionals who might work with Miller in the future; add to the small but growing pile of fragmented information we already had. And, hopefully, one day, all these bits of history could be put together, to create some sort of structured report that would form a timeline of his early life. In an ideal world this would have already happened. So much would have happened, to set him on a brighter path. But times were tough, money tight, children like Miller all too common. So it wasn't an ideal world, was it?

And perhaps Miller, muted by trauma, and deformed mentally because of it, was only now about to give up his secrets.

Chapter 18

Apart from emerging for food three minutes after the time I'd gone in and told the hole in the door what time it would be served, Miller spent the rest of the day and evening in his room. And, anxious not to welly in and potentially scupper what might well mark a vital watershed, I refrained from demanding that he come down unless he wanted to, and didn't ask him to expand on some of the chilling things he'd said.

And, having not received replies to either of my emails by mid-afternoon, I decided that I needed to be more proactive, leaving a brisk voicemail for Libby (who was out of the office) to demand that things were stepped up a gear, before the precious momentum (to quote Mr Hammond, my new favourite person) was lost. There was an urgent need, I told the answering machine, to get Miller some sort of regular counselling; to seize upon what had surely been his clearest cry for help yet. And in tandem with his endless talk of blood and gore and 'lucky' dead babies, it seemed to signify that there might be a very present danger of him wanting to do something to harm himself.

I disconnected in thoughtful mood. Or even us?

Because there was also the fact that my son had moved out, fearing the escalating tension. And, as far as I was concerned, Tyler's departure impacted on everything. Because, as Libby must surely realise – as should Christine Bolton, for that matter – if it came to a straight choice between Tyler's well-being and Miller's, there was *no* choice. They could push all they liked (and they had) for Mike and I to commit to Miller for the long term, but without a commitment from them to support him as well, both practically and psychologically, the question wasn't even worth asking; I had already made that commitment to Tyler, hadn't I? And I sure as hell wasn't about to renege on that.

And it seemed they got my point, because the next morning, bright and early, as per a text – a bloody text! – from Libby, the cavalry showed up. Not Christine – she was away dealing with an emergency elsewhere – but Libby, her supervising social worker, Jane, and a psychologist from CAMHS. They'd also brought another social worker, whose job it was to take Miller out for an hour while we thrashed out a strategy we were all comfortable with in the light of the new developments I'd outlined.

It started well, too. As in pleasingly *not* well. In that, despite all the training and tools he'd come equipped with, the young male social worker who'd come to take Miller off out somewhere was unable to even coax him from his bedroom.

A Boy Without Hope

I was keen to say 'See?' but I managed to restrain myself. It was sufficient that they'd noted this oh-so important point.

But the biggest point was a sticking point, as soon became obvious – when the psychologist, a stern-looking young man in a black funereal suit, voiced his professional opinion that there was no point in setting up one-to-one counselling with Miller till Miller was in a more stable situation. i.e. attending school regularly, by which he meant in September, and in a settled long-term placement. By which he meant with us.

So, like poker. The stakes raised. I'll call you. I'll see you. He would happily commit to helping, he said, as long as we were equally happy to commit to keeping Miller long term.

'But we're not prepared to do that,' I argued. 'Not yet. I mean, I know everybody wants us to give the reassurance that we can keep Miller in the longer term, but we just can't at this stage. I'm sorry, but we can't.'

'But he does need that stability,' the psychologist said. 'From what I've seen, a big *part* of the problem seems to be that Miller never knows where he will be living from one week to the next.' *Tell me something I don't know*, I thought. 'And until he feels comfortable,' he went on, 'and has a real sense of belonging, then we won't get very far trying to work with him, will we? In fact it's pointless if he's to be moving on again so soon. Like trying to put a Band-Aid on a broken leg.'

He looked at me pointedly. And might have meant nothing by it. It might just have been a simple statement of fact, which I understood. And, to a great extent, agreed with. At least, in principle. But I still felt that pressure – that what he was really saying was that the ball was in my court, and the decision was mine. That it would be my fault if Miller didn't get psychiatric help, so he could start getting better. I almost caved in at that point – God, I felt that as well, didn't I? And hadn't I already told Miller that the placement wouldn't end? Hadn't that been my exact point? That *he* couldn't control that? Yet here he was, it seemed, doing exactly that, even from his bedroom. Even so, something, some instinct, held me back; kept me going.

'As soon as I can tell you something different, I will,' I said. 'I'm afraid I can't do any better than that at this point. The sad truth is that if Miller is determined to end a placement, he will do so, by one means or another.' I glanced around the table. 'We all already know that. And frustrated as I am to admit it, we may not have any say in the matter.'

'I understand what you're saying, Casey,' said Jane, the supervising social worker. 'And I realise that this leaves us at a bit of an impasse.' She looked at the psychologist. 'So, how about, until we all know how this will pan out, Casey has access to your out-of-hours team? Perhaps she could make use of the service in the event of an emergency, or if she just needs some advice on something? Would that be something you could offer?'

'That seems reasonable,' the psychologist said. 'And, yes, I don't see why not.'

'Excellent!' Libby said, as if he'd offered me the moon on a stick. My 'thank you' was rather more muted.

But I at least got the Band-Aid. However, even as I made a note of the numbers he then gave me, I knew it would be highly unlikely that I'd ever use them. How could I be supported by people who knew nothing of Miller? His background, his psychological problems, his ongoing issues? What help could they possibly give me in a crisis situation?

But there was clearly nothing else on offer. And not much left to say. Except by the social worker who'd spent the meeting holed up in Miller's bedroom, and whose comment, when he'd been called down, when Jane asked him how things had gone, had only one word for her – 'hmm'.

But it seemed Miller himself *did* have something to offer me. Because, as soon as I'd waved the team off and closed the front door, I turned around to see the boy himself halfway down the stairs. He'd clearly been waiting and watching, having heard them all leaving. He also had some items in his hands.

'You alright, love?' I asked him, wondering at his strange expression as he came down the remaining half dozen. And I felt for him. How many children, as part of their everyday normality, had to cope with the knowledge that strangers (and they were, in many cases) sat around discussing their futures in the way we'd just done? Yes, it was what it was, and it had to be done. But, on the front line – there to mop up, once the professionals had swept out again – I never felt comfortable with it.

In reply, he held one hand out, and I opened my palm. He placed two things in it. Both plastic disposable lighters. Then the other hand. And, once again, I held a hand out. And in that one he placed a knife.

It was a slender chef's knife, and it was heavy. And doubtless sharp. And it wasn't mine.

'Where are these from, love?' I asked him.

He seemed happy to answer. 'I've had the lighters for yonks,' he said. 'I stole the knife off Jenny. I thought you might as well have them now, seeing as the police will prob'ly find them.'

'The police? There are no police coming.'

'There are *always* police coming.'

I turned the knife over in my hand. 'Why did you steal this from Jenny, Miller?'

He pulled a face – one that said, *Do you even need to ask?* 'For *protection*, of course,' he said.

'Protection from what, Miller? From *who*?'

He shrugged. 'Just in case,' he said.

'In case of what?'

A heavy outbreath. 'Just in *case*.'

'You haven't answered my question,' I said. 'What situation do you imagine where you'd need – or *want* – to use this?'

'I don't *know*,' he said. 'I just need to be able to defend myself.'

'Against what, *love*? Everyone around you – me, Mike, Libby … absolutely *everyone* – wants only what's best for you. No one wants to hurt you.'

'So you say …'

'But it's true, Miller. You *know* that.'

He shook his head. 'Well, just don't say I didn't warn you.'

'About what?'

'About a *raid*. About *everything*. You're on your own now.'

'Miller, there is not going to be police raid. Nothing bad is going to happen. There is no need for you to be frightened about someone trying to hurt you. *Or* us.'

He looked at me strangely. 'So *you* say,' he said again.

Then he turned on his heel and went back up to his room, leaving me at a loss to know what to do or what to say. But he was right about one thing, I thought, as I took the contraband into the kitchen. That's exactly how I felt. That I was on my own now.

* * *

Despite my resolution that he would have to earn back the TV remote, after our encounter I returned it to Miller's room. I'd been discomfited, to say the least, about his proclamations of impending danger, and was still chewing over the whys and wherefores of what he'd said. Mainly the whys. Why did he feel that he needed protection? There was nothing to indicate it in his records, but was it because of an incident that had happened with a removal from a previous placement? Or – more likely, I imagined – related to violence meted out to him while still with his parents? Either way, he clearly felt he was in danger – something clearly reflected in his obsession with disasters and death; his endless wondering what it might feel like to be fatally wounded. Yet he'd also spontaneously given up his 'protection', which, however garbled his thinking, felt like a big step towards trust.

Of course, it might just be that he genuinely believed that, as a result of the disclosures and the meeting, they'd have been searched for and found anyway. But even if that were so, it was still a considered action – one of taking control, yes, but of taking control in a positive way. A decision taken to perhaps minimise negative consequences. No, I wasn't sure that was quite how he'd seen it himself, but when I'd given it back I'd made much of the fact that he had taken control of a situation in a way that I definitely approved of. That he'd been a good boy, and had done the right thing.

Though, as I'd had to talk to the duvet in which he was currently rolled up, saying nothing, what he thought of my little speech, I had no idea.

* * *

At around three that afternoon, a young fire officer arrived at the house, armed with a small laptop and a big smile. He looked to be in his early thirties and was so tall that he had to duck his head as he entered the house.

'Well, I thought my husband was tall,' I said, as he bent even lower to come into the living room. 'I must look like someone from *Gulliver's Travels* to you.'

The fireman laughed. 'Not just you, Mrs Watson, I can assure you. I kind of have this dwarfing effect on most people. I blame my father. I'm David Helm, by the way,' he added, holding his hand out for me to shake. 'I trust the young man in question is ready to meet me?'

'It's Miller,' I told him. 'And please, call me Casey. But I'm afraid he's upstairs and I doubt he'll come down. He's not asleep – he's playing on his PlayStation – but I've tried everything to get him down here for your arrival, without success. I even told him you'd march up there and do the work right there on his bed, but he still won't come down, I'm afraid.'

'Well if you don't mind, that's exactly what I will do,' he said. 'When I'm right there in front of them, most boys tend to listen to what I have to say. Would that be okay with you?'

I had no doubt at all that most boys would listen to this imposing fellow, but would Miller? Though he was in the habit of listening more to males rather than females, he wasn't 'most boys' – far from it. Still, after the fraught, defeated expressions of my earlier visitors, this young man's demeanour was like a breath of fresh air. 'That would be great,' I said. 'Though you'll probably have to open his curtains, and please ignore the state of his room, but, yes, please, be my guest. Top of the stairs, turn right, second room. '

He patted his laptop. 'Leave it to me,' he said with a grin. 'All I need is this and my charming banter, and he'll be putty in my hands.'

Bolstered and inspired by his confidence, I left him to it, but still crossed my fingers for good measure. Perhaps a stranger of this kind coming in would flip some switch and get him to communicate properly, in a two-way conversation. But I wasn't holding my breath.

I'd been right not to, as well. Because half an hour later, David Helm was back downstairs, looking decidedly more frazzled than when he went up. 'Wow,' he said, shaking his head. 'That was a career first. What an odd experience.'

My heart sank. 'What happened?' I asked. 'He wasn't hiding in the wardrobe was he?'

'The wardrobe?' he shook his head again. 'Oh, nothing like that. He was watching TV, as you'd said.'

'And he was happy to listen to you?'

'Oh, more than happy. That's exactly my point. He listened more intently, I think, than any other kid I've ever talked to. Quite bizarre. He kept asking me to pause the video we were watching, so he could ask questions – which, of course, is normally a good thing – but Miller's questions weren't exactly what you'd expect. He wanted to know how the flames would make you feel, what the pain was like, how much it hurt. Wanted to know if I had I ever seen a dead, burned little child. Or a dead dog. I have to say, it was as if he was mesmerised. As if he was actually getting excited by the horrible scenes.'

'Well, that fits, I'm afraid,' I said. 'He is a bit overly obsessed by gore and death. Disasters of any kind seem to excite him, to be honest. So maybe this wasn't the best idea, after all.'

The fire officer nodded. 'I'm afraid I'm inclined to agree with you, Mrs Watson. The boy clearly knows the dangers of fire, and how fast it can spread. He knew all of that – he knows exactly how smoke and heat detectors work. He reeled all of that off to shut me up, I think. His only interest seemed to be about how much it might hurt to be burned in a fire, and he seemed to think I'd be able to describe that to him, which he was very keen for me to do. Is he having any counselling?'

I smiled a rueful smile. *Oh, if only*, I thought. Chance would be a fine thing. 'He will be,' I said, 'and thanks for coming anyway. It's ... well, it's at least ticked a box after what happened, which has to be a good thing. Let's just hope some of what you've told and shown him has sunk in somewhere.'

'Well, I'm only sorry I couldn't be of more help,' he said as I showed him out. 'And do give us a ring if you need us to do anything else, won't you? Though, to my mind, given his interest in people being burned, I'd suggest fire-proofing your home is the key priority.' He turned on the step. 'It's not too much of a cliché, Mrs Watson, to say with this one, you *could* be playing with fire.'

* * *

The fire officer's words, which had echoed Mike's, stayed with me. Was that it? Was Miller actually not just expecting some sort of Armageddon but welcoming one too?

One thing was for sure. Given this latest insight into Miller-world, school *had* to happen. He was a child with some very deep-seated psychological problems and things were fast becoming unsustainable as they were. So, after writing up yet another report and emailing it straight to Christine and Libby, I decided to get stuck into more practical matters, unwrapping, sorting out, labelling and ironing everything Miller was going to need for school.

The transport company had already confirmed that they would arrive at 7.10 a.m. on Monday morning, and that an escort would accompany Miller in the back seat to avoid any risk of him kicking off and distracting the driver. So at least all bases, it seemed, were covered. All that was left for me to do was to ensure he was up in time and in the mood to do what was expected of him – i.e. get into the car. I could only cross my fingers and pray. Though as I wasn't much of a praying type – at least not of the 'kneel down, hands together' variety. I instead raised my gaze to the kitchen ceiling and, since I was always told the universe provided, asked for some support there instead.

And the universe works in mysterious ways. Because I'd just put the ironing board back into its slot in the conservatory when I heard the doorbell. And was surprised to see an unfamiliar woman on my doorstep.

She had a sunny smile and a folded Tesco carrier bag in her hand. 'Hi,' she said, 'I'm sorry to call unannounced, but I'm Jenny, Miller's old foster carer? We spoke on the phone?'

'Oh, of course,' I said. 'Hello. Please. Come on in.'

She did so. 'I'm sorry to disturb you, it was just that I had an appointment to view a house over in this neck of the woods, and with Libby living all the way over the other side of town, it just seemed to make sense to come here instead. Sorry,' she added, seeing my evident confusion, 'I've got Miller's laptop for you. And I can maybe say a quick hello to him too. Well, if he's here, that is.'

'Oh, he's here alright,' I said. 'He's supposed to be starting at a school on Monday, but for the moment it's still very much business as usual, I'm afraid.' I rolled my eyes ceiling-wards to indicate and she shook her head.

'Well, you're a better woman than I am. I just couldn't ...' Another head shake. 'Well, I suppose it's done now. Some kids ... well ...' She seemed to shudder. 'And with my husband working away ... well, I don't need to tell you, do I? Anyway, all yours.' She handed the bag to me. 'To do with as you will.'

There was a part of me that wanted to sit down with her, ask her about Miller's curious openings-up, hear her take on it – *him* – find some common ground. Share our thoughts on him. But there was something about her manner, albeit that it was perfectly friendly (we were, after all, both batting for 'team fostering'), that stopped me. Perhaps, given that she'd passed him on to me, it wouldn't be appropriate. There is never any blame in such situations, and shouldn't be, but to quiz her now perhaps wouldn't result in gain. Besides, if there *had* been anything more she could tell me, it would have been in his notes or her email, wouldn't it? It hadn't been. He'd probably not been with her long enough to get that far.

So we chatted about this and that, about the school and my high hopes for it, and then I went and fetched the knife to return to her. Which she fell upon gratefully – it was an expensive chef's knife, after all. 'Good God, I knew it,' she said, accepting it. 'I *knew* it. The little ... You know, I searched high and low for this. High and low.'

'I imagine he kept it in his case,' I said. 'He said he took it for his protection.'

'Hmm ...' she said. 'I'm sure he did. A constant theme, that.'

'So I've noticed. And understandable, I suppose,' I said. 'Given everything that's happened to him.'

'And are you getting any help? That was my biggest, biggest bugbear.'

'Not as much as I could do with,' I told her. 'I'm hoping the school will prove to be my salvation.'

'From your lips to God's ears, eh? I'll keep my fingers crossed for you.'

And there was something *she* could do for me too I realised. 'You know,' I said, 'this laptop could be very helpful in getting him off to school on Monday morning. D'you mind if I hang onto it for a few days – use it as a bit of an incentive?'

'Oh, of course,' she said. 'Go ahead. It's all yours. I know how difficult he can be about getting into cars. Don't we all!'

So that was that. I had my power of persuasion right here in a Tesco carrier bag, thanks to the universe – well, and/or Jenny. And knowing it was within his grasp, give or take, Miller even deigned to come down to say hello to his former carer.

And although it was a bit of an awkward exchange, he did seem to be happy to have seen her, and even stayed downstairs for half an hour after she had left to reminisce in his own unique way about how brilliant his time with them had been. I thought back to what I'd been told about him kicking up such a fuss about leaving them, despite having told Jenny, day in, day out, that he couldn't wait to get away from them, and pushing them to the point that they agreed with him.

A Boy Without Hope

What a strange, strange boy. Even though I knew he was throwing in a lot of false memories, listening to him so animated was like listening to a different child; one sharing happy recollections that I knew differed wildly from the reality, but were told with such apparent pleasure and attention to detail that I could almost be convinced they were the real truth. It was almost as if he needed to create these alternative histories in order to locate them in a better place in his head. He was such a puzzle – a jigsaw puzzle that had been thrown on the floor, making it a mammoth task to work out what belonged where.

And where did Miller belong, as a consequence? Was he doomed to keep repeating the same process wherever he went? To destroy and, having done so, to reinvent history so it was more to his liking?

But what kind of future would that lead to? That was the real point. Because there wasn't much time between twelve and eighteen. And without some radical change, where would he be then?

Chapter 19

Just as I'd hoped, the promise of the laptop proved to be an excellent incentive.

Straight after Jenny had left and before he could escape back to his room again, I showed him the bag and told him what was inside it.

'But it's staying with me, Miller, okay? Remember what Mr Hammond said when we visited the school? About rewards having to be earned? Well, Jenny's brought this round for me to give back to you when you've earned it.'

'You can't do that,' he said, at once all spiky and confrontational. 'That's my property and you have no right to keep it from me.'

'Not exactly,' I said. 'It was confiscated, remember? And when something is confiscated that means it's no longer yours till you've earned the right to have it returned to you.'

'That's not true!' he said, and I could see he was eyeing it with a mind to grabbing it from me.

A Boy Without Hope

I tucked the bag under my arm, and smiled. 'Sorry, but you're wrong, love. It's in the social service handbook. I can show you the page, if you like,' I bluffed. 'But the main thing is that you really don't have to do too much to earn it back. Just be a good boy and get up for school in time next week.' I increased the smile wattage to brighter. 'And that won't be too hard, will it? Because it's *such* a nice school. And you're going to have such *fun* there. I know it's all very different and scary and new, but if you can manage that for me all next week, then this' – I patted the bag – 'will be yours again on Friday evening. So. Do we have a deal?'

'But –'

'A deal, Miller? Your choice. Your call.'

'But –'

'No buts, Miller. I said Friday.'

'Wednesday.'

'No, *Friday*.'

'Thursday, then.'

'No. *Friday*.'

'*Fine*, then!' he huffed, before stomping back to his room.

'Good lad,' I called to his retreating back. Then locked the laptop in the boot of my car.

* * *

And it worked. Although moody and extremely grumpy, he eventually came downstairs on Monday morning, dressed in his school uniform, which was a big tick on the relief front, but only about five minutes before the taxi was due to arrive. I still didn't want to count my chickens (so many chickens!), but I remained in a buoyant mood, because it was within the realms of possibility that, in a matter of minutes, I'd have a whole dozen hours to do whatever the heck I wanted. After the virtual house arrest of the last few weeks, freedom was finally becoming close enough to taste.

So I'd patiently ridden the whole 'down in ten minutes, no, I'll be down in twelve minutes' to-ing and fro-ing, and prepared to keep an even temper now he'd finally appeared.

'Would you like me to brush your hair, love?' I asked, noticing that he hadn't done anything with it. He wasn't so much rocking the 'dragged through a hedge' look as 'dragged behind a horse, for ten furlongs'. His hair, already unruly when he'd come to us, had noticeably grown now, a trip to the barbers, of course, having been impossible.

'No I don't,' Miller replied. 'If they don't like me as I am, then so what? I don't care. They can exclude me if they like. I'm not bothered.'

'You really could just run a comb through it, Miller,' I said. 'What will the school think of me if you go in unkempt? And you do look so smart in your new uniform, too.'

His withering look was all the answer I needed. How much did he care what the school thought of me? Not at all.

'Well, whatever,' I said, shrugging. 'I obviously can't force you, so if you're not bothered what your classmates might think, then it's up to you, love. Anyway, come on, eat something before the taxi comes, please. We've only minutes now before it gets here.'

Miller inspected the selection of offerings on the table: an array of fruits, yoghurts, cold meats and toast

– all of the things he usually ate. 'I want cereal,' he announced.

I bit my tongue, my lovely mood wilting rapidly. He never wanted cereal when it was offered to him. Never. Still, I refused to be agitated.

'That's okay then,' I said. 'But you'll have to be quick. We've got Rice Krispies, Coco Pops or Weetabix. Choose one, love.'

'I want porridge.'

'There's no time for porridge, Miller. I've given you the choices.'

'But I want porridge. I said cereal. Porridge is cereal.'

This was no time for a game of ping pong about the naming of various food groups. We both knew it. 'I *know* that,' I said. 'But I've told you what's on offer. Now which is it to be?'

'I want *porridge*.'

'Porridge isn't an option. Yes, it might have been if you'd come down for breakfast when I asked you. But now it's not.'

'Fine. I won't eat then.'

'Fine,' I parroted back. 'If that's your choice, so be it, love.'

'But I can't go to school on an empty stomach.'

'Well, actually, if you choose to, you can, Miller. But if you choose not to, then I suggest you either eat a bowl of cereal, or take a cereal bar and a banana to eat on the way. It'll be a long time before lunch, remember.'

'But I want porridge!'

Dear *God*.

The doorbell buzzed then, and I looked up to see a taxi parked on the street outside. 'Okay,' I told Miller. 'So your lift to school is here now. So it's cereal bar or nothing. Your call. And pop your shoes on too, please, while I go and answer the door.'

I left Miller huffing and puffing, and went out to do so, to be greeted by a cheerful couple – Chris the driver, and Joan the escort. I hoped their sunny smiles wouldn't be changed to grimaces too soon. 'He'll just be a moment,' I said. 'He's been stalling a bit. But he's almost ready now. He's just putting his shoes on.'

'No worries,' Chris said. 'First-day jitters and all that. He's obviously bound to be a bit nervous.'

At that precise moment, Miller barged a route through all three of us, in his seeming haste to be out of the door and gone. 'Fine, I'll go,' he hissed, 'and by the way, that laptop is mine. I know the law, and you can't use that against me. Only the stuff you've actually bought. Not my own stuff. That's got nothing to do with you. You're a liar!'

He then yanked the door open on the taxi, and hurled himself into the back, slamming the door with such ferocity that it sounded like a gunshot, causing the birds that had been roosting in the nearby trees to flutter into the air.

'But it's my bloody internet!' I muttered.

* * *

Twelve whole hours, though ... Just for me. Twelve solid hours of precious daylight, all to myself. Though, being human, I was still in a state of fraught tension, so I squandered the first half hour just calming down – trying to regain a sense of peace and equilibrium. It had been a long few weeks without much of either, after all.

Progress, with a child, is a bit like a drug. You get exposed to just the tiniest bit and it acts as a reinforcer. Despite knowing that there's likely to be further stress along the way, just that one hit to the brain's pleasure centres and you dig in and keep going.

I remember reading something about surfing once (definitely not a sport for me) and how a single second of success riding a wave was all it took. You were walking on water – flying, even – and there was no feeling like it. Which is why though surfing, dangerous at the best of times, was apparently one of the slowest skills to master, it was also so uniquely addictive.

Was that my core problem with Miller? That I just wasn't getting any fixes? Because I wasn't. I was just banging my head against a brick wall, and failing to dislodge a single brick. Yes, I'd learned a few things now. Got some sort of handle on his many demons. But with the child himself – the flesh and blood little human who was in my care – there wasn't so much as a flicker of connection, of warmth. Of the little signals – accepting a hug, a hand held, leaning into a goodnight kiss – that showed a child, however closed down, still needed affection. I had long sympathised with parents of severely autistic children, who so often couldn't bear to be touched, and how painful it must be for them to have such physicality rebuffed. I had also cared for children for whom normal physical gestures of affection were so alien as to be initially repelled. But I had always got fixes. Maybe tiny ones, to start with, but always just enough to keep me going.

And that just wasn't happening here. Miller, it seemed, could take me or leave me. But he didn't want me, and – Libby's words now had resonance – he didn't *like* me. Which shouldn't matter. It wasn't my job to be liked. It was to care. But could I care for him effectively if he didn't?

I must have sat there in my armchair for an hour, all told – something I almost never do, and when I realised the time, I also realised something else. That I had obviously chilled out, as the kids might have had it – that, apart from that first revelation, I'd sunk into a kind of fugue; I couldn't even remember the passing of the time. It unnerved me slightly – how do you lose a whole hour? But what unnerved me even more was the thought that suddenly jumped into my head then, which was *only eleven hours left now*.

Christine Bolton was due to arrive for our catch-up at 11.00 a.m., so I still had a couple of hours left to make myself presentable, and to make the house respectable, so that's what I did. I lost myself again, then, but in a good way – doing what I loved best – cleaning, disinfecting, bleaching, hoovering and polishing. I also stripped all the beds, and got the laundry done and out on the line, loving the fact that the sunshine had already warmed up the back garden so much that I could sit out and enjoy my mid-morning coffee. Even the different birds had joined forces to sing me a chorus of celebration!

I'd just finished it when Christine Bolton arrived, bang on the dot of eleven. And looking as sharp as I remembered, in a charcoal skirt suit. 'You're looking a lot better than you sounded on the phone,' she observed, as I led her straight out into the garden. .

'I feel it,' I told her. 'He's in school, and I'm free! And it's such a lovely sunny morning that I thought we'd have our meeting out here, if it's okay with you?'

'Bring. It. *On*.' she agreed, turning her face up to the sun. 'Best drug bar none.'

'Right,' I said. 'Grab a seat and I'll head in to make drinks. Tea for ma'am, yes?'

'Absolutely.'

I headed inside to make the devil's drink, and as I filled the kettle I could see Christine shrugging off her jacket, drinking the sun in as she did so. And, not for the first time, was enormously grateful that I no longer had the sort of job that required jackets, tights, laptop bags and suits – and all the other hateful trappings of a professional career.

I also saw her delve into her bag and pluck her phone out. Then take a call that, from her pained expression, definitely wasn't a welcome one. Another trapping of a job like Christine's – and John's, of course – was that you're on call for fire-fighting pretty much twenty-four seven. I felt for her. Wondered how she was settling in to her new role.

By the time I returned to the garden, the phone was face down on the table, and her own face didn't look quite as relaxed as before. In fact, despite the fact that she was wearing sunglasses, I could see she looked rattled.

'Can never get away from stuff with those things, can you?' I commented, nodding towards her mobile as I set down the tray. She scowled at it. 'You okay?' I asked. 'I saw you on the phone just then. Everything alright?'

'Oh, it's fine,' she said, though it was obvious that it wasn't. 'Just a bit of a domestic, that's all. Elderly parent stuff – sure you know how it goes.'

I did – well, only to a point, thankfully. I also remembered that Christine's elderly father-in-law had dementia. That it had been the reason she'd taken John's old job in the first place.

'Oh, I'm sorry,' I said, 'it must be so hard for you. How's your father-in-law doing?'

A grimace. Which she turned into a grim smile as she looked at me. 'Doing everything he shouldn't be, pretty much, at the moment. Everything he *wouldn't* be – wouldn't be *able* to if my sainted husband would simply accept that we need to put him into residential care, basically. Sorry. Enough of my moaning. So, how are things going with Miller?'

I got the sense that if given sufficient rein, she'd have much more to say. And I felt so sorry for her. Whole new area, out on a limb, no support ... 'No, it's fine,' I began, but then her mobile buzzed again. Deprived of its ringer – obviously set to 'off' – it was skittering its way over the glass top of the garden table.

Another scowl. She made no move to pick it up. Then thought better of it, looked at the display, then swiped across the screen. The 'not available' option, no doubt.

'Seriously, don't worry about me if you want to take that,' I told her, as I poured out her tea. 'I have all the time in the world today, remember?'

She shook her head. 'Sorry. Really, it's fine. It's only my husband again. Always has to have the last word.' Her shoulders slumped now. 'Thanks for this,' she said, lifting the cup. 'Just what I needed. 'Oh, Casey. It's just so … so *frustrating*. I mean, it's not as if I'm not supportive – God, I couldn't be more supportive – but he just doesn't seem to accept that *I* have a full-time job, too. That having to deal these daily crises with his father just isn't *possible*. I've lost count of the times when I've been interrupted in the middle of meetings – either a neighbour, of one of his home carers, or the police …'

I remembered something else she'd said. 'But your husband works from home, doesn't he? Can't he deal with most of them?'

'Oh, you'd think so, wouldn't you? But for all that he feels terrible about putting his dad in a home, he's also got that male thing of compartmentalising down to a T.' Another grim smile as she picked up her treacherous mobile. 'And of course, unlike *me*, he can switch his phone off.'

I tried to put myself in her shoes and could visualise myself there all too easily. Though it was a reminder of just how lucky I was; both my parents, so far, were healthy and mentally sound, and I knew that if either of them became ill in that way, I'd want to give up work immediately, so I could deal with it. Which was in itself a privilege. As was the knowledge that I'd have the support and help of both Mike and the kids. I felt for her. No children. And how much family were close by to support her? I suspected few or none. 'Things are that bad then?' I ventured. 'What about his wife – your husband's mother?'

'Oh, bad for definite. They're bad to awful. And sadly, she really can't cope with him. She's not quite ... well, let's say I suspect she might be heading down the same road. And, of course, she calls Charles endlessly. Day and night.' She sighed heavily. 'I mean we always knew it was going to get worse – that's the nature of the beast, isn't it? But the time is fast approaching when something really bad is going to happen. He'll wander off somewhere where no one can find him. Or have an accident. Or set the house on fire ... Does he *want* that to happen? Just because he feels too guilty to do what needs to be done?' She sipped her tea. 'But enough. More importantly, speaking of people who might burn down their houses, I've read the fire officer's report on Miller, and your emails about the knives and lighters. This is obviously a major red flag, Casey, isn't it?'

The subject duly changed, the conversation moved on to Miller and seeing her concern, it struck me just how 'normal' our abnormal lives with him had become. The sheer fact that Christine was taking the whole fire thing so seriously, when, to me, at least, it was just another item on the list of Miller-related anxieties. And I thought of Mike's words – 'he could have burned the house down, with us in it!' – and wondered if being cooped up with Miller for so long had dulled my sense, my appreciation, of the danger *we* might be in.

'All this fascination with death and destruction,' Christine was going on, reading from a report on her now open laptop. 'D'you think he intends to act on any of it? What's your take on his mental state currently? And these

disclosures he's been making – d'you think there's an esca-
lation in his need to vocalise things? If so that's progress,
isn't it?' (I'd talked a *lot* about my lack of progress.) 'Though
I worry that he might be unleashing something that might
precipitate a crisis …'

I nodded. 'The fascination with death is definitely
becoming more and more of a thing with him. As is the
twin obsession with babies. *Dead* babies – as I wrote in my
email. There is definitely a theme, one I presume has been
indoctrinated in his early childhood, not least by his grandmother, that there are too many babies in the world, and
that when they die it's a good thing. And that he's *definitely*
one too many …'

But then I stopped, transfixed. Because, from under
Christine's sunglasses there had appeared a tear. She was
still looking down at her laptop. Apparently reading one of
my recent emails, but that line of saline, tracking down her
cheek, to plop onto her keyboard, told a very different tale.

Or might it be hay fever? No. If it had been she would
have said so. Would have sniffled, would have started a
discussion about the misery of allergies. I might have
offered to go and fetch her an anti-histamine.

None of this happened. So I did nothing. Perhaps she
was hoping I hadn't seen it? But the silence lengthened,
and I was at a loss to know what to put in it. Should I
pretend I hadn't seen it? Let her regain her composure?
Yes, probably. But it was then joined by a second tear, rolling down her other cheek.

'Christine,' I said gently. 'Are you okay?'

In response she reached into her bag for a travel pack of tissues. Then she took off the sunglasses and dabbed at her eyes. 'Yes,' she said. 'Yes, I will be, just give me a minute.'

So I did that as well, sipping my glass of squash, while she delicately blew her nose. And, once again, I felt so sorry for her. Here was I, droning on, when she was clearly still struggling with the angry exchange she'd had with her husband. Still worrying about troubles she thought she'd left at home today. 'Look,' I said, eventually, because I could see she was still struggling, 'we can catch up another time, if you like. I know you have a lot on your mind. Let's just have another cuppa, hey? We don't have to do this today.'

She shook her head and straightened her back, 'No, Casey, it's okay. I'm so sorry,' she added. 'This is so unprofessional of me. It's just a culmination of things, to be honest. And reading about Miller's thing with dead babies …' A grimace. A wan smile. 'Just set me off again, that's all. Forgive me.'

'Of course it would,' I said. But her words confused me slightly. Surely, in her job, like mine, she'd heard worse. A lot worse. 'Like I say, you obviously have a lot on your plate.'

She nodded. And I realised she was nodding because she couldn't speak again. Had the proverbial lump still very much in her throat. And when she did speak, she said, 'God, Christine, get a bloody *grip*!' Then started furiously dabbing at her eyes again.

'Christine, *really*,' I said, 'if you need to leave and sort something out with your father-in-law, it's fine. This can wait. It's –'

She shook her head. 'It isn't that. It's just the whole thing with babies. Just today of all days ... Forgive me,' she said again. 'It's just touched a nerve, that's all. It's just my daughter ...'

'Your daughter?' But didn't she say she didn't have any children? Oh, *lord*.

Now she nodded. 'She died as a baby. Cot death.'

'Oh my God,' I said. 'Oh, I'm so sorry, Christine. I had no idea.'

She flapped a hand, almost dismissively. An action I recognised. As if to say 'no, please let's not go there'. Self-preservation. 'It was a long time ago,' she said. 'I'm fine. Really, I'm fine. It's just –' Unshed tears spilled from her eyes again. 'That today would have been her eighteenth birthday. Today, of all days, eh? And he's banging on about his bloody father, and, you know, sometimes it's just ... just ...

'Just that he didn't even say anything, not a word. Not a single word. I mean, I know people deal with grief in different ways, and I know it was a long time ago, but it's what it says, isn't it? Not that he's forgotten. I accept that. He moved on. It's fine. It's just that he knows how much it means to me. Just to *think* of her. To remember her. That's not too much to ask, is it? Just a hug. Just ...' She drew in an enormous breath, then exhaled. 'God, what am I *like*? Casey I really am *so* sorry ...'

I reached a hand across the table and gripped one of hers. 'Christine, stop *saying* that! Of course you're upset. You've every *right* to be upset.'

Another wan smile crossed her lips. 'But I'm supposed to be here for *you*. Not the other way around.'

My heart went out to her. To the human beneath the polished, sometimes brusque-seeming professional. Who clearly had her own heavy crosses to bear.

'Don't be so flipping daft,' I said. 'You just sit there for as long as you need. If you want to talk about it, we can talk about it. If you don't want to talk we won't. If you want to sit there and cry for a bit, I'll go get some bigger tissues.'

To my surprise, Christine then burst out laughing, even through her tears. 'Oh, Casey, bless you. You've cheered me up already. You really have. And I promise, no more tears now. Another cuppa and a couple of biscuits, and I'll be right as rain, honestly. Enough, enough, enough, now. Seriously. I'm *fine*. So, back to business.' She turned once again to her laptop. 'To Miller. I have some *extremely* good news for you.'

Chapter 20

Christine Bolton might not have realised it at the time, but even before she'd imparted her good news, she had cheered me up a good deal as well. Though it feels wrong to say that one person's traumas can lift another person's spirits, in this case there was an element of unexpected truth. Because I knew that one of the key issues I was wrestling with as I navigated Miller's place-ment with us was that constant feeling that I was going it alone. And that made me realise just what a big factor John Fulshaw's support had been – bigger even than I'd consciously known.

It's an often-used word, 'bonding', and a bit of a modern cliché, but in this case it felt like the right one. Just as Christine had bared her soul to me, showing me the woman behind the job title, so I suddenly felt I'd leapt the gap between our respective and different roles. And I'd seen that I'd made assumptions about her that were inaccurate, and slightly damning – seen a lickety-spit professional with lots of tick-boxes and targets but no understanding of the human challenges the job *I* did involved.

But I was wrong. I'd judged her harshly without knowing the whole picture, probably because I'd been too engrossed in my own woes. And now I did know it, not only did my heart go out to her, obviously, but I also felt we'd made an important personal connection.

And her 'extremely good news' sounded extremely good as well.

'It's quite a new initiative,' she explained, once things returned to more of an even keel and another pot of tea had been administered. 'But we have at our disposal, throughout the county, one or two older carers who are nearing retirement – in some cases retired, even – and who no longer wish to take on children for set lengths of time, but don't want to step out completely. In fact, in most cases, these carers haven't had a full-time placement for a few years. The kind who've been bobbing along, doing respite, and so on, but who'd prefer to channel their energies into a single child, for the long term. Sort of mentoring more than fostering, if you like.'

She went on to explain that this specific group of potential carers they were recruiting tended to come from a work background that favoured rather strict regimes, such as the military, the police or the prison service. They had then undergone further training within the fostering service to hone particular skills; those that would enable them to work with the most challenging children that came into care, to help support beleaguered full-time foster carers.

'So rather than doing respite as and when, as is the norm,' Christine explained, 'they are being partnered up with full-time carers who are in situations such as yours, where, without such continuity of regular respite, a long-term placement would probably prove unmanageable.'

'So kind of sharing the responsibility?' I suggested.

'Exactly. But more than that – this isn't just "holding the reins", like, say, a supply teacher or baby sitter might do – or playing gran, holding the fort, while mum and dad are away. Their role is also to work intensively with the children on their behaviour.'

'So no slipping them sweeties while mum's back is turned, kind of thing.'

'Precisely. It will be sort of on the same lines as the school Miller's started at today. With a strict "good behaviour means rewards" regime. They will have lots of fun – that's a given, and part and parcel of the set-up – but they have to earn it, and if they don't, then they will learn that they'll get nothing other than routine and a safe place to be for a couple of days. And, just as in school, the onus will be completely on Miller to have good or not so good days when he goes there.'

'*If* he agrees to go there,' I said.

'Well, he went to school this morning, didn't he? And, you know, if you look at the bigger picture, Miller does seem to love a challenge. I imagine that his curiosity will get him into the car, if nothing else.'

It was a good point. I hoped she was right. But the best bit was that they'd already identified such a person to work with us and Miller – a retired police officer who was childless, and had entered into fostering quite late in life, having been widowed very young. She had now decided she wanted to do more focused, behavioural-type work, one-on-one, and in short, regular bursts. She was called Mavis, which gave me confidence immediately. Surely no one would dare mess with a Mavis? She was in her mid-sixties, apparently, and lived out in the countryside with her three ex-police German shepherd dogs. Crucially, she had already offered to take Miller (and sight unseen, which also impressed me) every other weekend for as long as we needed it.

'And you do need it,' Christine had finished. 'As do we. Because there's clearly no way you're even going to survive the summer with him – let alone in the longer term, even if school pans out well. I know how intense it is at home with him. I also understand how much you need things put on a more even keel, so your son returns home. How are things there, by the way?'

Now it was my turn to feel tearful. Tyler had been great. Sending me funny texts, keeping me in the picture, sending silly pictures, too, of him and Dee Dee. Having fun. One thing was for sure. He was definitely singing for his supper on that front. But, much as he kept reassuring me that he'd be home again, and soon, every communication, however light-hearted, felt like a punch in the gut – because it just highlighted how isolated from my family I was feeling. And how beyond difficult it was becoming not to feel resentful about missing out, about not *being* there for them. And for me. How difficult it was to stop myself from thinking 'I don't need to *do* this.'

A Boy Without Hope

'It is what it is,' I said, trying to sound matter of fact. Then stopped, fearing the floodgates flying open. Fortunately, Christine had the wisdom not to pat me or try and soothe me, or I'd have been off to get the box of extra tissues myself.

'But it needs *sorting*,' she said crisply. 'You've been badly let down. Which is why I've fought so hard for you and Mike to be allocated this support.'

I smiled a wobbly smile. 'It's that obvious?'

She tapped her open laptop. 'You forget, Casey, I'm the one that reads your emails!'

So perhaps we'd both done a little bit more soul-bearing than we'd intended. And perhaps we were both all the better for it. And here was hope. No – more than that, here was tangible change for the better. No matter how bad things got at home, we would know that it would only be a matter of time before we got a break. There was light at last, at the end of the never-ending-seeming tunnel. And it was in touching distance. Finally.

* * *

I don't know if it was the thought of Mavis, of the perspective shift, having heard all about Christine's problems, or the fact that I was determined to get things on an even keel so that Tyler would come home pronto – probably a combination of all three – but following our meeting I seemed to get into gear and, with Mike's support, managed the next two weeks quite well.

And that despite Miller being in all-out campaign mode – both to keep upping the ante with our personal nonrelationship, and on a mission to get himself expelled. But from a school that was never going to expel him. What an incredible difference that made. I was very used to looking after children who'd repeatedly found themselves excluded from education, of course – and part and parcel of that would be giving it everything I could to avoid getting that dreaded phone call from a head teacher. But, thanks to Mr Hammond, with Miller I was Mrs Chillout personified. A walking incarnation of the word 'whatever'. Miller wanted control and, at last, I was happy to let him run with it. As long as he got in that car every morning – which, unbelievably, for the first two days he seemed more than happy to do – I had discharged my responsibility till the evening. Terrible to admit, but still true. That he was a problem I was happy to pass on.

Of course, key was that Miller didn't *know* he wouldn't be expelled. Or that Mr Hammond would be reporting to us daily on his progress initially, usually via a chat on the phone when he was travelling home. Indeed, Miller claimed on a daily basis that not only did he hate the school, but that that the school hated him too – and that he'd definitely be excluded before the end of term – now less than two weeks away. 'I'll make sure it happens today,' he would say every morning, before launching into all the details of his cunning plan to get chucked out.

On the third morning he declared he would set the fire alarms off. And he did. But rather than be excluded from school, he simply had to sit and study in the library while everyone else went out kayaking.

A Boy Without Hope

The next day he said he had found a code online that would allow him to hack into the school's servers and disrupt their intranet. Amazingly, he also managed to do this, and though no one had any idea how, and Miller naturally refused to say, to his frustration he didn't get excluded for that either. He merely missed an end-of-term trip to a theme park, remaining in school to do three hours of lines and maths tests.

Needless to say, by the time Miller returned home each night, he had a lot of pent-up anger about his inability to bend the school to his will, and though he only spent an hour downstairs with us before it was his bedtime, boy did we get to suffer for it. It was as if he realised that he was fighting a losing battle at school, so he had to cause a fight that he thought he *could* win at home.

And credit where credit's due – he took the task very seriously, getting all his emotional troops lined up meticulously for the war he would start the minute he walked in the door.

'You two hate me, I know you do,' he said on the first Thursday evening, before he'd even taken his shoes off. 'You shouldn't even be foster carers, sending me to school without making sure I brush my hair and my teeth, knowing that I'll get picked on by everyone!'

'Don't be daft, Miller,' Mike said. 'Casey tells you to do that several times every morning. And these are things you should do for yourself every day, anyway. As you often say yourself, you're not five, after all. Surely you shouldn't *have* to be told.'

He was only back-footed momentarily. 'Don't you think Casey sometimes lies to you, Mike? You know – to make her life easier?' He raised questioning eyebrows. 'She's lied to you before, you know. Like, I know for a *fact* that she doesn't tell you half of the things that I do and say. I've heard her tell you stuff. She skips out loads of things.'

I knew of course, that he was itching for an argument, but I couldn't help myself, and fell right into his trap.

'Don't be ridiculous, Miller,' I scolded. 'I've told you before that divide and conquer doesn't work in this house, so just knock it off and get your drink and supper and take your pills please.'

'There you go again,' Miller shot back. 'Trying to get rid of me. Trying to make me mad so I'll go off to my room. Out of sight, out of mind. Because you hate me so much. God! Why do you even foster kids at all? I told the taxi man that you both hate me, you know. And he agrees. He knows you only do it for the money.'

I felt an all-too-familiar irritation well inside me, even though I knew what his game was. He still seemed to crave making us dislike him more than anything. So I knew I mustn't rise to it, even as I felt it. It was becoming as knee-jerk as his *need* to be disliked. This isn't me, I kept thinking. This isn't *me*.

Thankfully Mike saw that too, and stepped in to save the day. 'You putting the kettle on, Case?' he asked. 'I'll have a coffee if you are. Oh, and some of that lemon drizzle cake that your mum sent up too?'

He then turned to Miller. 'You had a rough day, mate? Only school rang and said you'd got all your points today and got to go out on the motor bikes this afternoon.'

That stopped Miller in his tracks, as the penny finally dropped. Again, though, a quick regroup and he was off again. '*Yes*,' he huffed, 'but I was only good today for a *reason*. So I could go rallying. Tomorrow it's crappy swimming or something lame like that, so tomorrow I'll be bad. Tomorrow I'll be *worse*.'

But why? I pleaded silently. But Mike merely grinned. 'Got it all planned then, kiddo, eh? Well, that's fine. It's your choice. Yours and yours only. No one else gets to control if you get good things or bad things at the end of every day, do they? So yes, I imagine a few hours of maths or French or comprehension would be much better than splashing around in a lame pool.' He tapped Miller on the shoulder. 'Good thinking, kid.'

The confusion on Miller's face was priceless. But, yet again, I could see his mind whirring as he regrouped. 'Whatever,' he said. 'I don't care anyway. Because tomorrow you have to give me back my laptop. It's the *law*,' he added, as he picked up his milk and cookies, that vital last point having apparently been scored.

But as he left the kitchen, after us both agreeing that yes, of *course* we would, he had a distinct look of confusion on his face, as it he wasn't sure if he'd achieved anything much at all.

So. Miller – what now? Casey – what now? How was the score sheet panning out? Was he still keeping score, even? Or was it proving too complicated? After all, with the school in the mix things had definitely changed. It must feel that his control was being chipped away at every day. In fact it was. Because between us, we had at last found the means to make progress towards taking away his burning need to control absolutely everything. Towards helping him understand what he could and couldn't control, and working from there on what to do about it. In getting him to understand that precious link between actions and consequences.

It wasn't lost on me that, at other times, in other circumstances, with other children, I had been perfectly able to achieve such increments of progress on my own. But not with this child. And not just because we'd as yet failed to get our own rewards and consequences system up and running. It was because we'd yet failed to form even the slenderest of bonds. In that respect it was still very much Miller leading the league table. He did everything he could to actively make me dislike him. To find his presence irritating. To deal with him a burden. So I was grateful for any help the school could give me. And, at last, particularly seeing him now, I knew it was working. Even if it was painfully slow.

My only concern was that there was only a week of the summer term left now and I still hadn't told Miller what was to happen during the summer holidays. The little bit of extra help that Christine Bolton had promised me.

* * *

'I'm not going!' Miller screamed at Libby as she tried her very best to coerce him. 'I won't get in your stupid fucking car!'

A Boy Without Hope

It was the Sunday before the start of the long summer holidays – the day Libby was to collect him for an hour's visit with Mavis. After which, assuming no apocalypse happened during it, Mavis would start her fortnightly respite periods the following weekend. Well, if we could get him to her, that was.

It had seemed only sensible not to burden Miller with this development while he was still wrestling with his new school regime. I was just happy enough that he was still going every day without putting up too much resistance. Which, now he had his laptop, he wasn't. And even though I worried what he might be *doing* on his laptop, I reasoned that he had already long since opened most internet-based cans of worms. And that, because as smooth a transition into a school routine as could be achieved *needed* to be achieved, the end surely justified the means.

So it had only been on the Saturday that Mike and I had sat him down and told him that we had a little outing arranged for him, with a view to him having some regular weekends away over the summer. We'd taken care, too, to couch it in very specific terms – as something suggested by social services, that we'd been asked to agree to, in order to give *him* a break – from us.

'Because everyone needs a holiday, lad,' Mike pointed out. 'You included. After all, you must get fed up with rattling around with us two all the time – as you frequently tell us.' Pregnant pause. 'And Mavis' – who he'd painted rather colourfully, as a sort of cross between Mary Poppins and Bear Grylls – 'is so looking forward to meeting you, and has all sorts of fun things planned for you to do together.'

But, as expected, he'd dug in his heels. 'Not going,' he said. 'End of. She sounds like a witch. And you can't make me anyway. I do what *I* want. Not going. End of.'

And the conversation had been ongoing ever since. Because, of course it didn't take him long to see through our little ruse. 'You're just sick of me,' he insisted when I'd woken him up on Sunday morning. 'And sending me away just like everyone else does. I'm not *five*,' he pointed out. 'I'm not *stupid*.'

And as at least the sending away part *was* true – albeit for respite, not forever – I'd sat down on his bed and spelled it out.

'Okay, love,' I'd said. 'You're quite right, you're twelve now. Which means you're old enough to understand that I'm human, okay? Which means I'm not perfect. Which means *I* have feelings, just like you do. Which is why I think it's important for *both* of us that we have these little breaks. You, because it'll be good for you to make friends with someone else too. And have you heard the expression that absence makes the heart grow fonder? Well, perhaps spending some time away from us will work like that for you – make you feel less like fighting us all the time over everything. And that's true for me too, Miller – can you understand that? That's also why this is happening. So I don't get to the end of my tether, either, with all the arguments. So that *I'm* happier. So that I feel I *can* hold on to you.'

'So you *are* sick of me,' he'd retorted. 'I knew you were. Hah. And you just *said* it.' He crossed his arms over his chest. He sounded pleased with himself.

'No, I'm not,' I corrected. 'But I tell you what I am, Miller. I am at a loss. To understand why you *want* to make me sick of you. Why you keep wanting to stop people trying to help you.'

'I don't *need* help. I just want to be left *alone*!'

And, at that moment, it was the hardest thing not to grant him that very wish.

* * *

'I'm sure Casey will give you a little treat,' Libby was saying now, as she held the car door open. 'If you just do as you're told. And, you know, Mavis is *so* lovely, and she's really looking forward to meeting you.'

I wasn't sure I was that happy to hear Libby playing fast and loose with offers of 'treats' on my behalf. And Miller wasn't either. 'I don't want a fucking "treat"!' he retorted, putting the word in finger quote marks. 'She's probably an old bag! She's probably never had kids and won't even know where McDonald's is or something, and, as well, she probably locks kids in cages with her dogs or something.'

'Miller!' Mike was now walking up the front path towards us. 'Enough. Get in that car, right now. No more nonsense.' He walked towards Miller and put his hand on his shoulder. 'If I have to escort you into the car, I will do, lad. You know Libby, and you know she will stay with you. That's a promise. The truth is, kiddo, that we all need a little break every now and then – you included. This is just a little break for you to get to know Mavis before you start going to stay with her. You'll be right back.'

'You get in the car,' I whispered to Libby. 'Start the engine.'

She did this without saying anything and I walked over to Mike, and placed one of my hands on Miller's other shoulder. For any neighbours watching, as we escorted him all the way into the back seat, it must have looked like the two of us were officially detaining him.

'Listen love,' I said, poking my head in as I buckled his seat belt. 'I promise you'll be back here by teatime, so just try to be open minded and allow yourself to have some fun. This is not a punishment. It's going to be like a little holiday every couple of weeks, that's all, so do try to understand that and *enjoy* it.'

'I won't enjoy it,' he spat back at me. 'And you'll *pay* for this!'

I closed the car door and Libby drove off immediately. No further drama, thank goodness, and, thanks to the child lock, no leaping out of the fast-accelerating vehicle. Just his face scowling out, his eyes boring into me. Eyes which, despite the bile in his parting shot, held all the loneliness and unhappiness in the world.

'He'll be fine, love,' Mike said as he saw my crestfallen face. 'Tell you what, let's go grab Tyler – you badly need some Ty-time – and the rest of the crew too if they like, and we'll go out for lunch. Might as well make the most of it, hey?'

But it shouldn't be like this, was all I could keep thinking. We'd had Miller for over three months now. Surely by this time we should *all* be going out for lunch. Not having to pack him off out of the way. Not either/or when it came to having quality time with family. It felt like a failure. Because that's exactly what it was.

* * *

We did just that, though. Riley and the kids joined us, too, along with Kieron and Lauren and Dee Dee. We had a lovely Sunday roast at the local pub beer garden and forgot all our worries for a couple of hours. At least everybody else did. I couldn't get Miller off my mind; how frightened he had looked. How beaten. As if he'd known he'd reached the brink and toppled over.

I needn't have worried at all, however – at least not about the things I was concerned about. Indeed, when he arrived home, I realised that what I should probably be worrying about more were my many failings as a foster carer, because Mavis, it seemed, was the new superwoman. At the very least, according to Miller, the one that all foster carers should aspire to emulate.

'And, as well, she has chickens and ducks and a pond in her garden – which is miles bigger than yours,' he said. 'Miles bigger. And she has three dogs, but not house dogs – they wander the land and keep everybody safe. And, as well, they're like a *wolf* pack. Did you know about wolves? They're –'

'Wow!' I said. 'Sounds like you really got along with her, and, gosh, she must have a *huge* house. And land as well! Fancy that! Did you have something to eat there? Are you hungry?'

'It's not a *house*, Casey. It's a mansion, and it's *miles* bigger than yours. The bathroom is miles bigger than yours too, and guess what? I have an en-suite in my new bedroom' – or 'in suite', as he put it – 'and if I'm good she says I can have a TV in there too. I told her – hah! What's not to be good about? D'oh. She's like a *real* foster carer. A proper one. And, as well, no offence, but she's loads older than you are, so she's *much* more experienced. So it's not *your* fault,' he added soothingly.

It? As in *what*? As in everything, I imagined. And I wondered what Mavis might have to say about his estimation of our respective ages.

It made me smile at least. And provoked a highly unlikely phrase to spring to mind. One that Libby would have approved of. The little … monkey.

Chapter 21

As thrilled as Miller had been with his first visit to the wonderful Mavis, and the look he had given me as he had been, as he'd put it, 'packed off', the things I'd said to him beforehand clearly hadn't sunk in. But perhaps that was it. That he couldn't seem to help it. He said he'd make me pay, and he was going to.

After a mostly bedroom-based Monday, at around ten on the Tuesday morning, he came down to the living room in his Batman pyjamas. 'Phone Mavis,' he demanded. 'I want to speak to her.'

I was sitting with my laptop on my knees, dealing with emails. 'Why, love?' I asked. 'Is it something important? Because you'll be seeing her in just a few days now.'

'I just want to speak to her, and it's private,' he said. 'Why do you always have to make everything so *awkward*?'

'Well, I'll try and ring her in a minute or two,' I said. 'I just need to finish sending this report first. I won't be long.'

'Oh my *God*!' he yelled, instantly firing up on both cylinders. 'You don't want me to speak to her, do you? Phone her, phone her, phone her, go on, phone her, phone her now, you can still write your stupid email, just phone her, go on, phone her.'

'For God's sake, Miller!' I snapped back. 'I said give me a minute, and I *mean* give me a minute. Now go wait somewhere else please, while I finish this, or I won't phone her at all.'

But he clearly wasn't taking no for an answer. Before I could stop him, he lunged forwards and swept my laptop clean off of my knees, the power lead pinging out of it as it landed on the floor. I leapt up and picked it up, checking it was still on, then turned on him, silently cursing. 'What the *hell* are you doing, Miller? This laptop cost a lot of money and you've been told about messing with other people's things. How dare you!'

'So, phone her then,' he said, grinning right in my face. 'If you just *listened* instead of thinking you know best all the time, *that*' – he poked a finger at it – 'wouldn't have happened.'

I took a deep breath, not sure whether I wanted to cry or to scream at him, and when I had composed myself I looked him squarely in the face. 'Get up to your room, Miller. Now. Think hard about what just happened here. And I'm sure you'll be able to work out why I will not be phoning Mavis today. *Go*!'

Something in my voice must have touched a nerve with him because, though he didn't say a word, he just stood there and stared, before finally turning around and stomping back upstairs. He then slammed his bedroom door hard enough to make the house shake, but I was in no mood to race up there after him. I closed my laptop down and sat on the sofa for a full five or ten minutes before I felt able to get back up and do something. I didn't know why, but I was shaking. Was it anger or fear? I realised that actually it was fear. There had been something different in his eyes, only fleeting, but definite. As if he was considering attacking me before he ran off. Fight or flight. Thank goodness flight had held sway.

And something else. For the first time ever, I think, I was actually afraid of one of our foster children. And that wasn't a nice thought at all. I went into the kitchen and switched on the kettle, reminding myself that we didn't have long to go before we would get a whole weekend free from stress. Free from feeling constantly wired and wondering when the next attack would be. And, increasingly, what form it might take.

It was no better the next day, when I'd decamped into the garden, and, unusually, Miller had dressed himself and come out there as well, to kick a ball around – though where 'around', it soon became clear, meant 'at me'. I tried first to engage him. 'Shall we have a kick about together, love?' And when that was rebuffed, with a 'nope', to ignore him. As in both the ball, which kept banging against my shins, and the attendant 'oops, sorry' non-apologies.

Finally, I lowered the book I'd been trying to read. 'I wouldn't bother, love,' I said, after he'd kicked at my leg for the fifth time. 'I'm tougher than I look. Just be careful kicking that ball near the flowers please.'

Which was obviously an idiotic thing to say to him. The minute I'd said it, I knew that my flowers would be next, and, sure enough, my rose bush was the next casualty of the amazing straying football.

Now I put my book down on the table. 'Well, obviously the garden isn't big enough for you and your football,' I said evenly. 'So I tell you what. Why don't you and I take a walk down to the park with it?'

'Yeah, as if …' he began.

'Or it goes back in the shed, please. Before we have any more "accidents".'

'Why should I?' he asked, shoving the ball under his arm. 'It's not my fault you have such a crappy little garden. Why should I stop having fun just because of that?'

'I'm not about to have an argument with you, Miller,' I told him. 'I'm simply telling you, no more football in this garden today. And if you don't want to come to the park with me, there's a lovely big field at the bottom of the street. You can go play on that if you like.'

'Oh yeah, *right*!' Miller said. 'Like, where all the bullies play? No thanks. I know why you want me to go down there. Just so I'll get beaten up.'

'What bullies, Miller? Who are these bullies you speak of? As far as I can remember, you've not even been down there. Not once. So, do you want to come to the park then?' I said. *Keep trying, Case, keep trying.*

He looked as if I'd just suggested taking him for another spin around my favourite dress shop. '*No*! Oh my God. I can't wait till I get my weekend leave. It'll be like getting out of *prison*!'

He huffed off then, lobbing the ball onto the patio as he went, and I was tempted to shout, 'You and me both, kiddo!' Instead I ignored the temptation and took a few deep breaths. *Two more days, Casey*, I told myself. *Just two more days*. And those forty-eight hours couldn't go fast enough.

I'd just got back into my book when the phone rang.

'Speak of the devil,' I said, when Mavis introduced herself. 'Your ears must have been burning for a minute there.'

I'd tried to call her on the Monday, for a debrief after Miller's initial visit, but had had to leave a voicemail, so, given that it was now Wednesday, it was extremely good to hear her voice. Despite having no reason to – not via either Miller himself or Libby – I was still harbouring a fear that it might yet not happen. That, like Helping Hands Sheila, she had had second thoughts.

But not a bit of it. She told me she'd chuckled at my message. That yes, she indeed had a pond, and ducks and chickens. But that no, she didn't live in a mansion, with acres of land.

'I wish, but not quite!' she said, laughing. 'But at least it's good to know the lad has an imagination. And sorry to be so slow coming back to you, by the way. I've been off away at a dog show. I have dogs.'

'So I hear. Three – wow, that must keep you pretty busy!'

'Not as busy as a certain young man is keeping you, I hear.'

'Hmm,' I said. 'Well, I can't deny that I'm looking forward to a couple of days off duty. We've not had the best week. He's been sticky to cope with,' I added, looking out into the broken roses in my garden. 'Argumentative. Antagonistic.' There was no point in sugaring the pill here, after all. 'I hope he's not going to run you ragged.'

'Takes a *lot* to run me ragged,' she said. 'I've spent years wrangling with grown men with a far worse attitude, remember. So don't you worry about that. And I'm all genned up. Quite the back story, poor lad.'

'I just wish I could tell you we'd managed to make any progress. I can't even quite believe I'm in this situation with a child, to be honest. It's a first for me. It doesn't feel good, as you can imagine.'

'Oh, don't be too hard on yourself. Christine's filled me in and I totally understand why you'd feel so frazzled. I'm just glad I can step in and help. Get my teeth into him, so to speak.'

She sounded like she had the teeth for it, too. Perhaps Mike's description wasn't that far off the mark.

'That's reassuring to know,' I said. 'I just wish I could make more progress with him myself. He's just so angry all the time. Mostly with me, sadly. One thing I can tell you, at least – he definitely can't wait to get away from me.'

'Oh, I'll bet,' she said. 'But you know – and I got this impression last week – it's just his emotions getting the better of him, that's all. I've seen it before. Often, when they're ambushed by unfamiliar feelings, they fall back on the emotions that they're used to. Anger, defensiveness , rage –

anything that makes sense to them, really. Anything better than accepting that they're vulnerable. Odd and difficult for us to witness of course, but quite acceptable for them.'

She sounded like a very wise woman, I thought. 'That does make sense,' I admitted.

'It should,' she continued. 'It may be that Miller might be feeling that he's going to miss you, or that he's afraid you really *won't* want him back. Dealing with those thoughts is probably far too complicated for him so he reacts with what he knows. What he does best. Unfortunately, you're bearing the brunt of it. Sorry.' She laughed. 'I'm teaching my granny to suck eggs, aren't I?'

No, I thought, you're not. You're counselling me, actually. Because when exactly had I lost the ability to calmly analyse a Miller situation in that way? I really couldn't seem to see the wood for the trees these days, could I? Because here I was, feeling stupid, listening to an older woman giving me the explanations I should have been able to give myself.

'Not at all,' I said, grateful for her sage words. 'Thank you, Mavis. It makes so much more sense when a third party provides the clarity that's been evading me.'

'Oh please don't beat yourself up,' she said. 'I've worked with children like Miller for a while now, and I know how easy it is to be sucked into the here and now and then everything else, including the obvious, gets lost somewhere down the line. I've done it and worn the T-shirt, believe me. A step back – or in your case, a weekend every fortnight – might just be all that's needed to take stock and regroup. You'll see.'

Mavis was right. A mini break every so often would give me the opportunity to take a breath, forget all the nonsense and recharge my batteries. I'd be ready to face whatever was coming with renewed vigour after a weekend away from it all. That's what I told myself, anyway. And I was determined that's the way it would be. Or, at least, could be.

* * *

That Friday afternoon, for the first time in what seemed like ages, I switched on my radio and tuned it into my favourite oldies station, and sang along while I ironed and packed a little suitcase for Miller. I'd even bought him new pyjamas and slippers to pop in there.

'Anything you'd like me to pack in particular, love?' I called into the kitchen where he was sitting playing on his laptop while he ate his porridge. 'A favourite story book or something?'

'I'm not *five*,' came the reply. 'And I don't care what you pack. What time is the driver coming?'

'About an hour,' I called back, 'so make sure you're ready. I think Mavis has plans for taking you and one of the dogs to a lake or something, for a picnic.'

I heard a groan. Then, 'God, I'm not *five*,' again.

I rolled my eyes, but I didn't let it bother me. In an hour's time, this ball of worry tumbling around in my stomach would be gone, and I could once again relax.

I heard him head back up the stairs then, and finished packing the case. I was just putting it by the front door when he came back downstairs, dressed and ready, and with his PlayStation under his arm.

'Love, I don't think you'll have time to be on that,' I said. 'Mavis has lots planned this weekend, and besides didn't you say there wasn't a TV in your room?'

Miller shrugged. 'She said she was gonna get one if I was good, and I told her I'm gonna be good, so …'

I sighed. It was almost time for the taxi to arrive – was it really worth getting into it at this stage? Miller would probably kick off and refuse to go unless he got his own way. On the other hand, it was a bit of a cop-out me letting him take it and then leaving it to Mavis to deal with. I decided I had to at least try again.

'Look, love, why don't you leave it for this weekend, and see how things go, and then you can definitely arrange to take it the next time.'

'I want to take it!' Miller snapped. 'What if she hates me and makes me stay in my room all weekend? And, as well, what if I hate her and don't want to do what she wants to do? Least I'll have my gamer friends to talk to.'

I thought back to what Mavis had said about how Miller might be really worrying about going away, and I made the decision that I'd allow him to take it, but phone Mavis to explain after he'd set off. I knew it meant I'd still be leaving it down to her to sort out, and I felt bad, but I had a feeling she was resilient enough to deal with it.

'Fine,' I said. 'Take it, but don't be surprised if there isn't a TV yet. She can't just magic one up instantly you know.'

'So *you* say. But she will. You don't know *anything*.'

I had thought, at least for the preceding hour, if not longer, that the first thing I'd do when I saw the car turn the corner would be to punch the air. Yet he'd turned as they'd driven off, and actually waved. And again, despite the fraught few days we'd had, there was something about his expression that caused me to dampen my desire to do so. He looked so sad, and something else, as well, now – resigned. As though the fight had gone out of him. As though leaving places with a suitcase in hand was something he would just have to get used to. Rather than the euphoria I thought I'd be feeling at this moment, I just felt incredibly sad that it had come to this. I was past the point of admitting to myself that I couldn't manage this kid without regular breaks. That was already true; that was why we had arrived here. No, it was that horrible sense that I was a whisker away from failure. That, no matter what they threw at this, including the warm, sagacious Mavis, I simply didn't have the heart for it. That at some point, if not this point, I would be forced to accept defeat. Take my place on the long list of carers who'd given up on him. Passed him along.

It wasn't a nice revelation.

Chapter 22

I had watched the car pull up that Sunday afternoon braced for whatever was coming. My hope was that Miller would be somehow miraculously different. That he'd arrive full of stories about what a great time he'd had. And that the next two (long) weeks would be better. My fear was that I was living in cloud cuckoo land. That whether he'd had a good time or a bad time, the net result would be the same. Miller would still feel rejected by me – still struggle to adapt to his new reality.

And I'd been right to be fearful, because he was sullen and uncommunicative. Whether to punish me for what I'd 'done to him', or because he was genuinely happier with Mavis, it made no difference. Apart from telling me, sarkily, that he did have the promised TV, he seemed keen to shut me out of the whole experience. 'It's none of your *business* what I do there,' had been his last word on the subject. And, of course, I agonised because the guilt was so acute, made worse that my resentment levels were already so high. I felt isolated from my family, and I felt shut out by

him as well now. It was hard to get past that, however hard
I tried.

* * *

But if my next 'get out of jail free' card was a long two
weeks' distant, there had at least, on the Tuesday, been
some good news. The best news, in fact. That Tyler was
going to come home. This very night, in fact, after a trip to
the zoo with Dee Dee.

I'd phoned him the previous evening, as had become my
recent habit – more than anything just to check if he'd
heard back yet about his college place. I'd also waxed lyrical
about Mavis, and what a difference she was making. To me,
anyway, which was at least something, even if, Miller-wise,
it was still an unfinished story.

'That's great, Mum,' he'd said. 'I'll get packing then,
shall I?'

'You mean you're coming back?'

'If that's okay …'

'Shut UP! When – today?'

'Tonight. After my babysitting duties. Love her to bits
but, God, three-year-olds are full *on*. Dealing with Miller's
going to seem like a walk in the park now.'

* * *

I wasn't so sure about that. But it was now late morning on
Wednesday, and I had things to do. 'Miller,' I pleaded as I
leaned on his bedroom door frame, 'will you please get
dressed and come down so we can get to the shops?' It was

already 11.30 a.m. and I'd been trying to get him downstairs for the last hour, because I really did need to get out. For a start, I was out of coffee, and that was unthinkable for me. Even Mike would testify that it was actually dangerous to leave me without coffee for any length of time. I also needed a few other essentials before Tyler arrived back tonight, so, one way or another, I had to hit the shops today.

'I don't want to go anywhere,' he said. 'Why don't you just go by yourself? I'm old enough to be left. I told you – Mavis leaves me indoors. Why can't you?'

I knew this was true because she'd mentioned it herself, when she'd given me a debrief. And I'd thought, then as now, why indeed? Because I never had. And thought I never should. Because, unlike Mavis, I had assumed it would be inappropriate at his age. No, there were no laws about the age you could leave children – be they foster children or your own kids. People often thought there were, but the law was clear – there *wasn't* one. But for me personally, both as a mother and a foster mum, twelve had always seemed too young; a grey area that, for me, was on the wrong side of black. Kids of twelve could get into all sorts of scrapes.

But Mavis *had* left him. And more than once. To go to the post office, to walk her dogs. On the common-sense basis that he'd neither cause harm or come to harm if she left him alone for twenty minutes. 'You mean you haven't?' she'd asked, surprised, when I'd admitted that to her. 'Flipping nanny state nonsense. I don't hold with all that. The boy's almost thirteen!'

She was old school and then some. Perhaps I should be too. Desperate times called for desperate measures.

'Fine,' I said, decided. 'If you really don't feel like coming, then I'll go and leave you here. I'll only be about twenty minutes. Will you be okay?'

Miller sighed and shook his head, pausing his game to actually look at me while he spoke. 'I'm not a baby, Casey. You forget that I spent most of the time growing up being left on my own. I like being on my own, so just go. Do whatever you have to do and I'll see you when you get back. I'll still be here killing everyone online, so don't worry about me.'

My turn to sigh, as I walked out and closed his bedroom door. That was another thing that I didn't seem able to control: his obsession with violent games. PlayStations had evolved in the last couple of years and no longer needed actual physical games in order to play. At one time I could easily confiscate an inappropriate game by simply picking it up, putting it in its case, and removing it. But these days you could download a game instantly to the console and start playing it straight away. In Miller's case it didn't even require payment because, somehow, and don't ask me how, he knew ways in which he could get it for free. No one else in the family knew how he did it either but both Tyler and Kieron had said it was impossible, and that you couldn't do it without paying online. Well, impossible for most people, but clearly not for Miller.

I had, of course, reported it, because of it most likely being illegal, but nobody had been able to work out how it was happening, so nobody had been able to advise me on what to do about it. Other than take away the console, of course. The trouble was that Miller said he wasn't doing this, but that 'friends' were giving him codes, and it was all above board. And, without proof of it being otherwise, my hands were tied.

I grabbed my handbag, phone and car keys, and rushed out to the car. I'd be really quick, I told myself, still feeling guilty that I was leaving him home alone. I had no choice, however. With Riley, David and the kids off to the Lake District for a few days, and Kieron and Lauren at work, I had no one to call to come over and sit for an hour. Well, there was always Libby, but, tempted though I was to facilitate an improvement in their thus far rocky relationship, a twenty-minute jaunt to the shops hardly warranted calling upon a social worker to provide day care.

I was as good as my word too, despite the temptations of the great outdoors, and all too soon I was letting myself back into the house. 'Miller! I'm home!' I called up the stairs before taking the provisions through into the kitchen. 'I've got ice cream!'

It was an automatic thing to say. Most kids would come running down immediately given the promise of ice cream, but this was Miller, who only enthused about disasters. So, not expecting him, I quickly put the frozen things in the freezer, before going upstairs to check he was okay.

The door was shut, but there was no drone of the TV beyond it. I knocked. 'I'm back, love,' I called as I pushed it open. The room was in darkness, as per – he kept the curtains shut so he could see the screen better. But as light from the landing flooded in, two things became apparent.

That the TV wasn't on, and that Miller wasn't there. My heart sank. Had he been waiting for this very eventuality to happen to either scarper or get up to mischief? Or perhaps – a less unwelcome thought – he was in the wardrobe?

I could see a notebook open on the bed with a pen at the side of it, and, as my eyes adjusted, I realised I could see that he *was* there. But not in the wardrobe. He was standing behind his curtains. It wasn't as if he was hiding from me, however, as I could see he was facing out, towards the window. He was also talking softly to himself. Not a stream of consciousness however. Numbers. Was he counting?

'Miller? What are you doing, love?'

'Shush!' he said as he popped out from the centre of the curtains. 'Seventy-two seconds for subject twenty-three, and sixty-five seconds for subject twenty-four.' He then walked to his bed, picked up the notebook, and started to write.

I waited a moment for him to finish whatever it was he was doing, and asked again. 'Love, what are you doing?'

'An experiment,' he said, simply. 'It's been running for a couple of days now.' He waved the notebook in front of him. 'I'm keeping track of all the evidence and results in here. I'll soon have my conclusions and then I'm going to write it up. I'm going to do a talk about it in school in September.'

This was a surprise. Homework during the school holidays? I'd not been told he'd been given any. But he clearly had. I was impressed. Perhaps he liked school more than he had let on, after all. I watched him tuck the ballpoint pen behind his ear while he walked back towards his window. A cute gesture from a fledgling scientist? I hoped so. 'So what is the experiment, love?' I asked, keen to seize the moment. 'You studying something you can see from there? Is it an experiment on birds?'

Miller laughed then. But then my hackles rose immediately. Because it was a throaty, unnatural laugh. In fact, not what you would usually call a laugh at all. More like something you would do if you were reading a story to a child and you'd got a line where you had to provide the pantomime-style cackle of an evil villain. He then grabbed hold of one of the curtains and theatrically pulled it back along the rail, so he could reveal his experiment to me. 'Ta dah!' he exclaimed, sounding animated and proud now. 'Come look, Casey. You can watch me do subject twenty-five if you like. It's my last one. Come on. Come and see,' he added, gesturing.

I don't know why – perhaps that laugh, or the theatricals, or both – but even as I walked towards the windowsill to look, I already knew that I was about to witness something distasteful. I was also aware of Miller watching me intently, clearly expecting, and relishing, a reaction.

And as he opened the remaining curtain, all was revealed. There was a long row of what looked like dead wasps along his windowsill but, on closer inspection, I could see that one of them was still alive. Writhing around on its back, but alive. It hit me at once: this must be 'subject twenty-five'.

'Miller, what have you done?'

Again, that strange laugh. 'I told you, it's an experiment. An experiment on wasps. They're a pest to society and scientists experiment on pests all the time, like mice for example. And rats. This is no different.'

'Yes, but what have you done to them? You haven't killed all of these wasps, have you?'

'Not all of them. Not yet. *Obviously.*' He took the pen from behind his ear and, before my horrified gaze, poked the still wriggling wasp at the end with it. 'But it won't be long before this one goes, I think. I can't record his results though, because you interrupted my timing. But it doesn't matter,' he added brightly. 'Twenty-four results for today will still do.'

I had to sit down on the edge of the bed. I was literally lost for words and had to give myself a moment to think. Finally I looked at Miller. 'Love, this isn't right,' I said. 'Most boys your age would not want to kill defenceless wasps. They just wouldn't. This isn't *right*. Do you understand that?'

Miller raised his eyebrows. 'Defenceless? Are you kidding? These things are like flying snipers. Casey, they'd sting you in a minute. I've done you a favour by killing them, in fact. You should really be grateful.'

As I listened in stunned silence he went on to explain that his experiment was to see how long each wasp could live after he'd inflicted various forms of torture. He had pulled off legs and wings. He'd pulled one completely in half. He'd hit another with a book. Drowned another in a puddle of milk ... The horrible list went on and I couldn't listen to any more of it.

'How did you get them?' I interrupted. 'You never had twenty-five wasps flying around your room and caught them all. You can't have. So where did they come from?'

I suspected some trap somewhere. Some ongoing business. I didn't know what, but, eerily, like a villain in an Agatha Christie novel, he seemed keen to explain all. He turned around and reached behind the curtain at the far end of the window, then produced a paper cup. 'Not twenty-five,' he said, tilting the cup so I could see inside it. 'There's around sixty dead ones in here already – look.'

The cup was filled almost to the brim with dead, dismembered insects. I felt sick. 'So where, Miller? Where did you get them?'

'You have a nest outside my window,' he said. '*Surely* you knew that. I just leave my window open, and they fly in. Specially if I leave crumbs of biscuit on the windowsill. They've been doing it for weeks. Some of them get away, but usually I manage to stun them and catch them before they do.'

He leaned down and reached under his bed to produce a can of insect-killing spray. 'I use this. I found it in your conservatory and I thought, well the nest is outside my room, so it's only right I keep it up here, isn't it? For my protection.'

For my protection. That term again. But it wasn't for protection. It was to provide specimens for his 'experiment'. I didn't know what to say. All the time I had thought he was up here playing on his games, or sulking about one thing or another, or writing his endless lines of code, and all the time he'd been devising ways in which to kill wasps, and then recording how long they took to die using each method.

Why did he get such enjoyment out of things like this? *Because he's psychologically damaged, Casey, remember?* More pressingly, how could I put this right? Could it even *be* put right? I had no answers. But I finally found my voice.

'Close your window, Miller,' I said as I stood up. I took the spray from his hand, too. 'And I'll take that, thank you. This stops now. You can scoop all the rest of those wasps into that cup and take them down to the garden bin straight away. And I'll be checking up here daily. No more, do you understand?'

'But there's a *nest*. And they'd only die anyway. They don't live *forever*.'

'Mike will get someone up to sort that out,' I said. 'The nest will be gone.'

'But what about my talk for school?'

'Miller, school won't want to hear about experiments on living creatures.'

He looked genuinely perplexed. 'But scientists experiment on living creatures all the time!'

I had no answer to that. Not in terms I could explain without tying myself in moral knots. There was absolutely no point in trying to have a discussion with him, period. Certainly not about the more macabre side of what he'd done. He just didn't – almost certainly, given what I'd witnessed, *couldn't* – understand. He was proud of his experiment. And nothing I could say would change that. As he was quick to point out. He had found something to engage him that wasn't on a screen. I should be pleased about that, shouldn't I? He had at last found a hobby. Wasn't I *pleased* about that? I shuddered.

So instead, after telling him we would talk about it later, I went downstairs to do some recording of my own, and as I typed my emails to various people, detailing the experiment and our exchanges, the thought hit me that Miller was *our* experiment. He had been scooped up from an environment he had grown used to, thrown into the care system, into a world totally alien to him, and had been poked and prodded by professionals of one kind or another ever since, to watch his reactions and record their findings. I shuddered a second time as these thoughts joined the wasps buzzing round in my head.

And as they floated down and settled, a truth hit me, too. That this human experiment was happening in my home. Among my loved ones. And I wasn't sure if I wanted to continue to be part of it.

Chapter 23

Though I wasn't exactly having wasp-infested nightmares – I'd put enough jam jars out as wasp traps in my time, hadn't I? – Miller's experiment on defenceless insects had opened a whole new can of worms. If I'd been unsettled by his ghoulish attraction to news stories about violent death, and interest in how much it might hurt, I was much more disturbed by him personally administering it.

Though I didn't think I was being naïve. It was hardly unknown for children to go through a stage of casual cruelty – at least some of them, anyway. Particularly those who had suffered backgrounds of neglect and abuse. Neither was it news that cruelty to animals was part of the adult landscape either. Barely a day passed without some report or other of animals being abused, as the RSPCA would, I'm sure, readily testify. Then there was dog fighting, cock fighting and all manner of similar cruelties. So, no, I wasn't about to over-think it and make mountains out of molehills.

No, it was Miller's breezy attitude towards his grisly 'experiment'. This wasn't an immature, troubled twelve-year-old getting up to something that, at least on some level, they knew to be wrong. He didn't just think it wasn't wrong – he was on a whole other level. He'd really thought *I* was the mad one for thinking so. Something he'd reiterated when Mike had tackled him about it as well. Wasps were pointless, he'd told him. They were a stain on the earth. Why not experiment on them to find the best ways to 'off' them?

And, of course, we'd then had to 'off' them in any case. We'd called out an emergency pest-control firm, and had the nest removed that very evening – something Miller had been delighted to watch from his (firmly shut) window. 'But it's still a waste,' he'd commented, once they'd packed up and left. 'I could have done *loads* more experiments if you hadn't let them kill them.'

To use his own parlance: He. Just. Didn't. Get. It.

But Libby Moran needed to. CAMHS *definitely* needed to. By the time Tyler arrived home I was once again back at my laptop, typing up yet another urgent report. In which my number-one concern was that this showed he lacked empathy. Not headline news, obviously – he'd not shown much in the way of empathy at any point, but hadn't I read somewhere about how one of the indicators of possible psychopathy was a history of inflicting pain on defenceless animals? It certainly fitted – he'd been treated like an animal himself. And hadn't he said he'd been referred to as a runt?

In tandem with the growing pile of other kinds of evidence of Miller's disturbed state of mind, this new situation was a

definite concern. For the moment, however, my emails written and sent, all I wanted was to enjoy having Tyler back
with us, and for nothing else to blow up in the next ten days,
so that we could arrive at the next respite without further
damage – to either wasps or my flagging resolve.

* * *

To my relief, the next few days with Miller passed largely
drama-free. And I suspected that this might have had more
than a little to do with Tyler's presence once again in the
house. No, they didn't interact much – Tyler was out with his
friends most days, anyway – but I think both were more than
happy to give one another a wide berth, which was absolutely
fine by me. There was only one major revelation and, given
what had happened recently, it wasn't even major. The fact
that the following weekend, when clearing some of the
untamed undergrowth in the area of the back garden where
the pest control men had set up their ladders to get at the
wasps' nest, Mike had come upon something unexpected.

'Come look at this, love,' he'd told me, coming in
through the conservatory to find me. 'Seems to me laddo
up there' – because, of course, Miller was up in his bedroom
– 'has been pulling a fast one, and for some considerable
time by the looks of things.'

I followed him back out to the patch of flowerbed just
underneath Miller's window. He put a finger to his lips, and
pointed, mouthing 'down there'.

At the back of the flower bed was a runaway cotoneaster
– a spiky evergreen that had taken advantage of the sunny

spring to get seriously out of hand. Using his gardening gloves, Mike then pulled back the branches to reveal his find. Among and beneath what had remained of the torn pages of Tyler's burned college papers, there were what looked like dozens of white pills all around.

'The little s—' I began, before clamping my mouth shut, in case he heard us. 'But how?' I hissed. 'I've watched him take them – at least at the start – and so have you!'

But only at the start. When, wise to childish tricks, I'd asked him to stick his tongue out to prove he'd swallowed them. Which he had, with his usual whine: 'I'm not *five!*' After that, no, not so much, but I'd definitely seen him swallow them.

I whispered that to Mike. Who, in response, popped his tongue into his cheek. 'So *you* thought. And obviously thought wrong,' he whispered back.

He released the bushes. Rolled his eyes. 'So now we know why they weren't working, don't we?' he said, once we were back out of possible earshot.

Didn't we just? All that time he'd not been sleeping, and here, perhaps, was the reason. Perhaps he'd never taken the melatonin pills at all. Or, at least, since he was old enough to realise he didn't want to. So he'd taken control. And how many placements ago now? No wonder there had been no discernible difference between the real melatonin and the placebo.

Because he was now 'taking' the placebo anyway, there seemed little point in confronting him immediately. Our current priority – and everyone involved was agreed on that point – was to get Miller back to Mavis's for his next respite visit. If there was any prospect of things working long term, getting Miller into the routine of those fortnightly visits was key. I still wasn't sure things were going to work long term, and I was now more loath to commit to it than ever, but I had to give it my best shot over the school summer holidays, as once he was back in school I knew things would improve, even if only in that I got my days back once again.

But just as I was daring to make plans for our next respite weekend, Miller threw me another curve ball. Despite having told Tyler – if not me – how much he was looking forward to 'escaping prison' for the weekend, when I looked in on him to say goodnight on the Thursday evening – the night before he was due at Mavis's – he clearly had other ideas.

He was sitting on his bed, scribbling numbers on his pad, and he didn't even look up at me when I wished him a good night and dared to mention his upcoming mini-break.

'You think you've got a little holiday coming up, don't you?' he said, as he continued to write down numbers. 'Well, you haven't. Just so you know.'

'Miller, chop-chop. Time for bed,' I said, deciding to ignore it. He was just trying to wind me up – to punish me – and it was important not to react.

'I need three more minutes,' he said.

'That's fine, love,' I replied. 'Then into bed and off to sleep, okay?'

Now he did look up, presumably because he was surprised I hadn't taken the bait. I smiled at him. 'Sleep tight. Hope the bed bugs don't bite.'

'God. I'm not *five*,' came the muttered response.

* * *

And now it was Friday morning, and despite my spending the entire night with fingers, arms and legs crossed that that was all it had been, a wind-up, he was, it seemed, keeping his word. 'I'm not going! I am. Not. Fucking. Going!' he yelled, as I called upstairs that the driver had arrived.

And this despite him having dressed and had his breakfast. So was this part of an all-morning strategy to lead me to hope, or a spur of-the-moment reversal? I had absolutely no idea.

'Miller,' I called back up, 'if I have to ring Mike up and get him to come home from work, I will. And Tyler will be back any minute, so please don't cause a scene. Just come on down and get in the car, please.'

Although I knew Miller would perceive these bits of information as a warning, it was much more a cry for help – from *me*. Testing as it had been for Tyler to look after his little niece, I knew coming back home to a row – he'd only popped into town to pick up his weekly music magazine – would be the last thing we needed. Especially if he walked back in to see Miller screaming abuse at me.

Miller had by now come out onto the landing. 'Ignoring you! Ignoring you!' he yelled down from the top of the stairs. 'Just tell him to go. Because I'm NOT GETTING IN!'

Chris – now our regular driver – had by now come to the door. 'Don't worry. I can wait half an hour,' he reassured me. 'But no more than that, I'm afraid, because I have an airport run scheduled next.'

'Of course,' I said, with a great deal more confidence than I felt. 'Don't worry. I'm sure we can get this straightened out before then. I'll go see if I can talk him round again. Fingers crossed.'

Chris went back to his car, and now I had a decision to make. Did I try to talk him round, knowing that was exactly what he wanted? Knowing he wanted it so he could score that precious point off me?

Because instinct told me he *was* happy to spend another weekend having fun with Mavis. It just sat at odds with his fury at me for being the one to instigate the respite, and that whole 'loss of control' thing he struggled to get past. I was certain that, ultimately, he *would* get in the car. He would just first take it to the absolute limit. Yet more depressing evidence that I'd made not a jot of difference since the day he'd come to us. Just become another person for him to refuse to cede control to.

So how to play it? Did I take more decisive action, and call Mike? Given that the taxi clock was ticking I decided I'd better opt for the latter plan. I felt bad dragging Mike home from work, but I also felt powerless – and the last thing I wanted was to have Tyler get involved.

Mike told me he'd be home in ten minutes – thankfully, he'd just gone on lunch break anyway – and I spent the first five of them trying to convince myself I still *had* a vestige of control. Even if I didn't have much of a strategy.

All I had was an analysis. That he was willing to cut his nose off to spite his face just to punish me. Forget the new computer game we'd bought him, forget that we'd let him choose last night's takeaway, forget that we'd tried so hard not to rise to his goading. This was a power play, and he *knew* he was the one with all the power. Such was the excruciating nature of this kind of respite arrangement, and always had been. Perhaps always would be.

And I *got* that. This wasn't 'time-out' for a beloved toddler who's temporarily pushed all the buttons. This wasn't a parent saying to a cherished child, 'I love you dearly, but you need time alone, to reflect.' This was us, as a foster family, sending our foster child away. Yes, only for a weekend. But it might as well have been a month. The best option for us currently. And the least worst for Miller. But how did you build self-love, self-respect and self-esteem in a child if you are confirming their self-loathing by sending them away? No matter how sensitively handled, or how pressing the need, that was always going to be the elephant in the room – the thing that set foster children apart from flesh and blood or adoptive children.

Of course, often it wasn't like that. Respite might be needed and accepted by a child without distress. Say, if a family member fell sick, or foster parents were unexpectedly called away, or for a multitude of other, less damning reasons. But sometimes – and we often took on this kind of respite ourselves – it was because a carer couldn't cope with a child they'd been given. And there was no way of sugaring that bitter pill for them.

And in this case it was compounded by previous experience. Miller had been long enough in the system to understand that ours was a professional relationship. That, in fact, *we* held all the cards. We could *choose* who to foster. And, similarly, we could choose who to *stop* fostering as well. It was just wretched. For both of us. That was the painful, painful truth. I still had five minutes. I at least had to try.

'*Please* come down, love,' I said, walking up the stairs towards him. He turned around and walked back into his room. 'I know you're cross with me, but we really can't have all this fuss, love,' I said. 'And it's not fair on Chris. And Mike's missing his lunch break now, too.'

He was sitting on his bed, cross-legged and cross-armed, like a small angry Buddha. 'Oh, so big bad Mike is coming to get me now, is he?' he snapped. 'Well, good luck with that!'

'Love, I just don't understand what's going on,' I said, sitting beside him. 'I thought you enjoyed going to see Mavis. You loved it there last time. What's changed?'

'Nothing,' he huffed. 'I just don't want to *go*! She only lets me play on my PlayStation for how long *she* decides, and she hates takeaway food. I'm not going because I'm teaching her a *lesson*.'

This confused me momentarily. I'd been so wrapped up in the idea of Miller punishing me that I'd quite forgotten that he needed to control her as well. Was all of this actually about *her*?

'Well if all this is to hurt Mavis in some way, love, then it won't work,' I said. 'It just means that she will have a weekend without having to fight with you, won't she? And you will be the only one who suffers for it. She had plans to take you places, too – fun places – but, well, now …' – I added all this gently, as if explaining a maths equation to a struggling pupil – '... because of your behaviour today, here, with *me*, and causing Chris all this hassle, if you stay *here*, you will, of course, have to lose your PlayStation for the whole weekend, so ...'

'Except he won't be staying here, Casey.'

Mike had come up the steps and was now in the bedroom doorway. 'He's going to stay with Mavis, as per the plan, as will be the plan every two weeks from now on, and that's that.'

Miller scrabbled up to his feet, on the bed. 'I won't get in that car!' he told Mike.' 'I hate Chris as *well*! He drives like a lunatic!'

'Just as well I've sent him on his way then, hey?' Mike said. 'Poor guy has better things to do than hanging around while you play silly beggars. I'm taking you to Mavis's myself. Now off that bed, grab your hoodie, and *move*!'

Miller did move. He darted off the bed, dodged past both Mike and I and was off down the stairs like a lightning bolt. Mike followed. 'I'll get him, Case,' he shouted back up as he went. 'You put his bag or whatever in the back of the car – he's getting in it one way or another!'

Just as I'd rattled down the stairs into the hall, I saw Tyler coming in through the front door. 'Mum! What the heck's going on?'

I hurriedly explained. 'Grab his bag, love,' I said, 'and shove it in the back of the car. Your dad's chasing him down the street.'

'So I noticed! Should I go and help? What is *wrong* with this kid?'

I shook my head. 'No love, Dad's got this. Ah,' I pointed, 'and him. But that's certainly the million-dollar question.'

The commotion was the full audio-visual.

'Get the fuck off me!' Miller was screaming, as Mike frog-marched him to his car. 'I'm getting you done! You can't put your hands on me! I'm calling the fucking *police*!'

I could only imagine the twitching curtains in the neighbouring houses. And there was no let-up as they marched up the street. And worse still was that Tyler, unable to stop himself, scooted past me to join in the fray. 'Stop screaming *right now*!' he shouted. 'And get into that car before I personally drag you into it! I'm not your foster carer, Miller – *got* that? – so I'm not bothered *who* you tell!'

I could see Mike grip his arm, to try and calm him down.

Again. I thought, *a-bloody-gain*. The poor lad had only just come back home and now he was witnessing his parents being shown up on the street. But it had the desired effect. I watched Miller relax into Mike's grip. He even reached out to open the car door, then calmly got into it.

Well, apparently calmly. Hard to say at a distance. I wondered what kind of journey Mike had ahead of him. What state Miller would be in for poor Mavis.

And something else. What sort of state Tyler was in now.

All of these. Before worrying about poor Miller. But even as my brain clicked into normal fostering-thinking gear, I knew that, increasingly, it wasn't happening automatically. That I was having to *remind* myself to remember 'it's the behaviour, *not* the child'.

'I think I'm done,' I said to Tyler, as the car disappeared round the corner. 'I'm so sorry. I really didn't want you involved in all this, love. *Seriously*. I think I mean it. I think we're getting too old for all this stress, love.'

'Mum, don't be *daft*,' Tyler said. 'You're just stressed. Come on, come in, and let me make you a coffee. The weekend starts here, remember? And it's not even the weekend yet! And it's not you, Mum,' he added, as we went back indoors. 'It's not all kids. It's just *him*. I really don't think he wants to be liked by anyone. I swear. He really doesn't.'

'All the more reason to try and *change* that.'

'Mum, get *real*. There's only so much you can *do*.'

'Blimey, love. Quite the philosopher.'

'Yeah, well I have a lot of thinking time. Mum, the nicer you try to be to him, the worse he seems to treat you. Perhaps, I don't know, he just doesn't fit well in a family. Perhaps he needs not to *be* in one. Have you ever thought of that? Anyway, he's gone now,' he said, as he set about making coffee. 'And I'm off to meet Denver, so you can have some of your precious "me time". So will you go and grab your rubber gloves and cleaning bucket or shall I?'

I wasn't in swiping range, so I couldn't, but I shook my head anyway. 'No, you know what? I won't clean. I'm just going to sit down and relax. I'm just going to – what is it you young ones say these days? – watch Netflix and chill.'

Tyler's face was a picture. I didn't know why, quite, but it was. 'Please don't *ever* say that again, Mum,' he said firmly.

Chapter 24

I spent a lot of time thinking about what Tyler said, particularly about Miller perhaps not fitting well inside a family. Which, despite my wishing otherwise – family was all, wasn't it? Family, a loving family, was the gold standard, wasn't it? – did seem to hold a kernel of possible truth. But I had no idea that things would be taken so explosively out of my hands.

'Casey, Casey, wake up, love!' It was early on Sunday morning. And Mike was jiggling my shoulder, trying to drag me out of my lie-in.

'What? What is it?' I asked, turning over, and hoping for coffee. 'What time is it?' I asked as I propped myself up.

'Not quite eight,' Mike said, 'but you need to come downstairs and speak to the police. They're on the phone and want to speak to you. Seems that Miller is in some kind of trouble.'

'*What*?' I jumped out of bed and shoved my feet into my slippers. 'Is he okay? Is he with Mavis?'

'I think so,' Mike said, following me downstairs. 'I think the trouble is more of the criminal kind.'

I was in quite a panic by the time I'd rattled down the stairs to the house phone. We very rarely got a call on the landline these days but, when we did, it almost always spelt trouble. Same old, same old, I thought as I picked it up.

'Hello, this is Casey Watson,' I said into the receiver. 'Is Miller okay?'

'Oh yes, he's just dandy,' the officer on the other end said. 'Which is more than can be said for Mrs Postlethwaite's windows.'

It sounded surreally like we were having a conversation in a Sunday-evening cosy crime drama. Except, of course, that it was much more serious than that. The sergeant explained that Miller was currently being detained for criminal damage, at the request of his respite foster carer. Apparently he had been taunting her for a number of hours the previous evening in order to get her to allow him to play on her computer. She had apparently refused and ignored his constant taunting by picking up a book and reading it while he continued to rant. When Miller hadn't got the attention he wanted he had run out into the garden, picked up some large stones, and smashed in four of her downstairs windows. Luckily neither Mavis, nor any of her pets, were harmed in the ensuing chaos, but Miller had obviously caused a lot of expensive damage, so Mavis had called the police.

'And due to his behaviour when our officers arrived,' the officer continued, 'we detained him for his own safety as much as anything. He was picking up broken glass and threatening to cut himself with it, as well as saying he would stab Mrs Postlethwaite. It was for that as much as anything that we also encouraged her to press charges. These kids often need a night in a cell to show them where they might end up one day, and we thought that was the best course of action.'

'I see,' I said, feeling my mood drop to my slippers. No more Mavis doing respite then, no doubt. 'Thank you. So what's going to happen now, then? Do I pick him up from you directly? If so, what time?'

'Ah, well, you see, this is why I'm calling. Young Miller is apparently refusing to be released into your custody. Which, of course he can't do, seeing as you are *in loco parentis*, but since he's also insisting he will simply run away if we do so, I'm phoning for permission from you to hand him back into Mrs Postlethwaite's care.'

I tried to gather my wits. '*What?*' I almost spluttered. Not at the fact that he was refusing to come back to us – that was an often trotted path for him historically, after all. No, at the fact – could it be a fact? – that Mavis was willing to take him home again. 'You mean she's happy to have him back tonight?'

'Indeed she is. At least she says she is. That's right, Mrs Postlethwaite, isn't it?'

'You mean she's *there*?'

'Indeed she is.'

Wits half-gathered in, I then thought practicalities. 'Okay, so in that case I need to get in touch with the emergency duty team and put them in the picture. I'll –'

'No need,' the officer said. 'We've already logged the incident, so that his social worker will be up to speed when she logs into the system tomorrow morning. So for the moment there's nothing we need other than your agreement.'

'Well, yes, of course,' I said, trying to imagine Libby's reaction come Monday morning. 'So does she want us to collect him from her tomorrow?'

'She's suggested you chat on the phone later tonight about that, Mrs Watson. If that's okay with you?'

It was, of course, very much okay. Too much okay, I realised as I put the phone down and debriefed Mike. That old 'get out of jail free card', and for another whole day and night – it was feeling so good that it made me feel terrible.

There was also the small matter that, yet again, Miller had directed operations. He'd made something happen and all of us had agreed to it. Had caused maximum hassle (and a good deal of damage) for Mavis, and, having done so, had got to stay with her longer. To stay at a place he had categorically told me he didn't want to go to in the first place. That term 'head exploding from too much thinking'? I had that.

'Oh it's no problem at all,' Mavis said when I phoned her that evening. 'In fact he's fine to stay with me for another few days, if that'll suit you. It's the summer holidays after all and, what with everything that's happened, it sounds like you could do with a bit of a proper break, don't you think?'

'Well, that's ever so good of you,' I said, 'after what he did to your windows. Is there a lot of damage?'

'Nothing the insurance company won't deal with promptly, and you know, I'd never tell Miller this, but I had always planned on putting new windows in anyway, so not such a bad thing, after all.'

I wasn't going to argue. To my mind, it was a *very* bad thing, and one he shouldn't be rewarded for, but if Miller wanted to stay and Mavis was happy about it, then she was right, it would give us a real break. And precious time for me to decide if this was what I really wanted for us all. Something that was hard to do when Miller was actually with us. Distance would give me clarity – something I was sorely lacking. Time out might help me regain my perspective and compassion for this child.

So I told Mavis it was fine and that I'd ring social services in the morning, and she said she would do the same so we could have our plan officially sanctioned. I also said that I'd get some extra things packed up for Miller, more clothes, some toys and games, and his bits and bats of toiletries – if he was staying for a few days, he'd need more than he had there. Mike could then drive over with them later that afternoon.

'And his suitcase,' Mavis had said. 'The one he keeps under his bed? He'd be particularly glad of that, he tells me. I believe it holds all his very precious things. Oh, and he also mentioned a little toy train?'

And in the mention of it I felt a fierce little pang of regret. Had she now become Casey to my Jenny?

* * *

'Well, let's hope he stays the whole week,' said Tyler firmly. He'd returned from a sleepover with Denver to find me in Miller's bedroom, having had Mike give him the lowdown on what had happened. 'I'm not being awful, Mum, but it's just so stressful when he's here. It's like we all walk on eggshells wondering what he's going to do next. Gotta be honest,' he added, picking up Miller's pages full of numbers, 'he is one creepy kid.'

And he didn't even know about what had happened with the wasps. 'I know, love,' I said, as I added to the pile I'd made of clothing. 'D'you have a spare backpack I can use to put all this lot in maybe? He's already taken my little cabin bag with him.'

'I think I might have,' he said. 'But why don't you just use his own case?' He pointed to where it was peeking out from under the bed.

'Already full,' I said, pulling it out. Then remembering to rummage under his pillow for his little train. That was a thought, I realised. That he hadn't taken it with him. So perhaps he really had thought he'd be able to resist being taken there. Or, more likely, I decided, given everything that had happened since, he'd just failed to grab it in the heat of the angry exchange with Mike. Well, he could have it now, at least, I thought, popping it on top of the clothes pile.

But that suitcase. I remembered back to the knife and the lighters. Did I really feel comfortable sending his little box of tricks across to Mavis? Given his violent act of smashing her windows, and his threat to stab her with the resulting broken glass, who knew what his plan was now he was there?

Perhaps I should first satisfy myself as to what was in it. No, I didn't have a search warrant, but I did have good cause. He might well have other worrying items in there as well.

It was padlocked, as per, and I knew he'd have the key. But it was a cheap, tiny combination padlock. More a deterrent than anything. And, at Tyler's suggestion ('Mum, he's hacked into our flipping internet, so we can "hack" into his case'), I managed to prise apart the zip pulls to which it was attached in moments.

And, to put it in Ty's exact words, 'What the *hell*?'

Because beneath the innocent-looking contents I'd glanced at on several occasions – the tennis ball, the framed photograph, a sheaf of magazines and comics, a Premier League club scarf and a pair of pristine football boots, there was a piece of hardboard, under which there was more. A *lot* more.

There were printed-off pictures that I shuddered to even look at; the sort of images that, in news reports about shootings or war zones, no broadcaster would ever, ever broadcast. Plus a six-pack of matchboxes, still wrapped in their cellophane, a pair of what looked like surgical scissors, a pair of tweezers and a dozen or so small plastic takeaway containers, which, on closer inspection, were full of dead insects.

'OMG,' Tyler gasped, as he prised the lid off one of them, to find it half full with wasps. There were moths too, and spiders. Even a box full of dead bees. And in one, which Tyler opened, something flat, beige and furry. 'Mum, don't look,' he said, putting the lid back on swiftly. 'I think this is the remains of a hamster. God, it's *sick*.' He shook his head. 'Oh, Mum, what is *wrong* with him?'

I felt sick. And tried to think back to his notes. The stricken rabbit I remembered, but didn't I also read somewhere about one carer having bought him a hamster and it escaping? Yes, I was sure I had. Dear God. And to *here*.

I watched Tyler press the lid home on the box and its long-deceased occupant.

And felt the lid being put on for me too.

*   *   *

Even then, having removed all the more grisly contents from Miller's case, as I put the 'innocent' items and, and added the clothes and things I'd gathered, I wasn't done with him. Not quite yet. This was more evidence, or so my mind ran, of the urgent need for help. For a swift and robust psychological intervention. For help. As in *help*. As in *now*.

And I would have doubtless carried on along that more dispassionate line of thinking, had it not been, moments after I'd taken the case downstairs, for hearing Tyler, from upstairs, shouting, 'God! Mu-um!'

He was down the stairs before I could go up to him, guitar in trembling hand, fuming and tearful. 'Look what he's done!' he said. 'Look! The little *shit*!'

So I looked. And saw that all six strings on Tyler's guitar had been cut. He'd also scraped his initials into the wood of the body – 'MG' – so we'd be left in no doubt. I wonder if he'd known his parting shot would be just that? A parting shot.

Because after a long and difficult chat that night, Mike and I came to a decision. It wasn't an easy decision – how could it ever be, given the way Miller had come to us? But the only one we could make, for us as a family.

'So we're both decided then?' Mike asked, after our long, miserable talk. 'We end this placement, no matter how much pressure they put on you to change your mind?'

I nodded sadly, finally accepting that we had no choice. Things weren't going to change in the short term – I just couldn't see it – me! – so if Miller were to stay, it would mean making changes. And us as a *family* who'd be having to make the changes, to accept life Miller's way, to run with the daily madness and mayhem, to coax him through perhaps years of psychological interventions, and, even if he was in school, he would always be at the centre of my professional universe. But also in my home, in the centre of my family, and that was a price I was no longer willing to pay.

So, on Monday morning, Christine Bolton was my first port of call. I had no stomach for chatting to Libby about our 'little monkey', so I called Christine as soon as I knew the office opened. I then poured my heart out, in the ensuing conversation, trying to convey just how difficult looking after Miller was, and how it hurt me to admit it but we'd simply had enough. She listened and I talked, and I talked, and I talked, knowing I was just trying to offer reasons in mitigation of our decision, but doing so anyway, despite knowing I didn't have to.

'Casey,' she said, when I finally stopped talking. '*Stop*. You don't need to justify your decision, to me or anyone. To tell you the truth, I'm surprised that you've managed for this long. I know I haven't known you for long, so forgive me if I sound presumptuous, but I never thought Miller was the boy for you, not really. You've done so well with Miller – you really have – but, well, the cards were on the table from day one. He can't do long term and he won't. It's as simple as that. I didn't want to tread on toes by speaking out at the beginning, but he was never going to be suited to a family situation. You only needed to look at his history to know that.'

'But I just feel so *bad*,' I said. 'Here we are, doing exactly what Miller predicts all foster carers do – giving up on him. It will just reinforce his view that nobody wants him, that nobody cares. That nobody loves him.'

'Forgive my bluntness, Casey, but that's all true. They don't. Which is not to say society should, or *has*, given up on him. Just that, for some kids, other solutions, other situations, need to be found. If there's to be any hope of that sad state of affairs being corrected, that is. You know, I was a bit bemused that you seemed so keen to take him on, to be honest. I mean, I know it was an emergency situation, which tends to colour things. But, given your lovely family, and not least your commitment to your youngest son, Tyler, I was genuinely shocked that you were so keen to take him on.'

Where did I start? Because I was already doubting that I was in the right frame of mind? Because John was leaving? Because I wanted to prove to his successor that I was some kind of fostering superhero slash legend? Because I was trying to prove that to my flagging *self*?

I said nothing. I suspected she had wondered that already. Worked it through in her own mind as I'd bristled in front of her. She said nothing either. And she'd called Tyler my son. Not my foster son. My *son*. And in that instant I knew we would become friends.

Instead she said, 'Look, Casey, I have a germ of an idea. A bit radical and before I tell you, I need to speak to some other people. Can you give me half an hour and I'll ring you back?'

So I waited, and while I waited I took delivery of some new guitar strings, put a wash on and hauled the vacuum cleaner upstairs. I also found the link to a brilliant local Alzheimer's support group that I'd meant to pass on to her a couple of days back and hadn't. In short, got my day back on track.

And when she called back, it turned out that her plan was pretty simple. That, for the foreseeable, and with the amazing Mavis's full agreement, she and I would simply swap roles. What Miller thought of the arrangement I could only guess at, obviously, but spared the responsibility of wondering how to deal with it, I could only give thanks that it wasn't my problem. Well, at least till the weekend respites I was happy to agree to. One in two weeks' time and, then, because Christine felt it more sensible, once a month, going forwards – though with some flexibility, to fit in with Mavis's dog-show commitments.

'You know,' she said, 'I believe Mavis might be perfect for him. No, it's not what she originally thought she'd signed up for. But she's on her own, and can give him 100 per cent of her attention. And she tells me there's nothing he can do that will faze her. Did you know, by the way, that when she retired from full-time police work in her forties, she volunteered for a couple of years in a facility for the criminally insane?' Christine chuckled. 'So she doubts

Miller will be able to drive *her* insane. Early days, of course, but she's not worried in the least about how she'll handle him – as she says, she doesn't have anyone else to worry about, does she? And I have a hunch she'll be able to do some good.'

It was a genius plan, I thought – another borderline miracle. Cometh the hour, cometh Mavis. It also meant that Miller wouldn't feel so rejected; might feel he'd got things the way he wanted them, even. We would see. And at least he'd be granted some proper help from CAMHS.

And, of course, it left us free to take on another child. Full-time, if we wanted.

Which I *did* want, I shocked myself by thinking. I clearly wasn't done yet.

'But not just yet,' Christine said. 'Casey, I know I'm not your boss, exactly. But, as you might have realised, I *am* bossy. And I'm telling you here and now that you are taking a couple of weeks off. And now I'm off as well. D'you realise it's almost ten in the morning and I haven't even had my second cup of tea yet?'

'Ugh. The devil's drink,' I said laughing, as we said our goodbyes.

Some things are set in stone, after all.

Epilogue

Today's fostering is more fluid than ever before, I think. It has changed so much over the years that I've been doing it, and though budget cuts and new regulations often mean that we carers often get the thin end of the wedge, the changes have meant that we have become a lot more flexible in our approach. We have to be, because the children coming into care today are far more complex than the children I was asked to foster all those years ago.

Take our situation with Miller, for example. They say all political careers end in failure, don't they? But what they don't say, and perhaps shouldn't, is that sometimes fostering placements end in failure, too. At least, that's how I saw it for the first weeks after Miller officially 'left' us. That I was a failure, because I'd failed to keep my promise to him. I also thought hard about ending my own 'career' in fostering. If I couldn't make a difference, however small, then what was the point?

Happily, Mike had a stern word with me and told me to

stop being self-indulgent. I might be able to work miracles on a furred-up kettle, but there were no miracles in fostering. Just the daily slog of doing your best – with training, the right spirit and a heck of a lot of patience – and accepting that sometimes things didn't work out. I also accepted Christine's patient lectures about the importance of prioritising my family, too. For someone who's never had the chance to bring up her own child, she has spades of parental wisdom. She'd have made a lovely, lovely mum.

And who knew? So far, our shared arrangement has worked out. There is no pressure and the logistics of it are more or less left to us carers. If Mavis has plans for Miller on a particular weekend, she phones in advance and lets us know, and similarly if something comes up for us, we give as much notice as we can and rearrange. It also means that even if we've had Miller one weekend, if Mavis is having a struggle with him, she can ring us and ask for us to do an extra night or two.

And, to our delight and surprise, Miller seems to be thriving with this set-up. One might think that someone with such an appetite for control, would hate the uncertainty and the constant moving around, but he really doesn't. It seems he actually prefers to be in the midst of chaos. Organised chaos at least, at least when he's not in school, whose routines and order, and dependable structure, he seems to love. Nowt so queer as folk, eh? But perhaps the whole 'family as gold standard' idea isn't for everyone. When not in school, he is definitely still a paid-up member of the resistance, and this must be linked directly to his childhood. No matter how we professionals think that order and structure is the only way for some of these kids, it clearly isn't. They rebel against it because it isn't their norm; confrontation is their 'comfort blanket' and they still crave it, no matter how bad it seems to us.

So I'm very grateful for Christine Bolton's little flash of inspiration that day on the phone, because it has changed Miller almost beyond recognition. He still has his off days and no doubt he always will, and he still tries to control most situations when he can, but in himself, we can all see how much happier and less wound up he now is. We even saw an example of this last Christmas. Miller came to stay with us the weekend before and we'd arranged with Mavis to give him his gifts at that point, and she'd said he could open one of them while he was with us. His choice was a mobile phone (no surprise there!), which he was ecstatic about, truly thrilled – I even got an extremely rare hug. But what touched us most was his gesture towards Tyler.

He'd brought two Christmas cards with him, one for us and the family, and one just for Tyler, which he made him promise not to open till he'd left. Which he did, and as I watched him do so, to my surprise, he had tears in his eyes. It read:

Dear Ty

I hope you have a lovely Christmas and I bet Casey and Mike get you a well nice present. I wish I could buy you what I want to get you, Ty, I promise I do. And one day, when I'm rich through my hacking and stuff, I will get you the best new guitar that money can buy, I swear down! I have done a lot of bad things, and some of them to you and your family but my biggest mistake was cutting your guitar strings. I wish I had never done that. I wish I could take it back. If I could pick a brother it would be you. Merry Christmas and see you in the New Year.

Miller x

Oh, and I should add that Miller's handwriting, always erratic, was a dream to behold. Mr Hammond was (is) clearly doing a great job. And the best news (well, once we'd dried our eyes over the card) was that, as I write, he is top of the waiting list for a boarding place. So it's within touching distance. Keep your fingers crossed for him.

CASEY WATSON

*One woman determined to
make a difference.*

*Read Casey's poignant
memoirs and be inspired.*

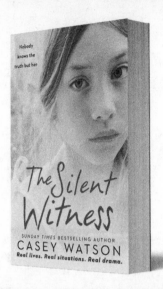

Bella's father is on a ventilator, fighting for his life, while her mother is currently on remand in prison, charged with his attempted murder

Bella is the only witness.

THE SILENT WITNESS

Adrianna arrives on Casey's doorstep with no possessions, no English and no explanation

It will be a few weeks before Casey starts getting the shocking answers to her questions . . .

RUNAWAY GIRL

Leo isn't a bad lad, but his frequent absences from school mean he's on the brink of permanent exclusion

Leo is clearly hiding something, and Casey knows that if he is to have any kind of future, it's up to her to find out the truth.

MUMMY'S LITTLE SOLDIER

Flip is being raised by her alcoholic mother, and comes to Casey after a fire at their home

Flip has Foetal Alcohol Syndrome (FAS), but it soon turns out that this is just the tip of the iceberg . . .

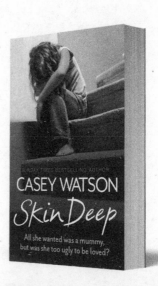

SKIN DEEP

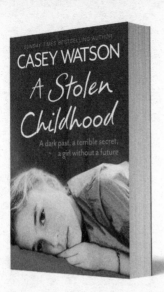

Kiara appears tired and distressed, and the school wants Casey to take her under her wing for a while

On the surface, everything points to a child who is upset that her parents have separated. The horrific truth, however, shocks Casey to the core.

A STOLEN CHILDHOOD

Eleven-year-old Tyler has stabbed his stepmother and has nowhere to go

With his birth mother dead and a father who doesn't want him, what can be done to stop his young life spiralling out of control?

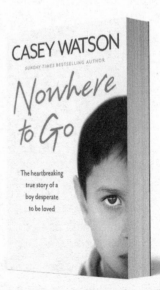

NOWHERE TO GO

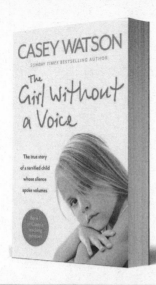

What is the secret behind Imogen's silence?

Discover the shocking and devastating past of a child with severe behavioural problems.

THE GIRL WITHOUT A VOICE

A teenage mother and baby in need of a loving home

At fourteen, Emma is just a child herself – and one who's never been properly mothered.

A LAST KISS FOR MUMMY

Two boys with an
unlikely bond

With Georgie and
Jenson, Casey is facing
her toughest test yet.

BREAKING THE SILENCE

A young girl secretly
caring for her mother

Abigail has been dealing
with pressures no child
should face. Casey has the
difficult challenge of helping
her to learn to let go.

MUMMY'S LITTLE HELPER

Branded 'vicious and evil', eight-year-old Spencer asks to be taken into care

Casey and her family are disgusted: kids aren't born evil. Despite the challenges Spencer brings, they are determined to help him find a loving home.

TOO HURT TO STAY

Abused siblings who do not know what it means to be loved

With new-found security and trust, Casey helps Ashton and Olivia to rebuild their lives.

LITTLE PRISONERS

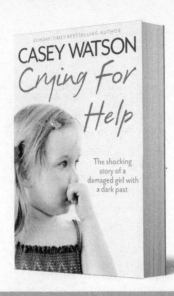

A damaged girl
haunted by her past

Sophia pushes Casey to
the limits, threatening
the safety of the whole
family. Can Casey make
a difference in time?

CRYING FOR HELP

Five-year-old Justin
was desperate and
helpless

Six years after being
taken into care, Justin has
had 20 failed placements.
Casey and her family are
his last hope.

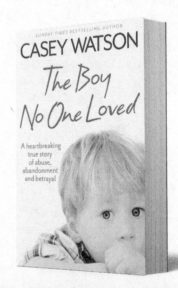

THE BOY NO ONE LOVED

AVAILABLE AS E-BOOK ONLY

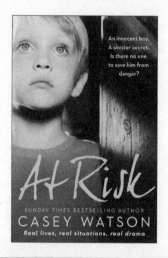

Adam is brought to Casey while his mum recovers in hospital – just for a few days

But a chance discovery reveals that Casey has stumbled upon something altogether more sinister ...

AT RISK

Six-year-old Darby is naturally distressed at being removed from her parents just before Christmas

And when the shocking and sickening reason is revealed, a Happy New Year seems an impossible dream as well ...

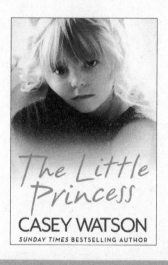

THE LITTLE PRINCESS

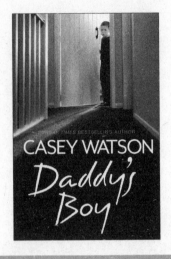

Paulie, just five, is a boy out of control – or is he just misunderstood?

The plan for Paulie is simple: get him back home with his family. But perhaps 'home' isn't the best place for him …

DADDY'S BOY

Angry and hurting, eight-year-old Connor is from a broken home

As streetwise as they come, he's determined to cause trouble. But Casey is convinced there is a frightened child beneath the swagger.

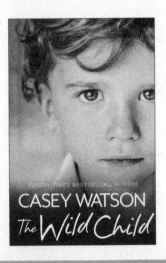

THE WILD CHILD

AVAILABLE AS E-BOOK ONLY

Nathan has a sometime alter ego called Jenny who is the only one who knows the secrets of his disturbed past

But where is Jenny when she is most needed?

Secrets always find a way of revealing themselves, sometimes you just need someone to talk to

No Place for Nathan

A SHORT STORY

CASEY WATSON

SUNDAY TIMES BESTSELLING AUTHOR

NO PLACE FOR NATHAN

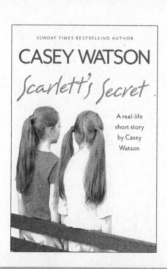

SUNDAY TIMES BESTSELLING AUTHOR

CASEY WATSON

Scarlett's Secret

A real-life short story by Casey Watson

Jade and Scarlett, seventeen-year-old twins, share a terrible secret

Can Casey help them come to terms with the truth and rediscover their sibling connection?

SCARLETT'S SECRET

AVAILABLE AS E-BOOK ONLY

Cameron is a sweet boy who seems happy in his skin – making him rather different from most of the other children Casey has cared for

But what happens when Cameron disappears? Will Casey's worst fears be realised?

CASEY WATSON
SUNDAY TIMES BESTSELLING AUTHOR

Just a Boy

An inspiring and heartwarming
short story

JUST A BOY

FEEL HEART.
FEEL HOPE.
READ CASEY.

Moving Memoirs

Stories of hope, courage and the power of love…

If you loved this book, then you will love our
Moving Memoirs eNewsletter

Sign up to…

- Be the first to hear about new books

- Get sneak previews from your favourite authors

- Read exclusive interviews

- Be entered into our monthly prize draw to win one
of our latest releases before it's even hit the shops!

Sign up at

www.moving-memoirs.com